Divided Allegiances

Divided Allegiances

Bertie County during the Civil War

Gerald W. Thomas

Raleigh
Division of Archives and History
North Carolina Department of Cultural Resources
1996

North Carolina Department of Cultural Resources

Division of Archives and History

North Carolina Historical Commission

CONTENTS

Maps and Illustrations

FOREWORD

Perhaps no period in American history excites more interest among readers than does the Civil War. Although North Carolina joined the Confederate States of America after the outbreak of the war, its citizens were far from unanimous in their support of the Confederate cause. In many areas of the state, neighbors became divided in their allegiances. Some inhabitants remained loyal to the Union and even joined the Federal military forces. Others steadfastly cast their lot with the Confederacy and marched in the ranks of its army.

One area in the Tar Heel State in which such a division occurred was Bertie County, which became a no-man's-land of mixed loyalties and military and civil conflict. In *Divided Allegiances: Bertie County during the Civil War*, Gerald W. Thomas has painstakingly identified those natives who served each side and graphically describes the battles and social upheavals that engulfed that eastern North Carolina county. His account of the Civil War on the local level represents a major contribution to the historiography of the sectional conflict.

Mr. Thomas, a graduate of East Carolina University, brings considerable knowledge of the Civil War to his work. His article "Massacre at Plymouth: April 20, 1864" (coauthored with Weymouth T. Jordan Jr.), which appeared in the *North Carolina Historical Review* in April 1995, received accolades from a number of prominent Civil War scholars. In the production of *Divided Allegiances*, Mr. Thomas was ably assisted by Robert M. Topkins and Lisa D. Bailey of the Historical Publications Section. Mr. Topkins edited the book and saw it through press; he also designed the cover. Ms. Bailey lent her proofreading skills throughout the project.

Joe A. Mobley, *Administrator*
Historical Publications Section

July 1996

"Ole Pap fought with the Yankees"

The impetus for this book began on a warm summer afternoon in 1979 while I was seated with my Aunt Nora Thomas Rose (now deceased) on the front porch of her home in Windsor, Bertie County, North Carolina, discussing our family genealogy. After graduating from East Carolina University in 1976, I had moved to the Washington, D.C., area and, like many people who relocate there, had begun researching my ancestry at the National Archives and the Library of Congress. At the time of my discussion with Aunt Nora, I was compiling information on my great-grandfather, William David Thomas.

William David Thomas was born in Bertie County in February 1845. He was sixteen years old when the Civil War began, making him of prime age for military service during the war. I had naturally assumed that he, being a native North Carolinian, served in the Confederate army; however, my research at the National Archives had failed to discover any Confederate military service records for him. Therefore, on that summer day in 1979 I asked Aunt Nora if she knew whether William David had "fought" during the war. Her answer, quite simply, astonished me. After informing me that as a child, she, along with her brothers, sisters, and cousins, had called my great-grandfather "Ole Pap," she stated: "Ole Pap fought with the Yankees."[1]

I could hardly believe what my aunt had said. I could not conceive that my great-grandfather, who was born, lived his complete life, and died in Bertie County, served in the Union army. While not a student of the Civil War, I had never heard, read, or envisioned that North Carolinians served in the Union military services. Now I realize that in

Union army veteran William David Thomas (1845–1925) eluded Confederate conscription officers in Bertie County and enlisted in Company B, Second Regiment North Carolina Union Volunteers, at Plymouth on October 10, 1863. He escaped capture by Confederate troops at the Battle of Plymouth (April 17–20, 1864) and on February 27, 1865, transferred to Company L, First Regiment North Carolina Union Volunteers, with which he served until June 22, 1865, when he transferred to Company I of that regiment. Thomas was mustered out of service at New Bern on June 27, 1865. In this photograph (ca. 1922) an elderly Thomas is flanked by his daughter and grandson. Photograph supplied by the author.

1979 I was not educated to the circumstances, political and regional differences, and other factors that led to the Civil War. In essence, I was naïve regarding the war, particularly of the dispositions, attitudes, contributions, and involvements of the people of North Carolina and Bertie County.

Shortly after the discussion with Aunt Nora, another relative informed me that John T. Cale, a brother of my great-grandmother, Amilia Jane Cale Thomas (wife of William David), had perished as a Union prisoner of war in the hellhole Confederate prison at Andersonville, Georgia.[2] That information also astonished me.

Subsequent research at the National Archives quickly confirmed that William David Thomas and John T. Cale had indeed served in the Union army. Further research identified other kinsmen of my Bertie County ancestors who similarly served. Those men served in two regiments of white Union soldiers raised in eastern North Carolina. After gathering this basic information, my interest and desire to obtain additional enlightenment regarding Bertie County men in the Union military was overwhelming.

I discovered that more than two hundred Bertie County men served in the First and Second Regiments North Carolina Union Volunteers.[3] Those men, degradingly called "Buffaloes" by the secessionists and Confederate soldiers, principally enlisted at Plymouth, North Carolina, a small town located immediately across the Roanoke River from Bertie County. Federal forces occupied Plymouth in May 1862 and immediately began enlisting North Carolinians into their military services. In April 1864 a Confederate force under the command of Brig. Gen. Robert F. Hoke captured the Federal garrison at Plymouth. I discovered that William David Thomas eluded the Rebel force at Plymouth, while John T. Cale was captured and transported to the Confederate prison camp at Andersonville, Georgia, where he perished in June 1864.

I conducted in-depth research on the North Carolinians in the Union army at the Battle of Plymouth (April 17–20, 1864) and prepared an account of the battle, in which I identified a number of Bertie County men who were captured and later died in Confederate prisons, primarily Andersonville. In August 1988 I presented a copy of my Battle of Plymouth document to Harry Lewis Thompson, a local historian in Bertie County, who, along with another local historian, Cullen Dunstan, was compiling a roster of Confederate soldiers from Bertie County. After several discussions with Mr. Thompson, I agreed to attempt to compile a roster of Bertie County's Union soldiers. Since my initial discussions with Mr. Thompson, I have strenuously endeavored to compile information on Bertie County and its citizens during the Civil War—not just a compilation of the county's Union servicemen. My endeavor has led to this history.

The citizens of Bertie County, for the most part, staunchly supported the Union and were adamant against North Carolina's secession until Fort Sumter was attacked and Pres. Abraham Lincoln called for troops from North Carolina to help quell the rebellion in the states of the lower South and blockaded North Carolina's coastline, waterways, and seaports.

My research in available military service and certain other records identified 1,425 Bertie County men who enlisted or served in the Confederate and Union military services. (Some men enlisted and were rejected by military surgeons, while others deserted before reporting for duty.) Eight hundred five individuals enlisted or served solely in the Confederate military services and the Bertie County militia/home guard. Another 557 men—black and white—served only in Union military forces, while 63 men served in both the Confederate and Union militaries.[4] The following table summarizes the military service of Bertie County men by race.

Table 1
Confederate and Union Military Service of Bertie County Men

Race	Confederate* service only	Union service only	Confederate* & Union service	Totals
White	804	159	63	1,026
Black**	1	398	0	399
Totals	805	557	63	1,425

*Includes service in the Bertie County militia (Eight and Ninth Regiments North Carolina Militia) and home guard
**Includes mulattoes

Throughout the war, Bertie County remained within Confederate lines and was governed by Confederate civil authorities; however, no sizable Confederate forces occupied the county.[5] Federal forces periodically carried out raids or "expeditions" in the county, from which the citizens had little means of resistance. In a number of instances, Bertie County natives who had joined the Union army actively participated in the raids.

To a certain extent, Bertie County became a no-man's-land during the war, and its citizens suffered greatly. After the spring of 1862 many men hid in the woods and swamps to avoid Confederate conscription officers. Men were "hunted down like foxes" and shot at by those officers, and at least one county resident, David Hoggard Jr., was killed near the present-day community of Elm Grove while trying to elude the conscription officers. Late in the war, armed bushwhackers and prowling bands of guerrillas "infested" the county, pillaging, robbing, and preying on defenseless citizens.

Hundreds of residents—black and white—left the county during the war. Certain whites (mostly non-slaveholders) and blacks fled to the Union lines—the former to escape conscription into the Confederate army and persecution by military and civil authorities and the latter to achieve freedom from the terrible bonds of slavery. Wealthy planters and their families fled inland into the state and southward as far as Georgia to escape the influence of Federal troops and to protect their personal property, including slaveholdings.

Commodities and foodstuffs became difficult to obtain, and martial law was imposed in the county. By early 1863 a substantial number of the county's citizens had become thoroughly disgusted with the war and longed for peace. By that time, more Bertie County men—black and white—were enlisting in the Union military forces than in the Confederate army. From January 1863 through March 1864, 375 Bertie

County men (black and white) enlisted in the Union military services, while 131 men enlisted in the Confederate army. Of the 375 Union enlistments, 141 were in the First and Second Regiments North Carolina Union Volunteers.

Bertie County men fought and died on battlefields scattered throughout the eastern theater of war, including Antietam, Maryland; Gettysburg, Pennsylvania; Reams Station, Chancellorsville, Spotsylvania, and Petersburg, Virginia; and Plymouth. Dozens of the county's men died of disease. They were incarcerated in the Union prisons at Fort Delaware, Delaware; Point Lookout, Maryland; Elmira, New York; Johnson's Island, Ohio; and Washington, D.C. They were likewise imprisoned in the Confederate prisons at Andersonville, Georgia; Salisbury, North Carolina; and Richmond, Virginia.

Bertie County natives served aboard Union gunboats of the North Atlantic Blockading Squadron, which enforced Lincoln's blockade of North Carolina. The county's sons participated in the famous Pickett-Pettigrew "charge" at Gettysburg on July 3, 1863, often referred to as the "high water mark" for the Confederacy. Former slaves from the county served as prison guards at Point Lookout while Confederate prisoners of war from the county were confined there. Some of the county's Confederate soldiers imprisoned at Point Lookout in early 1864 took the Oath of Allegiance to the United States and enlisted in the Union army, thereby becoming "Galvanized Yankees." Those men, members of the First Regiment United States Volunteer Infantry, were sent to the western frontier to fight Indians and protect settlers and their property. Bertie County men suffered intolerably in the trenches around Petersburg in 1864 and 1865. They laid down their arms with Gen. Robert E. Lee at Appomattox Court House, Virginia, on April 9, 1865, while others rejoiced as members of Gen. Ulysses S. Grant's conquering forces on that same day. In late April 1865 other county men surrendered with Maj. Gen. Joseph E. Johnston to Maj. Gen. William T. Sherman, whose forces included former Bertie County slaves.

This book brings to light much information that seemingly had "gone to the grave" with the Bertie County residents who lived through and participated in the most momentous event in American history. It has not been my intention to judge, condone, or glorify the actions of any of the county's citizens who participated in the war in whatever capacities they were involved. I sincerely hope that the information contained herein enlightens others who are unaware, as I was prior to my research, of the attitudes, conditions, and factors that caused the citizens of Bertie County to take the actions they did before and during the war. If my hope is fulfilled, then the innumerable hours incurred in reviewing records and documents, compiling information, and preparing this history will have been well spent.

I am not a historian, and I am confident that the material contained in this book could have been more comprehensively developed and presented had the research and writing been conducted by a professional historian. While I readily acknowledge my limitations as a historian, I just as readily accept responsibility for the information contained herein. As readers will quickly notice, I have prepared this document for the people of Bertie County and those who have an interest in the county's history. Whenever the evidence was sufficient, I have included details—names, dates, and locations—and I am sure that some readers of this book will be surprised, as I was, when they learn what their "great-grandfathers" did during the war.

A final prefatory comment: While conducting research, I often wished that more Bertie County citizens who lived through and participated in this tragic war had written and preserved their accounts and perspectives of the conflict. No research effort on the war, regardless of how comprehensively conducted, uncovers all existing records related to the topic under research. My point is that if the readers of this book have in their possession records relating to Bertie County during the Civil War, or know of someone who has such information, or in the future discover such records and would provide photocopies of them (the original documents are not needed) to the Hope Foundation (the historical society for Bertie County and the surrounding area), the North Carolina Archives, or the various universities within the state, then future researchers, casual readers, and "buffs" of the war will have a more complete resource of information about the war in Bertie County available to them.

Gerald W. Thomas
June 30, 1996

Notes

1. Nora Thomas Rose, interview with author, Windsor, N.C., August 18, 1979.

2. James Philip Hoggard, interview with author, Todd's Crossroads, Bertie County, N.C., September 15, 1979.

3. Compiled Service Records of Volunteer Union Soldiers Who Served in Organizations from the State of North Carolina, Record Group 94, National Archives, Washington, D.C. (hereafter cited as Compiled Service Records of North Carolina's Union Soldiers). Statistics presented throughout this book were developed by the author unless otherwise noted.

4. Statistics on Bertie County's Confederate and Union servicemen were developed from information obtained from a number of sources, primarily Louis H. Manarin and Weymouth T. Jordan Jr., comps., *North Carolina Troops, 1861–1865: A Roster*, 13 vols. to date (Raleigh: Division of Archives and History, North Carolina Department of Cultural Resources, 1966—); Compiled Service Records of Confederate Soldiers Who Served in Organizations from the State of North Carolina, Record Group 109, National Archives (hereafter cited as Compiled Service Records of North Carolina's Confederate Soldiers); Compiled Service Records of Confederate General and Staff Officers and Non-regimental Enlisted Men, Record Group 109, National Archives (hereafter cited as Compiled Service Records of Confederate Officers); Civil War Collection, Military Collection, State Archives, North Carolina Division of Archives and History, Raleigh; Roster of Bertie County Confederate Soldiers, Register of Deeds Office, Windsor; Militia Officer Roster, Records of the Adjutant General's Office, Archives, Division of Archives and History; Stephen E. Bradley, ed., *North Carolina Confederate Militia Officers Roster* (Wilmington: Broadfoot Publishing Company, 1992), 21–26 (hereafter cited as Bradley, *Confederate Militia Officers Roster*); Compiled Service Records of North Carolina's Union Soldiers; Compiled Service Records of Volunteer Union Soldiers Who Served in Organizations from the State of Virginia, Record Group 94, National Archives (hereafter cited as Compiled Service Records of Virginia's Union Soldiers); Compiled Service Records of Union Soldiers Who Served in Organizations from the State of Pennsylvania, Record Group 94, National Archives (hereafter cited as Compiled Service Records of Pennsylvania's Union Soldiers); Compiled Service Records of Union Soldiers Who Served in Organizations from the State of New York, Record Group 94, National Archives (hereafter cited as Compiled Service Records of New York's Union Soldiers); Compiled Service Records of Former Confederate Soldiers Who Served in the First through Sixth U.S. Volunteer Infantry Regiments, 1864–1866, Record Group 94, National Archives (hereafter cited as Compiled Service Records of U.S. Volunteer Infantry); Compiled Service Records of Volunteer Union Soldiers Who Served with the United States Colored Troops (USCT), Record Group 94, National Archives (hereafter cited as Compiled Service Records of USCT); Muster rolls for Union gunboats of the North Atlantic Blockading Squadron, Records of the Bureau of Naval Personnel, Record Group 24, National Archives; Index to Rendezvous Reports, Civil War (United States Navy), Record Group 24, National Archives (hereafter cited as Navy Rendezvous Reports). The author has found no records that identify the privates and noncommissioned officers of the Bertie County militia/home guard. His identification of Bertie County Confederate and Union servicemen was by necessity based on the information available from the various sources. The author is confident that he has not been able to identify all Bertie County men who served in the Confederate and Union military forces because of the lack of detailed data (such as place of birth, residence, or enlistment) in available records or because some records were lost or destroyed during or after the war. Moreover, some men enlisted at places outside Bertie County, including other states, which makes it difficult if not impossible to identify them with absolute certainty as Bertie County residents.

5. The Confederate forces that at various times occupied Bertie County were generally company-size organizations, predominantly Company B, Sixty-second Regiment Georgia Cavalry, and Company F, Sixty-eighth Regiment North Carolina Troops. Those units and others that visited the county principally performed picket, scouting, and foraging duties. The occupying organizations (such as the Georgia cavalry) were also involved in rounding up conscription evaders, deserters, and unionist citizens.

CHAPTER 1

In Favor of the Union

In the spring of 1860 the American nation—almost eighty-four years old—was on the verge of being torn apart. Thirty years of confrontations, crises, and compromises, primarily over the slavery issue, had culminated in ominous political and sectional differences. In April the Democratic Party split into northern and southern factions, primarily over dissensions regarding the question of congressional protection of slavery in the territories.[1] In May the Constitutional Union Party, formerly the American or "Know-Nothing" Party, with strong ties to the old Whig Party, nominated John Bell of Tennessee for president. The party, comprised primarily of Whig conservatives, took no stand on the pressing issues that divided the North and South but adopted a simplistic, two-paragraph platform "to recognize no political principle other than the Constitution . . . the Union . . . and the enforcement of laws." The party's platform emphasized devotion to the Union and avoided the controversial slavery issue.[2] Also in May, the young Republican Party nominated Abraham Lincoln of Illinois for president. The party's platform denounced the further spread of slavery and declared its preference for congressional prohibition of slavery in the territories.[3]

In June the northern and southern factions of the Democratic Party met separately. The "northern" faction nominated Stephen A. Douglas of Illinois for president and declared its intentions of leaving the question of slavery in the territories to the citizens in those areas or to the Supreme Court of the United States. The "southern" faction nominated John C. Breckinridge of Kentucky for president and maintained that neither Congress nor a territorial legislative body had the right to prohibit slavery in a territory. The southern delegates held that it was the duty of the federal government to protect slavery in the territories when necessary.[4]

The presidential campaign of 1860 evolved into two separate contests—Lincoln versus Douglas in the North and Breckinridge versus Bell in the South. Years of sectional tension had galvanized the people's beliefs and political ideals, and the political agitation came to a boil in the presidential campaign.[5] During the campaign approximately 14,300 residents of Bertie County, North Carolina, carried on with their daily lives as they and their ancestors had done for decades.[6] Bertie County's citizens, like those of other communities in the nation, were gravely concerned over the issues of the day but recognized that they had no control over their political fate as the nation of more than thirty-one million people moved to a critical crossroads.[7]

Bertie County, situated in the northeastern sector of the state, was thoroughly rural in 1860. Its inhabitants predominantly made their livelihoods by farming and primarily grew corn, cotton, and potatoes.[8] According to 1860 tax lists, there were 931 landowners in the county, of whom 655, or 70 percent, owned one hundred or more acres of land. Throughout the state, only 30 percent of the landowners owned as many acres.[9]

Table 2
Bertie County Landowners, 1860

Number of landowners	Percent of landowners	Number of acres owned
6	.6	4,000 or more
24	2.6	2,000–3,999
51	5.5	1,000–1,999
115	12.4	500–999
160	17.2	250–499
299	32.1	100–249
166	17.8	50–99
89	10.0	10–49
21	2.3	less than 10
Totals 931	100.0	

Source: Bertie County tax lists, 1860, State Archives, Division of Archives and History, Raleigh.

While almost 9 percent of the county's landholders owned one thousand or more acres of land and generally represented the upper echelon of the county's social and economic structure, many families owned exceedingly little property. According to the 1860 federal census, the county contained 1,210 free households, 165 (13.6 percent) members of which owned no real or personal property. Moreover, an additional 573 households (47.4 percent) owned less than one thousand dollars' worth of real and personal property. Many of the people who lived in those households were commonly considered "poor whites"— uneducated, poverty-stricken individuals who represented the lower end of Bertie County's social and economic structure.[10]

Table 3
Reported Property Values of Bertie County Households in 1860

Total value of real and personal property*	Number of households	Percent of total households
$200,000 and over	5	.4
$100,000–$199,999	15	1.2
$50,000–$99,999	28	2.3
$25,000–$49,999	47	3.9
$10,000–$24,999	84	6.9
$1,000–$9,999	293	24.2
$500–$999	134	11.1
$100–$499	328	27.1
$1–$99	111	9.2
$0	165	13.6
Totals	1,210	100.0

Source: Eighth Census of the United States, 1860: Bertie County, North Carolina, Population Schedule, National Archives, Washington, D.C.
*Personal property included slaves, vehicles, jewelry, stocks, bonds, and other sundry assets.

Table 4
Bertie County's Total Population, 1860

	Race White	Black	Mulatto	Totals	Percent
Free	5,821	73	232	6,126	42.8
Slave	0	7,864	320	8,184	57.2
Totals	5,821	7,937	552	14,310	
Percent	40.6	55.5	3.9		100.0

Source: Eighth Census of the United States, 1860: Bertie County, North Carolina, Population and Slave Schedules, National Archives.

Approximately 8,180 persons, or 57.2 percent of the total population, were slaves.[11] The county was one of sixteen in North Carolina in which slaves comprised more than 50 percent of the total population in 1860.[12]

Bertie County comprised part of North Carolina's cotton culture, producing 5 or more 400-pound bales per 100 acres of improved land. During the 1859 growing season, the county's farmers and planters produced 6,672 bales of cotton, of which thirty-nine growers produced 4,865 bales, or 73 percent of the total production.[13] Farming of cotton was labor intensive and required the use of large numbers of hands, principally slaves, to work the fields.

Slaves, while comprising a majority of the county's population, were owned by a minority of the county's households. In the summer of 1860 there were 462 slave owners in the county, with an average of 17.7 slaves per owner—almost twice the overall average of 9.5 slaves per owner in North Carolina. Of the total number of Bertie County slave owners, only 8 owned more than 100 slaves each, 28 owned 50 to 100 slaves, and 80 owned 20 to 49 slaves.[14]

Table 5
Slave Ownership in Bertie County, 1860

Number of owners	Percent of total owners	Number of slaves owned	Total number of slaves owned	Percent of county's total slave population
4	.9	more than 150	847	10.3
4	.9	100–150	463	5.7
28	6.1	50–99	1,971	24.1
80	17.3	20–49	2,633	32.2
97	21.0	10–19	1,329	16.2
88	19.0	5–9	596	7.3
161	34.8	1–4	345	4.2
462	100.0		8,184	100.0

Source: Eighth Census of the United States, 1860: Bertie County, North Carolina, Slave Schedule, National Archives.

Logically, the county's largest slave owners produced the most cotton. In 1860 Bertie County's eight largest slaveholders—those owning one hundred or more slaves—collectively owned 16 percent of the county's slaves and almost 11 percent of the county's land and had produced approximately 24 percent of the county's cotton in 1859.[15] They were some of the wealthiest men in North Carolina. In fact, the county's two largest slaveholders—Cullen Capehart and Joseph H. Etheridge—were among the fifteen largest slave owners in the state.[16]

Table 6
Cotton Production and Number of Acres of Land Owned
by Bertie County's Eight Largest Slave Owners, 1860

Slave Owners	Slaves owned	Bales of cotton*	County rank	Acres of land**	County rank
Cullen Capehart	258	425	1	8,431	1
Joseph H. Etheridge	248	165	7	2,375	18
Augustus Holley	173	176	6	7,579	2
William T. Sutton	168	197	5	2,830	10
William Moring	141	205	4	7,444	3
Stephen A. Norfleet	115	215	3	3,952	7
Lewis Thompson	104	118	12	3,849	8
Thomas H. Speller	103	78	25	1,771	40
Totals	1,310	1,579		38,231	

Source: Eighth Census of the United States, 1860: Bertie County, North Carolina, Slave and Agriculture Schedules, National Archives; Bertie County tax lists, 1860, State Archives.

*Represents cotton produced during the 1859 growing season
**Includes cleared and wooded lands

The county's large slave owners generally supported the ideals of the proslavery Democratic Party, while a large proportion of the citizens, owning no slaves and having little or nothing to gain from the perpetuation of slavery, supported the Whig Party. Indeed, many of the "poor whites" likely opposed the institution of slavery because it effectively excluded them from the labor market. Planters, relying on slaves as their primary source of labor, had little need or inclination to hire other county residents to work on their farms and plantations.[17]

As the political tensions of the presidential campaign increased, the Whigs, who more staunchly supported the Union than did the Democrats, aggressively cultivated a surge of unionist sentiment throughout North Carolina. Whigs had traditionally supported the ideals of the Union and actively promoted John Bell, the Constitutional Union candidate.[18]

In Bertie County the majority of the free citizens supported Bell and his party's unionist platform. But such support was not unusual for the county voters, as they had not once failed to provide a majority of votes to Whig or non-Democratic candidates in presidential and gubernatorial elections since 1848. Bertie County voters had continued to support the Whig Party during the 1850s, even though it declined in popularity and was not the majority party in North Carolina during that decade.[19]

Table 7
Bertie County Voting Results by Party Affiliation for Presidential and Gubernatorial Elections, 1848 through 1858

Year	Election*	Percentages Whig or Non-Democratic**	Democratic
1848	P	63.4	36.6
1848	G	58.6	41.4
1850	G	55.0	45.0
1852	P	52.9	47.1
1852	G	55.6	44.4
1854	G	54.4	45.6
1856	P	53.0	47.0
1856	G	53.7	46.3
1858	G	58.8	41.2

Source: John L. Cheney Jr., ed., *North Carolina Government, 1585–1979: A Narrative and Statistical History* (Raleigh: North Carolina Department of the Secretary of State, 1981), 1330, 1398, 1400.

*P: presidential; G: gubernatorial

**Percentages are for Whig candidates except 1856 gubernatorial election (John A. Gilmer, American Party) and 1858 gubernatorial election (Duncan K. McRae, Distribution Party).

In the midst of the 1860 presidential campaign, North Carolinians went to the polls in August to elect a governor. John W. Ellis, a Democrat, opposed John Pool, a Whig and former state senator from Pasquotank County with Bertie County ties.[20] In December 1857 Pool had married Mary Elizabeth Mebane of the influential Mebane family in Bertie County and presumably would have been the favorite candidate of the county's voters.[21] While Pool made a strong showing for the resurgent Whig Party and rekindled its members' hopes for the upcoming presidential election, he lost the election to Ellis by 6,093 votes (59,396 to 53,303), or 5.4 percent of the total votes cast.[22] Bertie County voters had maintained their preference for Whig candidates but gave Pool only a slight majority—51.7 percent of the votes cast, versus 48.3 percent for Ellis.[23]

By October the likelihood of a Lincoln victory in the upcoming election increased, and the national campaign became a question of union or disunion. In North Carolina, Whigs held numerous meetings to promote John Bell's candidacy, although they knew that in all probability he would not win the election.[24]

While the Whigs worked to build support for Bell, certain citizens began to view secession as the appropriate action North Carolina should take if Abraham Lincoln were elected president. On October 14 an undetermined number of Bertie County citizens, along with residents of the nearby counties of Halifax, Martin, and Edgecombe, attended a secessionist "convention" in the small community of Palmyra in Halifax County. The "delegates" to the "convention" were primarily influential men of the counties. According to an account of the gathering, "Crowds of men of all conditions and walks in life, from the great slaveholders of the Roanoke Valley to the humblest, poorest man in the neighborhood, thronged the village and the adjacent groves, manifesting deep and serious interest in the great momentous questions of the times." The "delegates" nominated as chairman of the meeting Thomas Jones of Martin County; Jones, in a "brief, incisive speech, pointed out the evils of the hours, and . . . portrayed in gloomy colors the threatening troubles hanging like a dark funeral pall over the institutions and the destinies of the Southern people."

Gen. David Clark of Halifax County spoke at the meeting and spiritedly predicted that Lincoln would be elected. The general declared: "The hour has struck. The enemy is upon us. The time for action, decisive action, is at hand. . . . We must act . . . with all the sublime courage of heroes and martyrs. There is nothing that stands between us now and our deadliest foes—the abolitionists and disunionists of the New England States, for the Democrats have played the devil and the Whigs have gone to hell."

Other men spoke and debated issues of importance until a committee was appointed to formulate a platform of resolutions of the views of the people. The committee developed a two-resolution platform that (1) upheld a state's right to secede, citing the fact that the New England states were the first to proclaim such a right during the Revolutionary period, and (2) renounced all allegiances to the United States government and appealed to the North Carolina legislature to call a convention for the purpose of withdrawing the state from the Union. The latter resolution also called for North Carolina to form an alliance with the southern states and the emperor of France. The "delegates" unanimously adopted the resolutions and adjourned the "convention."[25]

The majority of North Carolina's citizens did not share those views. Many people were seriously concerned over the prospect of Lincoln's being elected, but North Carolinians as a whole, including the majority of Bertie County's citizens, did not view Lincoln's election as sufficient cause for the state to break its bond with the Union.[26]

On November 6, 1860, 995 Bertie County white men went to the polls and cast their presidential ballots. John Bell received a majority, with 579 votes (58.2 percent). John C. Breckinridge received 399 ballots (40.1 percent), and Stephen A. Douglas received only 17 votes (1.7 percent). Abraham Lincoln was not on the ballot in North Carolina and thus received no votes.[27] Bertie County voters, in the midst of the political crisis, had once again voted non-Democratic and voiced a majority position of support for the Union.

Although Bell received a majority of the votes, the results within the county's districts were not consistent. Bell received majorities in five districts, including the county's largest districts of Windsor and Colerain. Breckinridge carried three districts—Salmon Creek, Snakebite, and Mitchell's—reflecting "pockets" of citizens within the county whose support of the Democratic Party and its ideals exceeded support for the unionist principles espoused by the Whigs in the guise of the Constitutional Union Party.

Table 8
Bertie County 1860 Presidential Voting Results, by District

District	Bell		Breckinridge		Douglas	
	Votes	Percentage	Votes	Percentage	Votes	Percentage
Colerain	135	71.1	52	27.4	3	1.6
Hotel	60	82.2	13	17.3	0	0.0
Mitchell's	16	25.4	43	68.3	4	6.3
Roxobel	36	62.1	20	34.5	2	3.4
Salmon Creek	51	46.8	58	53.2	0	0.0
Snakebite	15	18.8	65	81.3	0	0.0
White's	38	63.3	22	36.7	0	0.0
Windsor	228	63.0	126	34.8	8	2.2
Totals	579	58.2	399	40.1	17	1.7

Source: Bertie County 1860 Presidential Election Returns, State Archives.

While Bertie County's overall support for John Bell was consistent with its past voter preferences, its support for the Tennessean contrasted sharply with the overall voting pattern in North Carolina's high slave-owning counties (including Bertie)—those counties in which slaves comprised at least 50 percent of the total population in 1860. Overall, Bell received 38.2 percent of the vote in high slave-owning counties, whereas he received 54.8 percent in the low slave-owning counties.[28]

Bertie County's 58.2 percent for Bell—twenty percentage points higher than the overall results for him in high slave-owning counties—exceeded his overall support in the state's low slave-owning counties by almost 3.5 percentage points.[29]

Thirty-two other counties in North Carolina provided majority votes for Bell, but overall the state supported Breckinridge, providing him 48,533 votes (50.9 percent), while Bell finished a relatively close second with 44,039 votes (46.2 percent).[30] As most southerners had feared, Lincoln was elected president even though he did not receive a majority of the nation's popular vote and did not receive a single vote from ten southern states.

Immediately after Lincoln's election, South Carolina began making arrangements to secede from the Union. On November 10 the state's legislature enacted a law calling for a convention to meet at Columbia on December 17 to consider the question of secession. On November 13 the legislature resolved to raise ten thousand volunteers for the state's defense.[31]

The election of Lincoln created dismay among North Carolinians, but they did not propose to take part in initiating a destruction of the federal government. The North Carolina legislature assembled on November 19, and there soon appeared two distinct factions—the secessionists, who favored immediate action by North Carolina, and the unionists or conservatives, who saw no reason to withdraw from the Union. Two Bertie County legislators—Sen. David Outlaw and Rep. Peyton T. Henry—were among the leaders who staunchly supported the Union.[32]

During November and early December, Union meetings were held in various North Carolina counties, including Bertie. Overall, the state's citizens maintained a conservative attitude and were willing to await the course of events in the nation instead of actively campaigning for secession.[33] On December 8 Bertie County citizens assembled at the courthouse in Windsor, the county seat, "for the purpose of expressing their sentiments in respect to the present distractions in the country." Lewis Thompson, an old-line Whig and former state senator; Samuel Blount Spruill, a former state legislator; and John Pool, the unsuccessful candidate in the most recent North Carolina gubernatorial election, addressed the meeting, and a number of influential and respected citizens of the county, including planters Augustus Holley, James L. Mitchell, and John Perry, lawyer Thomas Miles Garrett, and physician William T. Sutton, attended. The participants formed a committee to draft resolutions representing their pro-Union position; the resolutions were to be "entirely without political party distinction."

While the committee retired to formulate the resolutions, John Pool "was called out" and made a strong speech supporting the Union. The citizens heartily approved of Pool's remarks and interrupted him on a number of occasions with "rapturous applause." According to an account of the event, Pool, "dispassionate, strong in argument and . . . with fervent patriotic sentiments," took issue with secession as being "unwarranted by the Constitution, as resolving itself in practice into revolution and unmanly desertion" of the citizens' rights in the Union. Pool particularly condemned the actions of South Carolina's leaders as "arrogant in the extreme toward some of her sister states" and as "rash and precipitate" in making no effort at reaching a peaceable solution to the difficulties confronting the nation. He appealed to the citizens present "not to yield their attachment to the Union, but to adhere to it until all possible peaceable means" were exhausted.

Next, Samuel B. Spruill "arose and made a short but very forcible speech," in which he depicted the "horrors of the civil war and bloodshed which seemed to be so near at hand." He denounced the doctrines of the "fanatics at the North" and the "disunionists of the South" as equally treasonable and argued that the best security for the people's liberties "was to be found in a quiet and orderly submission to the Constitution and the law." Both Pool and Spruill condemned the "scheme" of calling a convention in North Carolina to consider secession or to encourage South Carolina in its movement toward holding such a convention. "From the applause with which this sentiment was greeted, [it was judged] there was a pretty unanimous opinion . . . against any such measure."

After Pool and Spruill had spoken, the resolutions committee returned and submitted its "report," which was read to the citizens and "unanimously adopted." The resolutions proclaimed that Bertie County citizens were "devotedly attached" to the Union and the Constitution and considered them "sacred," that each individual was "bound by his allegiances to respect and maintain" the Constitution's authority, and that no state could "rightfully absolve the citizens from obligation" to the Constitution. The resolutions viewed any attempt at nullification or secession as "revolutionary in its character, of evil tendency, and . . . destructive to [the citizens'] liberty and happiness."

The report conveyed the citizens' position that secession or disunion was not the appropriate remedy for "any of the evils" under which the nation was laboring and that secession by any state, in the citizens' overall opinion, would embroil the nation in the "horrors of civil war and bloodshed" and lead to "common ruin." Bertie's citizens were not prepared "in mind or heart to embrace these consequences" and "hope[d]" that the members of the state legislature would oppose any scheme to commit North Carolina to secession.

Furthermore, the citizens of Bertie opposed the assembling of a convention to consider secession and in the resolution committee's report directed the county's representatives in the state legislature to vote against any "kindred measure" that might support such a convention. The citizens—although seriously concerned over Abraham Lincoln's election to the presidency—did not view Lincoln's election, in itself, as sufficient cause for dissolution of the Union but instead declared that dissolution "should be resorted to only because of actual oppression."

After the report was read, Lewis Thompson arose and supported it "in a very powerful speech," conveying his earnest concern for the fate of the country. According to a newspaper account, "there was no one present who was not carried away by the strong array of facts and arguments so admirably and clearly enforced." Thompson fully recognized "the perilous condition of the country and dwelt upon the danger of precipitate action, or hastening that issue, which must result in civil revolution before time can be given for that cool deliberation in which he founded his hopes for . . . safety."

Following Thompson's inspiring speech, the assembled group unanimously adopted the committee's resolutions; ordered that Thomas Miles Garrett, the meeting's secretary, furnish the proceedings of the meeting to the Raleigh *North Carolina Standard* and the *Raleigh Register* for publication; and directed that a copy of the resolutions be sent to each Bertie County representative in the state legislature, along with a request that the resolutions be presented to each house of the General Assembly.[34] Thus, in early December, before any state had withdrawn from the Union, the citizens of Bertie County voiced their sentiments, unequivocally supporting the Union and the Constitution.

On December 20, twelve days after the citizens' meeting in Windsor and slightly more than six weeks after Lincoln was elected, the fiery secessionist leaders of South Carolina withdrew their state from the Union.[35] Despite the deepening crisis and the gloomy prospect that additional states might secede, the citizens of Bertie County maintained their staunch support for the Union. Five days after South Carolina seceded, Kenneth Rayner, a former prominent Whig state senator and United States congressman, wrote to North Carolina chief justice Thomas Ruffin that the feeling of the citizens of Bertie County and other nearby counties was "in a great measure in favour of the 'Union at any and all hazards'—in other words, unqualified submission." Rayner informed Ruffin that he had heard from "several sources, that the people who did not own slaves were swearing that they would not lift a finger to protect rich men's negroes."[36]

The secession of South Carolina increased the anxiety of Bertie County residents. On January 3, 1861, Charles Smallwood, a prominent Bertie County citizen, privately recorded in his personal diary: "S. Carolina has seceded from the Union on account of Lincolns election & a civil war is expected. Well—none can tell what will be the end. Tomorrow Friday the 4th is the day appointed by the President as a day of fasting & prayer that God may avert such a calamity & restore unity & harmony."[37]

In January 1861 Mississippi, Florida, Alabama, and Georgia seceded from the Union. The rapid secession of those states increased pressure on the North Carolina General Assembly to call a convention to consider the question of withdrawal.[38] David Outlaw, Bertie County's state senator, believing that no state had the right to secede from the Union, vigorously opposed the bill to place the question of a secession convention before the people.[39] Peyton T. Henry, Bertie County's representative in the state house of commons, likewise opposed the calling of a secession convention. Addressing the house on January 17, Henry declared:

We need calmness and moderation. Let the head, heart and time unite, and I trust North Carolina may yet prove to be one to step forth with the olive branch of peace. My voice to-day is for conciliation and in this I speak the feelings of those whom I represent. I, . . . for my people, and myself, condemn the calling of a Convention for the open and avowed purpose to vote North Carolina out of the Union. . . . For eight days, I have quietly sat in my seat and listened to able speeches for and against the Union, while many noble things have been said for the Union, yet I have been pained to my very heart to hear the strains of ridicule and damning contempt heaped upon the Union.[40]

The citizens of Bertie County fully supported their elected representatives' positions. During January, Outlaw's and Henry's constituents met publicly and voiced their opposition to a secession convention.[41] The majority of North Carolina's legislators did not agree with Outlaw and Henry, however. On January 29 the General Assembly adopted a bill directing the people to vote on February 28 to consider whether a secession convention should be held.[42]

In early February, Peyton T. Henry appealed to the citizens of Bertie County to vote against the secession convention. In a passionate statement published in the *Raleigh Register* on February 6, Henry wrote:

You are [being] asked by your fellow countrymen what will you do to help save the State and the Union. That question is now put to you, and that question you must answer on the 28th day of February, 1861. I doubt not your response will be right, and in favor of the Union. You are called upon by an act of the Legislature to elect delegates to a Convention . . . for the purpose of deciding whether the State of N. Carolina shall remain longer a member of the Union, or, like other States, shall she drift off in an unknown and untried political field. All the States that have called Conventions, up to this date, have passed secession ordinances and left the Union. . . . [Y]ou cannot, and will not cast your votes on the 28th of February in favor of any man as a delegate to the Convention whose love for the State and the Union admit of the slightest shade of doubt or suspicion. . . . Entrust your safety in the hands of no man who refuses to openly and freely proclaim to you his attachment to the State and the Union.[43]

On February 28, 1861, 770 Bertie County men went to the polls and, by a vote of 632 to 138 (a greater than four-to-one margin), voted against a convention to consider secession. The voters elected two Union delegates—Lewis Thompson and Thomas J. Pugh—to represent the county at a secession convention if North Carolina voters decided that one should be held.[44] Thompson and Pugh never served as delegates to a secession convention, however. North Carolina voters defeated the convention proposal by 651 votes, or a mere seven-tenths of 1 percent of the votes cast. They cast 47,323 votes against a convention to 46,672 votes in favor of one. But, more indicative of the strong Union sentiment in the state, the citizens elected seventy-eight Union delegates (versus forty-two secessionist delegates) to attend a convention if one were to be held.[45]

After the convention vote, North Carolinians maintained their conservative "watch and wait" posture. As of the end of February, only states of the lower South, in which the plantation system was much more firmly entrenched in the social and economic order than in North Carolina, had withdrawn from the Union. On March 18, 1861, Arkansas withdrew and joined its sister states of the lower South in the Confederate States of America.[46]

Armed confrontation proved to be inevitable. At 4:30 in the morning on Friday, April 12, Confederate batteries around Charleston Harbor opened fire on federally held Fort Sumter.[47] The American Civil War officially began. As Confederate artillerists poured shell after shell into the besieged fort, the citizens of Bertie County, unaware that hostilities had commenced, still hoped that war would be avoided. On April 13 Charles Smallwood recorded in his diary the fear and sentiments of many of the county's residents: "War is thought inevitable. May God in mercy avert it."[48] Maj. George Anderson, the Union commander of Fort Sumter, surrendered the fort to the Confederate forces on that day.[49]

Smallwood traveled to Windsor on April 15 and learned from newspaper accounts that Confederate forces had attacked Fort Sumter three days previously. Everyone in Windsor was excited about the war news. Smallwood returned to his home near Woodville and, realizing that peaceful and joyful times were over, wrote in his diary: "Papers state the war began at Charleston[.] Fort Sumter was attacked the 12th[.] joy go[es] with it."[50]

News of the beginning of war at Charleston quickly spread throughout the county. Citizens gathered in the small communities of Windsor, Colerain, and Woodville and at crossroads throughout the county to read and discuss the newspaper accounts of the attack on Fort Sumter. They undoubtedly pondered what the future held for them and their country, a country whose dissolution they had opposed.

On April 20 Charles Smallwood again went to Windsor, where everyone was captivated by the "war news." The citizens were uneasy over the prospects of the escalation of hostilities and the uncertainty of the future. On that day, Smallwood wrote in his diary: "Will know in the next 10 or 20 days what to expect. Apprehend war in time."[51] In fact, North Carolina had already begun moving toward secession.

On April 15 President Lincoln had issued a proclamation calling for seventy-five thousand troops to suppress the rebellion in the lower-South states of South Carolina, Georgia, Alabama, Florida, Mississippi, Louisiana, and Texas. The president appealed to "all loyal citizens to favor, facilitate, and aid this effort to maintain the honor, the integrity, and the existence of our National Union." But the president's appeal fell on deaf ears in Raleigh, North Carolina's capital. On that same day, Secretary of War Simon Cameron telegraphed North Carolina governor John Ellis to request a quota of two regiments of militia to rendezvous in Raleigh. Ellis quickly and emphatically responded to the secretary that he could "be no party to this wicked violation of the laws of the country, and to this war upon the liberties of a free people. You can get no troops from North Carolina."[52]

The governor also ordered North Carolina citizens to seize Federal property in the state, including the coastal forts. He called the General Assembly into a special session for the purpose of authorizing a statewide election for a secession convention. Ellis also advised the Confederate government that North Carolina would unselfishly furnish troops for the Southern cause, pending approval by the General Assembly when it met. On April 25 Ellis advised Confederate president Jefferson Davis: "You are at entire liberty to open recruiting stations, as you may desire, in North Carolina."[53]

On April 17, two days after Lincoln's call for troops, Virginia seceded from the Union. On April 19 Lincoln declared a blockade of the states of the lower South, excluding the recently seceded upper-South state of Virginia, but on April 27 he expanded the blockade to include Virginia and North Carolina. Even though North Carolina had not left the Union, Lincoln decided to block the state's ports.[54] The citizens of Bertie County, like those throughout North Carolina, viewed the seriousness of the rapidly occurring events with grave concern. Charles Smallwood wrote in his diary on April 24: "War news getting quite serious. . . . Gov Ellis has called an extra session of the legislature to meet the 1st of May. What the end will be I cannot say."[55]

Many citizens of North Carolina already knew that the state would leave the Union and actively began efforts to raise troops. Overt unionism virtually ceased within Bertie County. On April 27 county citizens met in Windsor to issue a "call for volunteers" to serve in the Confederate army. Patrick H. Winston Sr., an influential Bertie County lawyer, presided over the meeting, during which he, David Outlaw, Lewis Thompson, Thomas Miles Garrett, Francis Wilder Bird, Joseph B. Cherry, and others made "Speeches of the strongest tone, in defence of our homes and firesides." Garrett, who only a few months

In December 1860 Thomas Miles Garrett, a Bertie County Whig and lawyer, was a staunch unionist, but by April 1861 he had reluctantly concluded that North Carolina must withdraw from the Union. Garrett, one of the first men in Bertie to volunteer for Confederate service, organized Company F, Fifth Regiment North Carolina State Troops, which was composed largely of men from Bertie. Engraving from Walter Clark, *Histories of the Several Regiments and Battalions from North Carolina in the Great War, 1861–'65,* 5 vols. (Raleigh: State of North Carolina, 1901), 1: facing 281.

previously had publicly supported the Union and who would later distinguish himself as a Confederate army officer, was one of the first men to volunteer.[56]

At the April 27 meeting the county raised its first company of Confederate soldiers.[57] Jesse Copeland Jacocks, a recent resident of the county, commanded the company. Jacocks, a twenty-seven-year-old planter and native of Perquimans County, had attended the United States Military Academy at West Point, New York, for five months in 1852 and 1853.[58] In early May, Jacocks traveled to Raleigh and tendered the service of his company to the state.[59] Governor Ellis granted him a captain's commission, and his company, which consisted of ninety-six men, including himself, became known as the "Bertie Volunteers."[60]

The "Bertie Volunteers," typical of military companies raised throughout the South during the early stages of the conflict, was comprised predominantly of young men. Twenty-one teenagers enlisted in the company, while seventy-four members—78 percent of the company—were under the age of twenty-five. In contrast to the youthful volunteers, one soldier—fifty-three-year-old Pvt. John H. Gilliam—was the "old man" of the company.[61]

The citizens pledged four thousand dollars at the April 27 meeting to help finance the cost of equipment and other necessities for the county's soldiers. The *Raleigh Register* later reported that the "most determined resistance to coercion is the settled course of every man in Bertie County without respect to party." Another meeting was scheduled to be held one week later, when about fifty more volunteers were expected to come forward.[62]

On May 1 the North Carolina General Assembly met pursuant to Governor Ellis's call and took only ninety minutes to authorize a secession convention for May 20 in Raleigh. The lawmakers set May 13 as the day North Carolinians were to vote for delegates to the convention.[63]

By early May the citizens of Bertie County were actively making military preparations. The Woodville militia met on May 4 and elected officers, selecting John G. Fraim as its captain. Over the next few days other units of the county's militia met, mustering some citizens for the first time in their lives.[64] On May 7 Col. Jonathan Jacocks Rhodes, commander of the Bertie County militia, wrote Governor Ellis that the county's militia was being organized and that "a good many young men" were "ready and willing to offer their services."[65] By May 8 the citizens of Bertie County, thoroughly aroused over Lincoln's actions, reportedly pledged ten thousand dollars for equipping the county's volunteers and supporting those soldiers' families that needed assistance.[66] Charles Smallwood reported approximately 175 volunteers—for both the militia and Confederate army—in the county.[67] He predicted that at the secession convention to be held on the twentieth, North Carolina would "slide out of the Union like a shot out of a shovel."[68]

Amid the excitement that prevailed throughout the county during the early days of May, some citizens continued to hope and pray that the dreadful crisis facing the country would somehow be averted. On May 4 and 5, members of Colerain Baptist Church fasted and prayed "to avert the impending crisis which pervaded the country."[69] Others appeared to be enthralled by the excitement of a pending confrontation with the "Yankees." Influential citizens of the county such as Jesse C. Jacocks, Jonathan J. Rhodes, and Thomas Miles Garrett urged the county's young men to enlist.

In addition to men, various other resources—clothing, food, horses, arms, and vessels—were needed from throughout the state to support the fledgling Southern cause. In a May 9 letter to Governor Ellis, Marshall Parks, president of the Albemarle and Chesapeake Canal Company, identified a number of privately owned steamers in the Albemarle Sound region that were suitable for conversion to gunboats. Parks advised Ellis that one such vessel, the *Alice*, was located on the Cashie River in Bertie County.[70] Balda Ashburn Capehart of Bertie owned the *Alice*, but Lafayette Thrower, a resident of Windsor, operated the vessel. Thrower used the boat to transport goods within the Albemarle Sound and connecting tributaries.[71] (The Confederate government later enlisted the services of Thrower and the steamer.)

On May 13 Bertie County voters went to the polls to elect delegates to the state's secession convention, which was to be held one week later. The voters chose Samuel B. Spruill, a fifty-year-old former Whig state representative, and James Bond, a thirty-year-old planter, to represent the county. Both men had originally opposed secession.[72] At the convention the delegates quickly consummated the urgent business of the day and by unanimous consent withdrew North Carolina from the Union.[73] No other decision ever had such dire consequences for the people of Bertie County.

Heavy rain fell in Bertie County on May 20, as if to mark the beginning of dreary times for its citizens.[74] It was only the first of many "dark and gloomy" days that the county's citizens would endure during the next four years. The nation was at war with itself.

Notes

1. Robert Underwood Johnson and Clarence Clough Buel, eds., *Battles and Leaders of the Civil War*, 4 vols. (New York: Century Co., 1884–1888), 1:1 (hereafter cited as *Battles and Leaders*); William H. Price, *Civil War Handbook* (Fairfax, Va.: L. B. Prince Co., 1961), 2.

2. *Battles and Leaders*, 1:1; James M. McPherson, *Battle Cry of Freedom: The Civil War Era* (New York: Oxford University Press, 1988), 221; Frontis W. Johnston, ed., *The Papers of Zebulon Baird Vance* (Raleigh: State Department of Archives and History, 1963), 1:68–69 (hereafter cited as Johnston, *Vance Papers*).

3. *Battles and Leaders*, 1:1.

4. *Battles and Leaders*, 1:1.

5. McPherson, *Battle Cry of Freedom*, 223; Wayne K. Durrill, *War of Another Kind: A Southern Community in the Great Rebellion* (New York: Oxford University Press, 1990), 21.

6. Eighth Census of the United States, 1860: Bertie County, North Carolina, Population, Slave, and Agriculture Schedules, National Archives, Washington, D.C. (hereafter cited as Eighth Census, 1860: Bertie County, with appropriate schedule or schedules).

7. Charles H. Wesley and Patricia W. Romero, *Afro-Americans in the Civil War: From Slavery to Citizenship* (Washington, D.C.: Association for the Study of Afro-American Life and History, 1976), 18.

8. Eighth Census, 1860: Bertie County, Agriculture Schedule. During the 1859 growing season Bertie County planters and farmers produced, among other commodities, 718,000 bushels of corn, 108,000 bushels of sweet potatoes, 81,000 bushels of peas and beans, and 6,670 four-hundred-pound bales of cotton. County residents owned approximately 65,700 head of livestock (horses, cows, oxen, swine, and so on).

9. Bertie County Tax Lists, 1860, State Archives, Division of Archives and History, Raleigh (hereafter cited as Bertie County 1860 Tax Lists); Cornelius O. Cathey, *Agriculture in North Carolina Before the Civil War* (Raleigh: State Department of Archives and History, 1966), 44.

10. Eighth Census, 1860: Bertie County, Population Schedule; Joseph Carlyle Sitterson, *The Secession Movement in North Carolina* (Chapel Hill: University of North Carolina Press, 1939), 7–8.

11. Eighth Census, 1860: Bertie County, Slave Schedule.

12. Sitterson, *Secession Movement in North Carolina*, 5.

13. Rosser Howard Taylor, *Slaveholding in North Carolina: An Economic View* (Chapel Hill: University of North Carolina Press, 1926), 49; Eighth Census, 1860: Bertie County, Agriculture Schedule.

14. Eighth Census, 1860: Bertie County, Slave Schedule; Cathey, *Agriculture in North Carolina*, 44; Taylor, *Slaveholding in North Carolina*, 46. According to historians' definitions, "planters" were considered slave owners with twenty or more slaves, while "large planters" owned fifty or more slaves. (Those definitions appear in William C. Harris, *North Carolina and the Coming of the Civil War* [Raleigh: Division of Archives and History, North Carolina Department of Cultural Resources, 1988], 6.) Using those defi-

nitions, 110 Bertie County slave owners can be considered "planters"; of that number, thirty-six can be characterized as "large planters."

15. Eighth Census, 1860: Bertie County, Slave and Agriculture Schedules; Bertie County 1860 Tax Lists.

16. Eighth Census, 1860: Bertie County, Slave Schedule; Taylor, *Slaveholding in North Carolina*, 46.

17. Clarence Clifford Norton, *The Democratic Party in Ante-Bellum North Carolina, 1835–1861* (Chapel Hill: University of North Carolina Press, 1930), 203, 205–207; Cathey, *Agriculture in North Carolina*, 44.

18. Harris, *North Carolina and the Coming of the Civil War*, 11, 31–33.

19. John L. Cheney Jr., ed., *North Carolina Government, 1585–1979: A Narrative and Statistical History* (Raleigh: North Carolina Department of the Secretary of State, 1981), 1330, 1398, 1400.

20. Harris, *North Carolina and the Coming of the Civil War*, 30.

21. Bertie County Marriage Certificates, Register of Deeds Office, Windsor. John Pool married M. E. Mebane on December 15, 1857.

22. Cheney, *North Carolina Government*, 1401.

23. Cheney, *North Carolina Government*, 1400.

24. Harris, *North Carolina and the Coming of the Civil War*, 32–33.

25. Unidentified newspaper quoted in James H. McCallum, *Martin County During the Civil War* (Williamston: Enterprise Publishing Company, 1971), 6–8.

26. John Gilchrist Barrett, *North Carolina as a Civil War Battleground, 1861–1865* (Raleigh: Division of Archives and History, North Carolina Department of Cultural Resources, 1980), 1; W. Buck Yearns and John G. Barrett, eds., *North Carolina Civil War Documentary* (Chapel Hill: University of North Carolina Press, 1980), 5.

27. Bertie County Presidential Election Returns—1860, North Carolina Division of Archives and History (hereafter cited as Presidential Election Returns—1860).

28. Daniel W. Crofts, *Reluctant Confederates: Upper South Unionists in the Secession Crisis* (Chapel Hill: University of North Carolina Press, 1989), 46.

29. Presidential Election Returns—1860.

30. Cheney, *North Carolina Government*, 1330–1331.

31. E. B. Long, *The Civil War Day by Day: An Almanac, 1861–1865* (New York: Da Capo Press, 1971), 4–5.

32. Yearns and Barrett, *North Carolina Civil War Documentary*, 8; John G. Barrett, *The Civil War in North Carolina* (Chapel Hill: University of North Carolina Press, 1963), 3–5; Sitterson, *Secession Movement in North Carolina*, 182.

33. Sitterson, *Secession Movement in North Carolina*, 195.

34. *Raleigh North Carolina Standard*, December 20, 1860.

35. Long, *The Civil War Day by Day*, 12–13.

36. Kenneth Rayner to Thomas Ruffin, December 25, 1860, quoted in Norton, *The Democratic Party in North Carolina*, 204–205.

37. Diary of Charles Smallwood, January 3, 1861, Southern Historical Collection, University of North Carolina Library, Chapel Hill (hereafter cited as Smallwood diary).

38. Barrett, *Civil War Battleground*, 6.

39. Sitterson, *Secession Movement in North Carolina*, 182; Joseph G. de Roulhac Hamilton, *Reconstruction in North Carolina* (1914; reprinted, Freeport, N.Y.: Books for Libraries Press, 1971), 17.

40. *Semi-weekly Raleigh Register,* January 30, 1861.

41. Sitterson, *Secession Movement in North Carolina*, 206.

42. Barrett, *Civil War Battleground*, 6.

43. *Raleigh Register*, February 6, 1861.

44. Crofts, *Reluctant Confederates*, 150; Marc W. Kruman, *Parties and Politics in North Carolina, 1836–1865* (Baton Rouge: Louisiana State University Press, 1983), appendix B; Bertie County Convention Vote Returns, February 28, 1861, State Archives.

45. Sitterson, *Secession Movement in North Carolina*, 223–224.

46. Long, *The Civil War Day by Day*, 50.

47. Arthur M. Wilcox and Warren Ripley, *The Civil War at Charleston* (Charleston, S.C.: the *News Courier* and the *Evening Post*, 1991), 15.

48. Smallwood diary, April 13, 1861.

49. Wilcox and Ripley, *The Civil War at Charleston*, 19.

50. Smallwood diary, April 15, 1861.

51. Smallwood diary, April 20, 1861.

52. *The War of the Rebellion: A Compilation of the Official Records of the Union and Confederate Armies*, ser. 3, 1:67–69 (hereafter cited as *Official Records . . . Armies*); Simon Cameron to John W. Ellis (telegram), April 15, 1861, and John W. Ellis to Simon Cameron (telegram), April 15, 1861, in Noble J. Tolbert, ed., *The Papers of John Willis Ellis*, 2 vols. (Raleigh: State Department of Archives and History, 1964), 2:612 (hereafter cited as Tolbert, *Ellis Papers*).

53. Harris, *North Carolina and the Coming of the Civil War*, 50–54; John W. Ellis to Jefferson Davis, April 25, 1861, in Tolbert, *Ellis Papers*, 2:678–679.

54. Long, *The Civil War Day by Day*, 60–62, 66. Realistically, Lincoln had no choice but to blockade North Carolina's coastline and ports once Virginia seceded, inasmuch as the Old North State's neighbors to the north and south had withdrawn from the Union. If North Carolina's coastline had not been blockaded, the state would most certainly have served as an easily accessible conduit for goods and supplies to the Confederate states.

55. Smallwood diary, April 24, 1861.

56. William A. Ferguson to John W. Ellis, April 29, 1861, in Tolbert, *Ellis Papers*, 2:694; Smallwood diary, April 27, 1861; *Semi-Weekly Raleigh Register*, May 18, 1861.

57. William A. Ferguson to John W. Ellis, April 29, 1861, in Tolbert, *Ellis Papers*, 2:694; *Semi-Weekly Raleigh Register*, May 18, 1861.

58. Susan P. Walker, United States Military Academy Archives, West Point, N.Y., letter to author, May 14, 1992; application papers of Jesse C. Jacocks, United States Military Academy Cadet Application Papers, 1805–1866, Record Group 94, National Archives; William Picard Jacocks, *Descendants of Thomas Jacocks who died in 1692 in Perquimans Precinct, North Carolina* (privately published, date and place missing), 27–28.

59. *Raleigh Register*, May 8, 1861.

60. Manarin and Jordan, *North Carolina Troops*, 3:57–58.

61. Manarin and Jordan, *North Carolina Troops*, 3:57–61.

62. William A. Ferguson to John W. Ellis, April 29, 1861, in Tolbert, *Ellis Papers*, 2:694; *Semi-Weekly Raleigh Register*, May 18, 1861. The author has been unable to determine whether or not such a gathering took place on May 4, 1861 (one week after the April 27 meeting).

63. Barrett, *The Civil War in North Carolina*, 14–15.

64. Smallwood diary, May 4, 8, 1861.

65. J. J. Rhodes to John W. Ellis, May 7, 1861, in Tolbert, *Ellis Papers*, 2:730.

66. *Raleigh Register*, May 8, 1861.

67. Smallwood diary, May 8, 1861.

68. Smallwood diary, May 3, 1861.

69. Colerain Baptist Church Records, 1821–1909, May 1861, Special Collections Library, Duke University, Durham.

70. Marshall Parks to John W. Ellis, May 9, 1861, in Tolbert, *Ellis Papers*, 2:733.

71. *"Confederate Tax Census" for Bertie County, North Carolina, 1862* (Windsor: United States history class, 1975–1976, Roanoke Chowan Academy, n.d.; hereafter cited as *Bertie County Confederate Tax Census*); Eighth Census, 1860: Bertie County, Population Schedule.

72. John G. McCormick, *Personnel of the Convention of 1861* (Chapel Hill: University of North Carolina Press, 1900), 78–79.

73. Sitterson, *Secession Movement in North Carolina*, 247.

74. Smallwood diary, May 20, 1861.

CHAPTER 2

Volunteers and "play soldiers"

In May 1861 Bertie County's military-age men, having never experienced hostile military action, had no realization of the tragedy of war or the hardships that accompanied military service. Dozens of the county's sons, youthfully enthusiastic and patriotic to the Southern cause, began volunteering for the military companies being organized in Bertie.

Capt. Jesse C. Jacocks's "Bertie Volunteers," having received orders from the North Carolina Adjutant General's office on May 24, marched out of Windsor on May 29 destined for the recently established camp of military instruction at Garysburg in nearby Northampton County. The company marched to Colerain, on the Chowan River, where on May 30 it boarded the Albemarle Steamboat Company's steamer *Sea Bird* for the trip up the Chowan and Blackwater Rivers to Franklin, Virginia. From Franklin the company traveled by train to Garysburg, where it was eventually assigned to the First Regiment North Carolina Infantry and designated Company L.[1]

In mid-June, as recruiting efforts were under way in the county, news arrived that on June 10 a small Confederate force commanded by Col. John B. Magruder had defeated a much larger Federal force led by Maj. Gen. Benjamin Franklin Butler at Big Bethel, near Yorktown, Virginia. That news buoyed the citizens' hopes for a quick Southern victory. While the affair at Big Bethel was not militarily significant, Bertie County citizens viewed it as "quite a battle," in which the "enemy retreated."[2] The news was encouraging.

Throughout June, Thomas Miles Garrett, the thirty-one-year-old Colerain lawyer who only six months previously had publicly opposed secession at a citizens' meeting in Windsor, recruited Bertie County men for a volunteer company he was organizing. On May 16—four days before the state seceded—Gov. John W. Ellis granted Garrett, a graduate of the University of North Carolina, a captain's commission. On June 20 a "general muster" of county men was held in Windsor to recruit volunteers.[3] Garrett obtained only seven recruits on that day, but by July 3 he had enlisted seventy men, including four from Hertford County.[4] That number was sufficient to constitute a company.

At Colerain on July 5 Garrett and his volunteers boarded the steamer *Sea Bird*, which five weeks earlier had taken the "Bertie Volunteers" away from the county. Like the "Bertie Volunteers," Garrett and his company traveled to Franklin.[5] From Franklin, Garrett's company traveled overland to Camp Winslow, Halifax County, where it was assigned to the Fifth Regiment North Carolina State Troops and designated Company F.[6] Sixteen days after departing the county, Garrett's company was at Manassas, Virginia, and, as part of Brig. Gen. James Longstreet's brigade, came under Federal artillery fire. The members of the company sustained no casualties but had quickly been exposed to the hostilities and perils of combat.

After Garrett had organized his company, two Northampton County residents—John Randolph and Henry B. Hardy—came to Bertie County and recruited men for a cavalry company they were organizing. Between July 3 and 9, Randolph and Hardy enlisted thirty Bertie County residents for their company, which became Company H of the Nineteenth Regiment North Carolina Troops (Second Regiment North Carolina Cavalry). On August 30, 1861, the North Carolina legislature authorized Samuel B. Spruill of Bertie County to be colonel of that regiment.[7] By the middle of July the initial flurry of enlistments in the county had ended. From late April through mid-July, approximately 220 Bertie County men volunteered for Confederate service and left for state camps of military instruction.[8]

Simultaneously with the organization of volunteer companies for Confederate service, county officials began reorganizing and revitalizing the civilian militia. By the spring of 1861, the Bertie County militia, along with similar organizations in other North Carolina counties, had deteriorated into a state of disarray and military uselessness, primarily from years of inactivity. North Carolina still retained the enrolled militia system, which relied upon the outdated and increasingly impractical concept of mandatory service. By the time the Civil War erupted, the state's militia had declined to "a condition of utter impotence," having "no actual practical existence" except on paper. Indeed, two years earlier North Carolina's adjutant general, Richard C. Cotten, had reported that the state's militia system was in a "greatly disorganized condition" in the majority of the counties and that his office had received no reports or returns from any of the militia regiments.[9] As part of the reorganization of the militia, the state's Adjutant General's Office on August 16 granted officer's commissions to twenty-four Bertie County men.[10]

Organizing, equipping, and maintaining companies of soldiers was costly. While the state of North Carolina initially assumed primary responsibility for financing its military units, the Confederate government eventually undertook such responsibilities—although communities in which companies were organized often assumed some financial responsibility for their soldiers. Such responsibility could become quite a burden, particularly for communities such as Bertie County, in which many citizens barely had sufficient resources to supply their basic needs. Nevertheless, in June Bertie officials realized the necessity of providing some finances for the county's companies. On June 13 the county magistrates met in a special session at Windsor to address that issue. Recognizing the need for sources of revenue other than subscriptions from the public at large, the magistrates authorized the county government to issue bonds to pay for equipment and provisions for the county's volunteer soldiers. On that date, the county sold four thousand dollars' worth of bonds to William Moring, Whitmel T. Sharrock, and Miss Emily Ryan, all affluent citizens of the county.[11]

The eastern sector of North Carolina is punctuated and indented by five sounds into which flow the major rivers of the Coastal Plain. The sounds—Albemarle, Currituck, Pamlico, Core, and Bogue—in conjunction with the primary rivers—Chowan, Roanoke, Tar, Pamlico, Neuse, and Trent—provide navigational access to almost one-third of the state. Bertie County is situated at the confluence of three of those waterways—the Albemarle Sound and the Roanoke and Chowan Rivers. Early in the war, Federal commanders clearly realized that military control of the eastern sector waterways would drastically impede the ability of North Carolina and the Confederate government to transport military supplies, men, equipment, and stores. Likewise, Confederate and state leaders realized the strategic importance of those waterways to their cause.

Bertie County, in the northern Coastal Plain of eastern North Carolina, is situated at the confluence of three of the state's most important waterways—the Albemarle Sound and the Roanoke and Chowan Rivers. That location quickly made the county important strategically to Union and Confederate forces, which contended for control of the adjacent waterways.

Shortly after North Carolina seceded, the state's leaders began preparing to defend the state's coast and eastern waterways. Fortifications were constructed and strengthened along the Outer Banks. Two fortifications—Forts Hatteras and Clark—were constructed at Hatteras Inlet, as were similar facilities near Oregon and Ocracoke Inlets. Forts Hatteras and Clark were the most important of those installations because they were intended to guard the main inlet into the sounds north of Beaufort.

During the summer, as construction of the forts was progressing, Union general Benjamin F. Butler proposed to the United States War Department that a military expedition be sent to Hatteras Island to destroy a supply depot established there. While the War Department apparently gave little consideration to Butler's proposal, Federal navy commanders viewed it with interest. Eventually, Federal authorities decided that a joint army-navy expedition should be sent to the island with the primary objectives of destroying Forts Hatteras and Clark and obstructing the Hatteras Inlet channel.

On August 26 a Federal squadron of seven warships accompanied by a fleet of transports carrying almost nine hundred soldiers departed Hampton Roads, Virginia. In the afternoon of the next day, the Federal ships arrived off Hatteras Inlet. Commanding the Confederate forces in the immediate area, numbering fewer than four hundred men, was Col. William F. Martin of the Seventeenth Regiment North Carolina Troops. When the Federal fleet appeared, Colonel Martin requested reinforcements from Col. G. W. Johnson, who was sixteen miles away at the community of Portsmouth. On the morning of the twenty-eighth, the warships—mounting 149 cannons—began bombarding Fort Clark. Before noon the Confederates, unable to endure the heavy shelling and having consumed all of their ammunition, abandoned the fort and retired to Fort Hatteras. Federal soldiers landed and immediately occupied the abandoned facility.

During the night, the chief of Confederate coastal defenses, Commodore Samuel Barron, arrived with about 230 reinforcements and replaced Colonel Martin as commander at Fort Hatteras. At daybreak the Federals commenced shelling the fort. The Confederates were unable to withstand the Federal assault and bombardment. Commodore Barron surrendered the fort and its garrison of more than seven hundred men during the morning of the twenty-ninth. The Federal military had achieved its first significant victory of the war.

News of the capture of Hatteras Island was received with great rejoicing in the North, but in the South the loss angered Confederate officials. The Confederate Congress demanded a "truthful account" of what had transpired at Hatteras Island, while North Carolina officials scurried to assign blame for the loss.[12]

In Bertie County, news of the Confederate defeat was received with disgust and sorrow. Charles Smallwood traveled to Woodville on September 1 and learned of the capture of Hatteras Island. Smallwood was particularly moved by the news because two groups of soldiers from neighboring Martin County—Companies F and G, Seventeenth North Carolina—had been involved in the action on the island and had suffered casualties. (Five Bertie County men who had enlisted in several companies of the Seventeenth North Carolina, a regiment whose organizations were raised in the Albemarle Sound region, were captured at Hatteras Island.) Rumors concerning two Confederate officers from Martin County—that Capt. John C. Lamb had had "his arm shot off" and that Capt. Henry A. Gilliam was badly wounded—reached that county.[13] The rumors were false but nonetheless demoralizing to the citizens.

The news of the Confederate defeat at Hatteras Island and the casualties reportedly suffered by the Martin County soldiers brought a somber realism to Bertie County's citizens. No Bertie men had yet been killed or wounded in battle, but it seemed inevitable that some of the county's sons would shed their blood and sacrifice their lives for the Southern cause. The fighting at Hatteras Island prompted the commander of the Bertie County militia, Col. Jonathan Jacocks Rhodes, to call the county's militia to a muster at Windsor on September 4. Charles Smallwood, a member of the militia, viewed that show of militarism with skepticism, sarcastically noting that he did not know what the colonel intended to do.[14]

Rumors circulated within Bertie County that Gov. Henry T. Clark was expected to send the county's militia to Hatteras Island. Charles Smallwood viewed that prospect with grave concern. Smallwood was not impressed with the military capabilities displayed by the county's militiamen, or "play soldiers," as he termed them, and concluded that they would be an inadequate fighting force for confronting Union troops. He recorded in his diary in early September: "I should hate badly to go into battle under such Captains as I see mustering rather play soldiers."[15] Smallwood's fears were not realized, however, inasmuch as the governor did not order the county's militia to go to Hatteras Island.

After capturing the forts at Hatteras Island, General Butler decided that Federal troops should occupy the area. In September he placed Col. Rush C. Hawkins of the Ninth Regiment New York Infantry in command of the Union forces at Hatteras Island.[16] Upon assuming command, Hawkins established a policy of creating friendly relations with the "loyal inhabitants" of the Outer Banks and verbally agreed to provide them protection. Hawkins's policy yielded immediate positive results. By September 7, 250 North Carolinians had reportedly taken the Oath of Allegiance to the United States at Hatteras Island, and others were "still coming in." The people who took the oath agreed to keep Federal military authorities apprised of Confederate movements in the area.[17]

The citizens of Hatteras Island, prior to the war, had exhibited strong Union sentiments when the question of secession had been placed before them during the convention vote of February 1861. At that time, three-fourths of the voters of Hyde County, which included

Hatteras Island, supported the Union and opposed secession.[18] While undoubtedly there was a predisposition among certain citizens to support the Union, the actual occupation by Federal forces made the outright expression of such support much easier and less risky. The news of hundreds of North Carolinians taking the Oath of Allegiance to the United States prompted Governor Clark to inform acting Confederate secretary of war Judah P. Benjamin that the people had taken the oath "under the fear of the enemy's guns."[19] On September 27 Benjamin advised Clark that anyone known to have sworn the Oath of Allegiance to the United States should be indicted for treason.[20]

Hawkins quickly surmised that Hatteras men would also enlist in the Union army. On September 11 he wrote to Maj. Gen. John E. Wool, commander of the Union army's Department of Virginia, that he believed Union troops could be raised at Hatteras Island if assurances could be given that they would not be sent out of the state. Five days later, President Lincoln directed the War Department to prepare an order authorizing the Federal army to recruit North Carolinians at Hatteras Island. The following day, the War Department authorized the commanding officer of United States forces at Hatteras Inlet to accept the services of loyal North Carolinians in the army. The order stipulated that no more than one regiment be recruited and that the recruits, depending on their number, would be formally organized into a battalion or regiment.[21] In spite of the order and for undetermined reasons, no formal efforts to raise a regiment of such soldiers occurred until approximately nine months later.

With Federal forces in control of Hatteras Island, confining them to that immediate location became the desire of North Carolina citizens. On September 11, 1861, the *Raleigh Register* observed:

as long as we can confine [Maj. Gen. Benjamin F.] Butler and his thieves to Hatteras, their victory there amounts to nothing, for they cannot harm us, and the expenses [to them] of keeping the place . . . will be immense, and there they must be kept. . . . If the State authorities will only do their duty and give us the means of defending the coast and protecting the citizens and property thereon, the people will do it. We call upon the Legislature, thereof, not to wait for everything to be done by the Confederate States government, but to take steps themselves to prevent the advance of the invaders.[22]

The Federal military's capture and occupation of Hatteras Island created consternation and anxiety within North Carolina and the Confederate government. Confederate and state officials, along with the citizens of eastern North Carolina, intuitively realized that Roanoke Island, strategically located for controlling navigation in Albemarle and

Pamlico Sounds, would be the Union military's next objective in eastern North Carolina. On September 23 acting Confederate secretary of war Benjamin wired Governor Clark that Pres. Jefferson Davis desired that Clark "call out" the militia of twelve eastern North Carolina counties, including Bertie County.[23] The objective of such a summons is not clear, and, in any event, Clark failed to act upon the president's request.

By October 19 rumors circulated within Bertie County that thirty Union naval vessels with "8,000 Yankees aboard" had entered Pamlico Sound through Hatteras Inlet, intending to attack Roanoke Island.[24] The rumor was false—no Federal fleet had entered Pamlico Sound—but the citizens of Bertie County were thoroughly aroused over their vulnerable location at the head of Albemarle Sound and the rumored existence of Union men-of-war in a connecting waterway.

In September 1861 the North Carolina legislature had passed and Governor Clark had signed a bill to organize the state's militia regiments into brigades. Two regiments—the Eighth and Ninth—were designated in Bertie County and made part of the Second Militia Brigade, which also included the Fifth (Chowan County), Sixth (Hertford County), and Seventh (Gates County) Regiments. The law provided that the governor could draft any militia regiment to fulfill requisitions for troops made by the Confederate government. Additionally, the law made "all free white men and white apprentices," except ministers and certain other designated professionals between the ages of eighteen and fifty, liable for militia service. Any individual who was liable for such service was required to enroll immediately with the militia captain of his district and, within one month after enrolling, to arm himself with "a good musket, smooth bore gun or rifle, shot pouch and powder horn."[25] The citizens were thus expected to expend their personal resources for military purposes.

In early November another rumor spread throughout Bertie County: that the county's militia had been ordered to go to Roanoke Island to meet an expected advance by Federal forces. The rumored deployment created anxiety among the county's citizens. On November 7 Charles Smallwood, believing that as a member of the militia he would be sent to Roanoke Island, wrote: "[I] shall have to go, but hope the [Federal] fleet will give it a wide berth while I am there."[26]

On the morning of November 12, Smallwood left his home near Woodville and was traveling toward Windsor when he met fellow county resident Allen Smith, who informed him that the Bertie County militia had been ordered to Roanoke Island. The militia was to assemble at Windsor at ten o'clock on the next morning. Smallwood returned home and packed provisions, which included boiled ham and biscuits, for the expected trip.[27] The county's militiamen assembled in Windsor on the morning of the thirteenth fully expecting to be sent to Roanoke Island. About ten o'clock, however, news arrived that the order directing them to proceed to Roanoke Island had been revoked. The militiamen disbanded and returned to their homes.[28]

About mid-November, Capt. Jesse C. Jacocks's "Bertie Volunteers" returned to the county, having been mustered out of service at Raleigh on November 13. The company had enlisted to serve six

Twenty-two-year-old Calvin J. Morris enlisted in Capt. Jesse C. Jacocks's "Bertie Volunteers" (Company L, First Regiment North Carolina Infantry) on May 1, 1861, and served with that unit until it was mustered out of service on November 13, 1861. He reenlisted in Capt. Joseph B. Cherry's cavalry unit (Company F, Fifty-ninth Regiment North Carolina Troops [Fourth Regiment North Carolina Cavalry]) on August 9, 1862, and was present or accounted for through October 1864, the date of that company's last available muster roll. Photograph courtesy Mrs. Henry Lyon.

months and, having fulfilled that term, had been mustered out. The "Volunteers" had been involved in no battles or skirmishes and, therefore, had few exploits to convey to their family and friends back home. The company had spent its time primarily in the Yorktown area performing picket and fatigue duty.[29]

By December 1861 the aroused mood of Bertie County citizens appears to have been calmer. The Federal military had made no movement toward Roanoke Island, and, with winter fast approaching, the opportunity for active military operations was apparently passing. While a lull existed in Federal military activity within North Carolina, residents of Bertie County began to be concerned over the prospect of much harsher times ahead. In December, Charles Smallwood privately recorded his fear that "we shall have a long ruinous war & possibly become divided among ourselves." In a prayerful wish, he also wrote: "May God take the management of the affairs of our country in his hands & drive them to a speedy peace."[30] The year closed with no Bertie County men having been killed or wounded in battle. The only deaths of county soldiers had occurred as the result of disease and illness. On December 31, 1861, approximately 125 county men were serving in Confederate army units, excluding the militia.[31]

As the year ended, Federal authorities were organizing another military expedition to eastern North Carolina. As early as September 1861, those authorities had decided to commit more troops to the state. Maj. Gen. George B. McClellan had assigned to Brig. Gen. Ambrose E. Burnside the task of raising a coast division of fifteen thousand men for service in North Carolina. Annapolis, Maryland, was selected as the rendezvous location for units to be assigned to that division. By early January 1862 Burnside's troops had been assembled and were ready to embark for North Carolina, although the need for secrecy prevented them from knowing their destination. Adm. Louis M. Goldsborough of the United States Navy was assigned command of the squadron of transports and gunboats that was to convey and accompany Burnside's ground forces to North Carolina. On the evening of January 11 the "Burnside-Goldsborough Expedition" set sail from Hampton Roads, Virginia. The expedition's first objective, unknown to North Carolina authorities and citizens, was Roanoke Island.[32]

The fleet reached Hatteras Inlet on January 13 but because of the large size and displacement of a number of the vessels did not immediately pass through the inlet into Pamlico Sound. Soon afterward, extremely poor weather prevented the vessels from passing through the shallow waters of the inlet. Not until late January did most of the vessels able to navigate the inlet enter Pamlico Sound.[33]

While the Federal expedition was stalled at Hatteras Inlet, the second surge of enlistments for Confederate service occurred in Bertie County. During January approximately 120 county men enlisted for Confederate army service. On January 23 the Bertie County militia assembled at Windsor, and some of its members were reportedly "drafted" for active military service. During that assembly, Francis Wilder Bird, a Windsor lawyer, enlisted more than eighty men for a company he was organizing. Bird had served as a second lieutenant in the "Bertie Volunteers" and had received authority from the state of North

Edward Ralph Outlaw, a student at the University of North Carolina when the Civil War began, abandoned his studies and enlisted in the "Bertie Volunteers" (Company L, First Regiment North Carolina Infantry) at the age of twenty on May 1, 1861. Engraving from Clark, *North Carolina Regiments*, 1: facing 583.

Carolina to raise a company of soldiers. Bird selected four other Bertie County men as his lieutenants. Three of them—Edward Ralph Outlaw, Thomas Watson Cooper, and Clingman Craig—had also served in the "Bertie Volunteers." Bird's fourth subordinate officer was Edward Averett Rhodes. Additionally, twenty other men who had served in the "Bertie Volunteers" enlisted to serve again with Captain Bird. Bird's company was later assigned to the Eleventh Regiment North Carolina Troops and designated Company C.[34]

During the January 23 meeting at Windsor, approximately a dozen men enlisted in an artillery company being formed by Thomas Capehart of Hertford County. Capehart's company was eventually assigned to the Third Battalion North Carolina Light Artillery as Company C. Four days later an additional sixteen Bertie County men enlisted in another artillery company being organized for the same battalion by William Badham Jr. of Chowan County. Badham's company was later designated Company B. Four Bertie County men—David J. Gaskins, John M. Sutton, John G. Fraim, and John R. Powell—became officers in those two companies.[35]

While a considerable number of men enlisted in Bird's and Capehart's companies during the January 23 meeting, some members of the "drafted militia" paid men to enlist in their places. Charles Smallwood attended the meeting and hired Richard "Dick" Owens to "take [his] place." Owens, who had served as a private in the "Bertie Volunteers," enlisted in Bird's company.[36]

The January 23 meeting was apparently quite a festive affair and likely included boisterous and challenging rhetoric by the men, particularly with the awareness that Burnside's and Goldsborough's forces were at the state's doorstep. According to Charles Smallwood, who attended the meeting, "so many drunk men" had never before been seen in Windsor.[37] In two and a half weeks, Windsor would once again be the scene of heavy drinking: Burnside's and Goldsborough's forces were about to move on their first and most strategic objective— Roanoke Island.

Notes

1. Smallwood diary, May 30, 1861; Adj. Gen. J. F. Hoke to Capt. J. C. Jacocks, May 24, 1861, Records of the Adjutant General's Office, State Archives; Confederate Vessel Papers (microfilm M909), Record Group 109, National Archives; Compiled Service Records of North Carolina's Confederate Soldiers (service record of Capt. Jesse C. Jacocks, First Regiment N.C. Infantry); Manarin and Jordan, *North Carolina Troops*, 3:67.

2. Smallwood diary, June 17, 1861; Long, *The Civil War Day by Day*, 84.

3. Smallwood diary, June 20, 1861.

4. Compiled Service Records of North Carolina's Confederate Soldiers (Fifth Regiment N.C. State Troops).

5. Confederate Vessel Papers.

6. Manarin and Jordan, *North Carolina Troops*, 4:196.

7. Compiled Service Records of North Carolina's Confederate Soldiers; Manarin and Jordan, *North Carolina Troops*, 2:98, 157–164. On March 29, 1862, Spruill resigned his commission as colonel of the regiment. Because he was a member of the North Carolina Secession Convention, he had divided his responsibilities between legislative duties in Raleigh and leading his regiment. See W. A. Graham, "Nineteenth Regiment (Second Cavalry)," in Walter Clark, ed., *Histories of the Several Regiments and Battalions from North Carolina in the Great War, 1861–'65*, 5 vols. (Raleigh and Goldsboro: State of North Carolina, 1901), 2:81, 83 (hereafter cited as Clark, *North Carolina Regiments*).

8. Compiled Service Records of North Carolina's Confederate Soldiers.

9. Wilson Angley, "A Brief History of the North Carolina Militia and National Guard" (unpublished research report, 1985), North Carolina Division of Archives and History.

10. Militia Officer Roster, Records of the Adjutant General's Office, State Archives; Bradley, *Confederate Militia Officers Roster*, 21–26.

11. Minutes of the Bertie County Court of Pleas and Quarter Sessions, June 13, 1861, State Archives (hereafter cited as Bertie County Court Minutes).

12. Barrett, *Civil War Battleground*, 17–18, 21.

13. Smallwood diary, September 1, 1861. The Bertie County men (and their companies) of the Seventeenth North Carolina captured at Hatteras Island were: Com-

pany D—William Thomas Brooks, James M. Madison, John R. Matthews; Company F—William J. Pugh; and Company H—George W. Hodder. See Manarin and Jordan, *North Carolina Troops*, 6:118, 142, 145, 155, 165, and 177. The companies of the regiment were raised in Pasquotank, Hyde, Pitt, Hertford, Currituck, Martin, Washington, Perquimans, and Beaufort Counties.

14. Smallwood diary, September 1, 1861.

15. Smallwood diary, September 1, 4, 1861.

16. Barrett, *Civil War Battleground*, 21.

17. Col. Rush C. Hawkins to Maj. Gen. John E. Wool, September 7, 1861, *Official Records . . . Armies*, ser. 1, 4:607–609; Barrett, *Civil War Battleground*, 22.

18. Kruman, *Parties and Politics*, appendix B.

19. Henry T. Clark to J. P. Benjamin, September 25, 1861, *Official Records . . . Armies*, ser. 1, 4:658.

20. J. P. Benjamin to Henry T. Clark, September 27, 1861, *Official Records . . . Armies*, ser. 1, 51, pt. 2:319.

21. Col. Rush C. Hawkins to Maj. Gen. John E. Wool, September 11, 1861, *Official Records . . . Armies*, ser. 1, 4:609–610, 613.

22. *Semi-weekly Raleigh Register*, September 11, 1861.

23. J. P. Benjamin to Henry T. Clark (telegram), September 23, 1861, *Official Records . . . Armies*, ser. 1, 4:655.

24. Smallwood diary, October 19, 1861.

25. *Public Laws of the State of North Carolina Passed by the General Assembly at Its Session of 1862–63* (Raleigh, W. W. Holden, Printer to the State, 1863), 7–10 (hereafter cited as *North Carolina Public Laws, 1862–63*).

26. Smallwood diary, November 7, 1861.

27. Smallwood diary, November 12, 1861.

28. Smallwood diary, November 13, 1861.

29. Manarin and Jordan, *North Carolina Troops*, 3:2; Smallwood diary, November 17, 1861.

30. Smallwood diary, December 2, 1861.

31. Compiled Service Records of North Carolina's Confederate Soldiers. No rosters or compiled service records, other than for officers, exist for members of Bertie County's militia. The officers are listed in the Militia Officer Roster, Records of the Adjutant General's Office, in the State Archives. Because of the lack of records, the strength of the county's militia during the war cannot be determined.

32. Richard A. Sauers, "Laurels for Burnside: The Invasion of North Carolina, January-July 1862," *Blue and Gray* 5 (May 1988): 9–10. Most historians have referred to the Federal incursion in eastern North Carolina in January 1862 as the "Burnside Expedition." Since the Federal navy played an extremely significant role in the expedition—and Burnside's army force could not have achieved the success it did without Admiral Goldsborough's cooperation and assistance—this study refers to the incursion as the "Burnside-Goldsborough Expedition."

33. Sauers, "Laurels for Burnside," 10–11.

34. Smallwood diary, January 23, 1862; Manarin and Jordan, *North Carolina Troops*, 3:57–61, 5:32–40; Compiled Service Records of North Carolina's Confederate Soldiers.

35. Manarin and Jordan, *North Carolina Troops,* 1:346–371; Compiled Service Records of North Carolina's Confederate Soldiers.

36. Manarin and Jordan, *North Carolina Troops,* 3:60, 5:37; Compiled Service Records of North Carolina's Confederate Soldiers (service record of Richard Owens, First Regiment N.C. Infantry); Smallwood diary, January 23, 1862.

37. Smallwood diary, January 23, 1862.

CHAPTER 3

Gunboats, Runaway Slaves, and Conscription Refugees

During the morning of February 7, the Federal fleet transporting General Burnside's soldiers approached Roanoke Island from the south. About eleven o'clock, the gunboats began to bombard the Confederate forts on the island and the small fleet of Confederate gunboats in the area, known as the "mosquito fleet." During midafternoon, as the Northern gunboats fired away at their Southern adversaries, Burnside landed his infantry at Ashby Harbor on the western side of the island. By nightfall those troops had secured their onshore position, and early the next morning they attacked. Before the day's end, the Confederates surrendered Roanoke Island. As at Hatteras Inlet five and one-half months earlier, the Confederate forces at Roanoke Island were grossly inadequate for defending their position and were easily pushed aside by the amphibious Union forces.[1]

Facing a vastly superior naval force and certain annihilation, the heavily outgunned "mosquito fleet" under the command of Commodore William F. Lynch withdrew up the Pasquotank River to Elizabeth City. Two days later, Admiral Goldsborough dispatched Commodore Stephen C. Rowan toward Elizabeth City with fourteen gunboats to search for the Confederate vessels. Rowan's flotilla appeared near the town about 8:30 in the morning and quickly destroyed, captured, or sent fleeing the Confederate ships. The gunboat *Commodore Perry*, under the command of Lt. Charles Williamson Flusser, attacked Lynch's flagship, the *Sea Bird*. Flusser steered his vessel straight into the *Sea Bird*, striking it amidships and quickly sinking it. After the gunboats dispatched the "mosquito fleet," Federal troops easily occupied Elizabeth City.[2]

On February 10 the Bertie County Court of Pleas and Quarter Sessions convened in Windsor.[3] As usual during "court week," county citizens came to Windsor to transact business, serve as jurors, and attend the court session. On this day, as Rowan's force occupied Elizabeth City, news of the capture of Roanoke Island reached Windsor. The citizens' thoughts quickly turned from their personal agendas and the business of the court to the distressing news of the day. Bertie County, situated at the upper end of Albemarle Sound, was now highly vulnerable to raids by Federal gunboats and troops. During the day, the citizens in Windsor, concerned over the recent military developments, consumed "quantities of whiskey" as they discussed and pondered the worrisome state of affairs in their region.[4]

In January Commodore Lynch had advised Stephen R. Mallory, the Confederate secretary of the navy, that if Federal forces captured Roanoke Island, they would have a "great thoroughfare" in Albemarle Sound and its tributaries to execute their operations.[5] Immediately after the capture of Roanoke Island and the occupation of Elizabeth City, Federal gunboats began to utilize the "great thoroughfare," advancing up the sound toward its confluence with the Chowan and Roanoke Rivers. The linear distance from the Bertie County shoreline of the Chowan River to Elizabeth City is approximately thirty miles. By water the distance is almost doubled but was still a mere few hours' cruise for Union steamers. News of the capture of Elizabeth City and the Federal gunboats' advance up Albemarle Sound reached Bertie County during the morning of February 11.[6]

During the early morning of the following day, four gunboats (the *Underwriter*, the *Commodore Perry*, the *Lockwood*, and the *Louisiana*) under the command of Lt. Alexander Murray appeared off the town of Edenton, immediately across the Chowan River from Bertie County. Union troops landed and "had undisturbed possession" of the village as the few Confederate soldiers in the area fled. The Federals found no fortifications at Edenton during their two-hour stay but discovered and destroyed eight cannons and one schooner and seized six bales of cotton.[7] Admiral Goldsborough's gunboats were making a poignant show of force up Albemarle Sound.

When Federal troops occupied Elizabeth City and Edenton, citizens of those areas immediately approached the troops and expressed support for the Union cause. As on Hatteras Island, residents of the

Albemarle Sound region had exhibited strong Union sentiments during the secession crisis. Now Federal forces were finding sympathizers in the areas they visited and occupied. Indeed, a number of Confederate sailors captured at Elizabeth City on February 10 refused to accept paroles to return to their homes, electing instead to remain with the Federal forces and "positively" declining to "return again to the rebel service or country."[8]

With the arrival of Federal vessels at Edenton, rumors circulated in Bertie County that Federal gunboats were at the mouth of the Roanoke River and that firing had supposedly been heard in the direction of Plymouth.[9] The Union vessels that visited Edenton did not approach Plymouth, several miles up the Roanoke from that waterway's confluence with Albemarle Sound. But to the secessionist citizens of Bertie County, it was now depressingly clear that the North Carolina and Confederate governments had committed inadequate military resources in defending North Carolina's coast and connecting waterways. The Albemarle Sound region was entirely exposed to the Federal forces, which could now use the sound as a launching point for expeditions and raids into the interior regions of the state and to impede the transportation of Confederate stores and supplies toward Norfolk, Virginia, and Chesapeake Bay.

While it was still relatively early in the war, North Carolina officials were acutely aware that the Wilmington and Weldon Railroad was a vitally important supply link between the state and Confederate forces operating in Virginia. Federal disruption of transportation on the railroad would surely have detrimental consequences on the Confederate government's ability to supply its army in Virginia. The Roanoke River, which forms the southern boundary of Bertie County and empties into Albemarle Sound, was navigable by light-draft vessels to Weldon. On February 11, three days after Burnside's forces captured Roanoke Island, the Halifax County militia was engaged in "devising ways to blockade" the Roanoke River to prevent Union gunboats from ascending it to Weldon and its critical juncture with the Wilmington and Weldon Railroad. The militia's efforts to develop impromptu defenses against gunboats inspired one Halifax County planter's wife to observe: "what trouble [the] neglect of the defenses at Roanoke Island has cost us."[10]

On February 13 Governor Clark wrote Confederate secretary of war Judah P. Benjamin that the Weldon and Seaboard Railroad, a primary transportation link between Weldon and southeastern Virginia, must also be defended and that he had called the North Carolina militia together for that purpose. Clark also advised Benjamin that the militia was insufficient to provide the needed protection and that troops from Virginia were necessary for that purpose.[11]

Many North Carolina citizens felt that Confederate authorities had inexplicably neglected the state's coastal defenses. Although North Carolinians had volunteered in great numbers immediately following the outbreak of war, most of the state's troops were in Virginia when Federal forces invaded their home state.[12] One North Carolina official, writing to Secretary of War Benjamin on February 13, remarked:

The fall of Roanoke Island, the key to all the rich northeastern counties of the State, has made a most profound and sad and discouraging impression on our people. Without the means of full information, they think they have been neglected by the authorities at Richmond. . . . The enemy can, and doubtless will, commit depredations to the extent of many millions in value of property in the rich country on the sounds, and will at his ease and with impunity where he can obtain any amount of supplies for his army. . . . [H]e can destroy Washington, New Berne, Plymouth, Edenton, and other towns on the two sounds of Pamlico and Albemarle, or advance from them at his leisure.[13]

Charles Smallwood initially surmised that the Federal forces advancing up Albemarle Sound intended to land at Colerain and launch an overland expedition toward Weldon and the crucial railroad bridge over the Roanoke River.[14] Only the county's inept militia was available to forestall a landing of Federal troops at Colerain, but the Federal gunboats that appeared off Edenton on February 12 departed after a short visit and returned back down Albemarle Sound.

The Federals' capture of Roanoke Island and incursion into the Albemarle Sound region greatly disturbed the citizens of North Carolina as they sought to ascertain the true objective of Goldsborough's and Burnside's mission. On February 18, in response to the heightened anxiety of the populace, the two officers issued a joint proclamation "to the people of North Carolina" that declared: "The mission of our joint expedition is not to invade any of your rights, but to assert the authority of the United States and to close with you the desolating war brought upon your State by comparatively a few bad men." Goldsborough and Burnside further proclaimed: "We shall inflict no injury unless forced to do so by your own acts, and upon this you may confidently rely."[15]

On the day that Goldsborough and Burnside issued their proclamation, they dispatched another major expedition from Roanoke Island up Albemarle Sound. Eight gunboats (the *Delaware*, the *Commodore Perry*, the *Commodore Barney*, the *Hunchback*, the *Louisiana*, the *Morse*, the *Lockwood*, and the *Whitehead*) under the command of Commodore Rowan and with Col. Rush C. Hawkins's Ninth Regiment New York Infantry aboard advanced during the day to Edenton Bay, where the fleet anchored for the night.[16] For the second time in a week, Federal gunboats were at the "doorsteps" of Bertie County.

Early on the morning of the nineteenth, Rowan dispatched the *Lockwood* up the Roanoke River to reconnoiter in the direction of Plymouth. Because no Federal forces had visited the town, Rowan had no knowledge of whether or not Confederate troops were present in the vicinity. The *Lockwood* slowly steamed up the river until it was within sight of Plymouth, where it found conditions to be quiet and "all rite." The gunboat returned to the Federal fleet, which then began to ascend the Chowan River.[17]

Unknown to Bertie County's citizens, the objectives of this expedition were to visit the village of Winton, about twenty miles up the Chowan from Colerain, and ascertain the validity of rumors that citizens in the area entertained Union sympathies and desired to meet with Federal forces. More important militarily, Rowan and Hawkins's plan was to advance further up the Chowan and enter the Nottoway and Blackwater Rivers to destroy railroad bridges across those tributaries.[18]

Shortly after Rowan's gunboats began their ascent, a courier departed from near the mouth of Salmon Creek in Bertie County carrying intelligence to North Carolina officials that eight "large steamers [were] going up the Chowan" and that six of the vessels were "apparently loaded with troops." About two o'clock in the afternoon, the Federal fleet passed Colerain and observed that the wharf was burning, having been set afire by the citizens of the area.[19] The citizens, apparently believing that Federal troops might land at their town, set fire to the wharf to forestall such a course of action.

The gunboats did not veer toward the blazing wharf but steamed past the village and later in the day approached the little town of Winton. As the *Delaware*, Rowan's flagship, with Colonel Hawkins posted in its crosstrees as a lookout, led the fleet and neared the town, the ship's occupants sighted a Negro woman at the wharf beckoning the vessel to approach. As the *Delaware* steered toward the dock, the vigilant Hawkins spotted the glint and gleam of bayonets of a battalion of Confederate infantry stationed on the bluff overlooking the wharf. The woman had been sent to the dock as a decoy to lure the gunboat into rifle range of the pre-positioned Southern soldiers. Hawkins emphatically shouted for the pilot to steer away from the shore. The Confederates—Col. William W. Williams's First North Carolina Battalion—

immediately opened a heavy musketry fire on the *Delaware*, striking the vessel with approximately 185 projectiles. Nonetheless, the barrage killed or wounded no Federal servicemen. The *Delaware* backed off from the town, and, upon the arrival of the *Commodore Perry*, Rowan ordered his cannoneers and those of the latter vessel to shell the town. The engagement had begun in the late afternoon, and with darkness fast approaching, Rowan and Hawkins decided that it was not judicious to attempt to land the New York infantry. After a relatively brief bombardment, the fleet withdrew down the river about two miles and anchored for the night.[20]

That evening Rowan conferred with Hawkins and the commanders of the other vessels in his fleet, and they decided that the flotilla should return to Winton the following day. The next morning, the gunboats returned and began to shell the town, driving Williams's North Carolinians into the surrounding countryside. Colonel Hawkins landed his infantry and, upon inspecting the buildings, found "Plenty of evidence . . . that the place had been recently occupied by a strong force, and that it was a depot of supplies for the Confederate army." Hawkins then ordered his men to burn the town. The resulting inferno reduced most of the town to ashes. Hawkins's soldiers reboarded the gunboats. The rumors of Union sympathizers at Winton proved to be false—at least no such loyalists were found.[21]

Rowan and Hawkins realized that they could no longer operate effectively in the area, having lost the element of surprise. Therefore they decided not to proceed further upriver and attempt to destroy the railroad bridges over the Nottoway and Blackwater Rivers. Rowan's gunboats returned to Roanoke Island, where Hawkins's troops joined other soldiers preparing for military operations in other sections of eastern North Carolina.[22] It would be more than two months before Union gunboats would again visit the upper Albemarle Sound region.

With Union gunboats able to control the waterways from Hatteras Inlet to the Chowan River, Confederate authorities decided to commit a token force of troops to the Bertie County area. On February 24 they sent a four-company detachment of cavalry to the county. Col. Samuel B. Spruill of Bertie led that force, which was detached from the Nineteenth Regiment North Carolina Troops (Second Regiment North Carolina Cavalry), which he commanded.[23] The purpose of Spruill's mission to Bertie County was to "harass the enemy and assist the inhabitants." He and his detachment spent approximately two weeks in the area but encountered no Federal raiders, who had departed after burning Winton. By March 13 Spruill and his entire regiment,

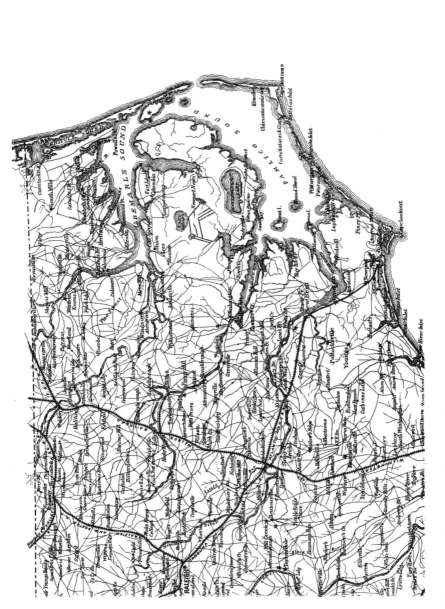

This Civil War-era map of eastern North Carolina shows the numerous waterways that punctuated and dissected much of the region and afforded navigational access to nearly one-third of the state. Early in the war, Federal military commanders employed naval gunboats and occupying army forces to seize and maintain control of the waterways.

along with other Confederate troops, were in the vicinity of New Bern to counter Burnside's advance there.[24]

March 15 was cloudy, damp, and dreary as the Bertie County militia assembled at Windsor. About eleven o'clock a steady rain set in, and the militiamen "got really wet playing soldiers." On that dreary day, more gloomy news arrived in Windsor: Burnside's forces had attacked New Bern.[25]

On the nineteenth, news reached the county that Federal forces had captured New Bern and that the Confederates had made a stand at Kinston, "only to fall back to Goldsboro." Federal troops were methodically capturing and occupying more areas in eastern North Carolina. Charles Smallwood, disappointed and concerned over the continued advance of Burnside's soldiers on North Carolina soil, sarcastically surmised that "falling back's [the] policy" for the Confederate forces in eastern North Carolina.[26] Other Bertie County secessionists likely entertained similar views.

As Burnside's forces continued to achieve military successes by occupying Washington (March 20), Carolina City (March 21), Morehead City (March 22), and Beaufort (March 25), Bertie County citizens attempted to organize additional companies of soldiers for Confederate service.[27] The people of Bertie undertook to raise several companies but actually organized only one such unit during March. Within the county, ninety men were recruited for a company that was initially intended to serve in a battalion of North Carolina Light Artillery. Solomon H. Whyte, a Bertie County planter, was elected captain of the company. In May 1862 Whyte's company was transferred from the artillery to the infantry service and assigned to the Thirty-second Regiment North Carolina Troops as Company G.[28]

By March 1862 conditions in Bertie County had deteriorated to the point that officials imposed martial law in the county, making it necessary that citizens "almost had to have a pass" to travel. Some men, unless they were legally exempted from militia duty, became somewhat reluctant to travel, apparently because of the fear of being summarily drafted, inasmuch as "the country's call" for their services was "quite loud" at that time.[29] While the Confederate government had not yet decided to conscript men for military duty, the North Carolina militia law basically required all white men between the ages of eighteen and fifty to serve in the militia. The governor could then draft militiamen for Confederate service.[30] Naturally, some men felt that it was in their best personal interests to refrain from traveling and stayed near their homes.

Bertie County's exposure to Federal raiding parties necessitated that militia patrols be established to provide some protection to the citizens and notification to officials in case Federal troops invaded the county. In addition, such patrols were intended to enforce martial law and provide protection to the citizens from unruly whites and runaway slaves. Generally, the militia was an infantry-type organization whose patrols were carried out on foot. On March 27, however, the North Carolina Adjutant General's Office provided that in counties in which patrols were deemed necessary, the commanding general of the militia could direct that detachments of mounted men be organized for patrol duty in lieu of infantry. The men who formed such mounted patrols were required to furnish their own horses, forage, and rations.[31] On April 11 North Carolina adjutant general James G. Martin granted Col. Jonathan J. Rhodes, commander of the Bertie County militia, permission to "use pistols and sabers on the patrol if it should be deemed necessary."[32]

By April 1862 approximately 390 Bertie County men were serving in Confederate army units, excluding the Bertie County militia. Of the 510 men who had enlisted by that date, 67 (predominantly members of the "Bertie Volunteers") had been mustered out and had not re-enlisted; 16 had been discharged, primarily because of disabilities; and 32 had died of disease. Five county soldiers had deserted. The war had been ongoing for one year, and still no soldiers from Bertie had been killed in battle.[33] The county's soldiers had seen very little action. At that time approximately 44 percent of the county's military-age men were serving in the army.[34] Bertie County men had volunteered in respectable numbers, but a significant resource of manpower for potential army service remained.

Throughout North Carolina and the South, substantial numbers of men were available for military duty. Although the war was only one year old, obtaining sufficient military manpower solely through volunteerism was becoming a problem for the Confederate government. Therefore, to maintain its army, on April 16, 1862, the Confederate government passed its first conscription law.[35] In Bertie County that law became one of the most detested statutes enacted by the Confederate government.

The law, the first in American history providing for the conscription of troops, granted the president authority to draft for three years' service all white males aged eighteen to thirty-five years who were residents of the Confederate states. Conscripted men were allowed to hire substitutes to assume their places in the army and were also granted a brief grace period in which to volunteer in companies of their choice. Men liable for conscription were to be enrolled in their residential districts by state officials under Confederate supervision. All enrollees who were not assigned to companies were subject to call by the president to fill vacancies in old regiments, but the enrollees could remain at home until called.[36]

Within one month after passage of the conscription act, opposition to the legislated military service began forming in Bertie County in the guise of substitution. By the middle of May, substitutes were "in demand" in Windsor, with some receiving as much as four hundred dollars, or an equivalent of almost three years' private's pay, to enlist in the place of other men.[37] Only the more affluent citizens were financially able to hire substitutes, however. In general the wealthier citizens, those who owned substantial amounts of property and economically had more to gain from the Confederacy's successful prosecution of the war, hired less affluent countrymen to serve in the army. While in many respects the war was a rich man's contrivance, it had been quickly transformed into a poor man's fight.

Some Confederate officers considered those Southerners who would not fight for the South's independence as the lowest form of humanity. Maj. Gen. Daniel Harvey Hill, former colonel of the First Regiment North Carolina Infantry (in which the "Bertie Volunteers" served) and commander of the Department of North Carolina during part of 1863, referred to men who hired substitutes as cowardly "dogs."[38]

The conscription law had the potential to decimate the North Carolina militia, inasmuch as its members were not exempt from Confederate military service under the act. Maj. Jesse H. Bunch of Bertie County's Ninth Militia Regiment was concerned over the detrimental effects that conscription would have on his unit. On April 26 Adjutant General Martin advised Bunch that his office had "nothing to do with the conscription law" and that Bunch's regiment would probably not suffer any more than other state militia regiments. Martin advised Bunch that "In times like these, each one that remains at home must try and do double duty by looking after the interest of his friends and neighbors who are in the field."[39]

While Bertie County officials and militia officers were concerned over the welfare and safety of the county, General Burnside's forces were still advancing in eastern North Carolina. On April 25, following a two-week siege, Burnside's troops captured Fort Macon near Beaufort Harbor.[40] The Federals now had a much safer port to the Atlantic

Ocean to remedy logistical problems caused by the treacherous and shallow waters of Hatteras Inlet, the only other federally controlled outlet to the ocean. With the capture of Fort Macon, Federal forces virtually controlled all of the major waterways in eastern North Carolina except the Cape Fear River and its outlet to the Atlantic Ocean. For the remainder of the war, Federal forces retained control of those vital navigational corridors.

On April 29 Commodore Rowan ordered Lt. S. P. Quackenbush, commander of the *Delaware*, to make another show of force to the citizens of the Albemarle Sound region. Rowan directed Quackenbush to proceed up the sound in the company of the gunboats *Ceres* and *Whitehead*; visit the towns of Hertford, Edenton, and Plymouth; and destroy any vessels under construction. Rowan cautioned Quackenbush to "Use good discretion. . . . Say to the people . . . their safety depends on their neutrality and good conduct." He directed his subordinate officer to "Promise nothing in the way of protection" and "keep your people [sailors] in hand, that they neither scatter nor do violence to private property." Rowan did, however, order Quackenbush to seize and destroy public property but cautioned him against allowing the gunboats to remain in the rivers overnight within musket range of the shore.[41]

The following day, Quackenbush began executing Rowan's orders and visited Hertford. He then struck a course for Plymouth, where the three gunboats arrived about 3:30 in the afternoon. Quackenbush, along with some of his men, landed and delivered Rowan's proclamation to members of the town's council. In surveying the area, the lieutenant spotted a vessel under construction; but the townspeople assured him that it was private property, and he did not have it destroyed. After remaining at Plymouth about one hour and fifteen minutes, Quackenbush and his men reboarded the gunboats. The three-vessel flotilla then weighed anchors and steamed toward Edenton, where it arrived before darkness and anchored for the night out of musket range. About eight o'clock the next morning, Quackenbush left the Edenton area without going onshore, having made the ordered show of force.[42]

On May 5, as Federal naval forces were initiating military activity in the Albemarle region, Bertie County soldiers suffered their first battle casualties of the war. On that day, Capt. Thomas M. Garrett's company (F), Fifth Regiment North Carolina State Troops, as part of Brig. Gen. Jubal A. Early's brigade, Maj. Gen. Daniel H. Hill's division, was shockingly baptized to Federal fire at Williamsburg, Virginia. Early's brigade formed Hill's front line as the Confederates moved on a Federal battery strongly supported by infantry. In the resulting charge Garrett, 1st Lt. Joseph S. Hays (his half brother), and ten other Bertie County men were wounded and captured. Five other county soldiers were captured and two wounded.[43] A year had passed since the war began, and now the blood of Bertie County men had been spilled in combat.

In the predawn hours of May 14, Lt. Charles W. Flusser, acting under Rowan's orders and commanding three gunboats—the *Commodore Perry*, the *Ceres*, and the *Lockwood*—entered the Roanoke River and steamed up to Plymouth, where the vessels arrived at five o'clock in the morning. The naval authorities had received information that Rebel steamers were transporting goods and supplies on the river. Flusser stopped at the town briefly, examined some wagons and found "nothing suspicious," and then continued steaming up the river. At or near Jamesville, citizens on the bank informed Flusser that the steamer *Alice*, under the command of Capt. Lafayette Thrower of Windsor, had passed by only an hour before, ascending the river toward Weldon. The Confederate government had contracted for the *Alice* to transport supplies and stores up the Roanoke River to the depot at Weldon. On that particular day, Thrower's vessel, which had been loaded at Windsor primarily with lard and bacon, had steamed down the Cashie River and passed into the Roanoke River.[44]

Approximately two miles above Jamesville, Flusser dispatched the gunboats *Ceres* and *Whitehead* to pursue the *Alice* while he, having been informed by his pilot that his command vessel, the *Commodore Perry*, could navigate no further up the river without grounding, returned to Jamesville. About two hours later, the *Ceres* and the *Lockwood* overtook the *Alice* approximately three miles below Williamston and fired a cannon shot over it. Captain Thrower, fully cognizant that his loaded boat could neither evade nor defend against its pursuers, turned the *Alice* toward shore and abandoned it, escaping into the surrounding swamp.[45]

Flusser, "hearing the sound of a great gun up the river" and concerned that his dispatched vessels might have run into a Rebel ambush, immediately began ascending the Roanoke. The *Commodore Perry* proceeded up the river at full speed for several miles and met the *Ceres* and the *Lockwood* returning downriver with their prize in tow. Flusser had the *Alice* towed to Plymouth, where he had its cargo confiscated and the food items distributed to vessels of his fleet. Aboard the Rebel steamer, Flusser also found church bells from Plymouth that the Confederate government had confiscated and ordered to be melted down and cast into artillery pieces.[46]

Flusser, aware that the *Alice* had been loaded at Windsor, decided that a visit to the town was in order. Early the next morning he took command of four gunboats—the *Ceres*, the *Lockwood*, the *Shawsheen*, and the *Whitehead*—and departed Plymouth. The Cashie River, along which Windsor is situated, is a deep but exceedingly narrow and remarkably crooked waterway, particularly for several miles below the town. Despite the somewhat treacherous trip, during which the sailors had to cut away overhanging limbs, Flusser's force arrived off Windsor at 4:20 in the afternoon. The townspeople "were astounded" when Flusser's vessels appeared off the village. The citizens had received news that the gunboats were in the river, but, according to Flusser, they did not believe that the vessels "could reach so high a point" up the waterway.[47]

Flusser and his marines landed and searched the town for United States property but found none. The only Confederate property found was an undisclosed "quantity of black beans, stowed in bulk" and approximately three hundred pounds of loose cotton. "The cotton was of little value and the beans were worthless." Nevertheless, Flusser considered destroying the items by setting them afire but restrained himself "by the tearful prayers of a poor widow who had lived hard and whose house might have been destroyed by the conflagration."

Before sunset, Flusser and his men reboarded the gunboats, turned the vessels around in the narrow waterway, and began descending the river. The gunboats progressed only about a mile when darkness forced them to halt and anchor for the night. During the night, Bertie County citizens and the militia did not harass the vessels. The following morning (May 16) the gunboats completed their descent of the river and returned to Plymouth.[48]

Overall, the Union gunboats' visit to Windsor was militarily insignificant; nevertheless, the foray acutely brought to the citizens' attention the fact that their town was not immune from raids by armed Yankee vessels and troops. Flusser apparently observed some Union sympathizers at Windsor: three days after the visit he reported to Commodore Rowan that "the loyal people are two to one against the disloyal" at Elizabeth City, Plymouth, and Windsor. Flusser concluded that if the people were provided Federal arms, "the State would soon return to her allegiance."[49]

Flusser's arrival at Plymouth in the middle of May marked the beginning of Federal occupation of the town. Plymouth, located a few miles from where the Roanoke River empties into Albemarle Sound, was strategically situated for military purposes, as well as for navigational

The Union gunboats *Ceres* (top) and *Shawsheen* (bottom), two of four warships under the command of Charles W. Flusser of the United States Navy, ascended the Cashie River from Albemarle Sound and visited Windsor on May 15, 1862. Drawing at top from Fred W. Smith Sketchbook, Tryon Palace Manuscripts Collection, New Bern; photograph at bottom courtesy U.S. Army Military History Institute, Carlisle, Pennsylvania (reproduced from Richard A. Sauers, "Laurels for Burnside: The Invasion of North Carolina, January–July 1862," *Blue & Gray* 5 [May 1988]: 17).

control of the Roanoke. Federal occupation of the town effectively sealed the river to Confederate traffic seeking routes to Norfolk, the Chesapeake Bay, and the Atlantic Ocean.

Flusser dispatched the gunboat *Whitehead* to patrol the Chowan River. Flusser's command, part of the North Atlantic Blockading Squadron, was charged with preventing trafficking in contraband and illicit trade in the Albemarle Sound region. The Chowan River became the unofficial demarcation line between Confederate- and Union-controlled territories. The counties east of the river—Chowan, Perquimans, Pasquotank, and Currituck—came under Federal domination, while the counties to the west, including Bertie, Gates, and Northampton, remained under Confederate influence.[50] Citizens who resided on both sides of the Chowan were not allowed to transport goods across or upon the waterway without official permission from Federal authorities. In effect, the Chowan River and other watercourses in the area were blockaded.

On May 17 Commodore Rowan visited Plymouth, where he learned that the "most rabid secessionists" had left and that Maj. Henry A. Gilliam, a paroled prisoner from the Battle of Hatteras Island, had reportedly violated the terms of his parole by harassing Union men in the area and attempting to raise a company of soldiers for Confederate service. Lieutenant Flusser arrested Gilliam, and Rowan decided to station a naval force at Plymouth. Writing to Adm. Louis Goldsborough on this date, Rowan noted that "at the earnest entreaty of the Union inhabitants of Plymouth," he had decided to keep a vessel stationed in the waters there.[51] Rowan appointed Lieutenant Flusser to command the Union naval forces in the Albemarle and Croatan Sounds region. Flusser established his headquarters at Plymouth, and for the remainder of the war Union gunboats constantly patrolled the various waterways bordering and intersecting Bertie County—Albemarle Sound and the Chowan, Roanoke, and Cashie Rivers.

Lt. Charles W. Flusser, who subsequently became an "institution" in Plymouth, was an extremely energetic and capable naval officer who was highly respected by his men, fellow officers, and superiors. Years after the war, one of his colleagues characterized Flusser as "one of the most gallant spirits in the War of the Rebellion." Flusser was born in September 1832, resided as a child with his family in Kentucky, and was appointed to the United States Naval Academy by Pres. James K. Polk at the age of fourteen. He graduated sixth in his class in 1853 at the age of twenty-one. When the war erupted, he remained in the

Lt. Charles W. Flusser led Union naval forces in the Albemarle region of North Carolina from his headquarters at Plymouth. Flusser strongly urged the recruitment of North Carolinians for the Union army and worked strenuously to enforce his naval blockade of area waterways. On a number of occasions, Union sailors and marines under his control landed on Bertie County soil and undertook "expeditions" against secessionists and supporters of the Confederate government who resided in Bertie. Photograph courtesy U.S. Naval Historical Center, Washington, D.C.

Union navy, while his two brothers became Confederate army officers. Flusser was promoted to lieutenant commander in September 1862.[52]

On January 9, 1862, navy officials had assigned Flusser to command the *Commodore Perry*, a New York ferryboat converted to a warship. He accompanied Adm. Louis Goldsborough's fleet on the Burnside-Goldsborough expedition to North Carolina in January 1862. Of significant importance to Federal military actions in the Albemarle Sound region, he participated in the Battle of Roanoke Island (February 8), the action at Elizabeth City (February 10), and the Rowan-Hawkins expedition to Winton (February 18–20).[53]

Flusser, intensely loyal to the Union, was extremely confident in his military abilities and privately egotistical. As commander of naval forces in the Albemarle and Croatan Sounds, he viewed the fight for possession of those waterways and the stringent enforcement of the blockade as serious business. From his headquarters at Plymouth, he effectively executed his duties, directing his gunboats to roam the waterways, break up contraband trade, rescue runaway slaves and Rebel conscription evaders from the swamps and woodlands, and cooperate with Union army forces on expeditions and raids. The Confederate leaders and secessionists in the Albemarle Sound region faced a most challenging and determined adversary in Lieutenant Flusser.

Less than nine months had passed since Maj. Gen. Benjamin F. Butler's forces had overwhelmed the Confederates at Forts Hatteras and Clark. Now Union gunboats occupied Plymouth. Possibly the worst fears entertained by Bertie County's secessionist leaders—other than the outright occupation of county soil by Union soldiers—had materialized. Residents of Bertie County who harbored Union sentiments and sympathies and desired to leave the county to avoid persecution and Confederate conscription could now easily reach Union forces operating on area waterways. In almost every eastern North Carolina town Federal forces had visited, local citizens had come forward and expressed sympathies for the Union cause. Plymouth would be no different.

By May 19 one hundred people had reportedly approached Flusser and conveyed their desires to take up arms in their own defense on behalf of the Union. Flusser wrote to Commodore Rowan and requested that an army recruiting officer be sent to the town. Flusser advised Rowan that otherwise the men, if not accepted for service in the Union military, would be conscripted into the Confederate army. Flusser informed his superior officer: "Men from 20 odd miles around have come to see the gunboats, and all are anxious to enlist." He felt, perhaps overconfidently, that if the Federal government provided protection and aid to the Union men of eastern North Carolina, then the area could "readily be brought back to [the] allegiance of the United States."[54] Indeed, Federal authorities were already taking steps to establish a form of Union government in eastern North Carolina.

On May 20, exactly one year after North Carolina seceded, President Lincoln appointed Edward Stanly as the Union's military governor of North Carolina. Stanly, a native North Carolinian who had been residing in California, returned to the state and established his "capital" in Federally controlled New Bern. Federal authorities gave Stanly no specific instructions about his position other than urging him to maintain peace and security for loyal inhabitants until a new Union government for that sector of the state could be established.[55] The future was looking even more uncertain for the secessionists of eastern North Carolina.

Bertie County's white citizens, as well as the thousands of slaves who resided in the county, monitored with great interest the incursion of Union gunboats into Albemarle Sound. No day ever dawned bright and hopeful for Bertie's people of bondage, but the news of Yankee vessels in the waters surrounding the county brought a degree of hope and optimism to the slaves. To many of them, freedom seemed as close as the nearest gunboat flying the Stars and Stripes in the waterways of the Albemarle region.

In less than three weeks of the Union navy's occupation of Plymouth, Bertie County slaves began running away from their masters and overseers in hopes of reaching Union forces. By June 2 three Bertie County slaves—Henry Sharp, John Sharp, and Haywood Sharp—had made their way to the shore of the Chowan River, where they hailed the gunboat *Whitehead* and were picked up. The three men had gained their freedom and immediately enlisted in the Union navy.[56] They were the first of hundreds of Bertie County slaves who would seek and win their freedom, and many of the former bondsmen enlisted in the Federal military services.

By running away from the plantations and seeking freedom, slaves risked their personal welfare and lives. But the risks, no matter how great and imposing, were worth taking to many slaves who had only dreamed of being free. In early June four slaves belonging to J. Powell and a Mr. Ruffin of Bertie County ran away and attempted to reach the Yankees at Winton. Those slaves were not as fortunate as Henry, John, and Haywood Sharp. According to an account of their attempt, the "Yankees . . . refused to take them." The citizens of Winton captured three of the runaway slaves and confined them in jail. The fourth slave, the property of J. Powell, "jumped in the river" to avoid being captured and drowned. That unidentified slave's quest for freedom cost him his life, but such were the risks for a slave who decided to run away. The three slaves captured in Winton were returned to Bertie County.[57]

On June 12 Commodore Rowan and Colonel Hawkins visited Plymouth and met with "the country people," who numbered as many as 250. The two officers informed the citizens that the Federal government was prepared to aid them in "throwing off the tyranny that now oppressed them, and to put arms in their hands to defend and assert their rights, if they would organize into companies and come under military discipline." Rowan and Hawkins apparently were not interested in forming guerrilla organizations but desired to raise regular army units. Twenty-two men signed their names to enlistment rolls at the meeting, and more men were expected to enlist the following day. At Rowan's suggestion, General Burnside authorized Hawkins to station a company of his regiment at Plymouth.[58]

On June 15 Company F of Hawkins's Ninth Regiment New York Infantry, under the command of Capt. William W. Hammell, arrived at Plymouth. Soon afterward men of the area began professing

Union sentiments and a desire to serve in the Union army. Lieutenant Flusser stressed to Hawkins the importance of enlisting those North Carolinians, most of whom were from the poorer, non-slaveholding portion of the populace, which was resisting Confederate conscription. According to Hawkins: "Very few of them were slave-owners, and consequently had little interest in aiding the rebellion. They worked in their fields in groups, with arms near at hand during the day, and at night resorted to the swamps for shelter against conscripting parties of rebel soldiers. . . . Commander Flusser . . . urged me in the strongest manner to occupy the town of Plymouth, and to organize the Union men of that vicinity into a regiment of soldiers."[59]

Although the War Department, under direction from President Lincoln, had authorized the recruiting of a regiment of soldiers at Hatteras Island in September 1861, no such unit had been organized. In early May 1862, however, General Burnside had authorized creation of the First Regiment North Carolina Union Volunteers, an action initiated by the desires of Union citizens in the vicinity of Washington, North Carolina.[60] Therefore, Burnside granted Colonel Hawkins permission to enlist Union soldiers at Plymouth for the newly authorized North Carolina regiment. Captain Hammell immediately began organizing a company of such soldiers, which subsequently became Company C, First Regiment North Carolina Union Volunteers.

On June 22, one week after Captain Hammell arrived at Plymouth, he enlisted his first Bertie County men—twenty-one-year-old Miles Mizell and twenty-year-old John M. Todd. Within five weeks Hammell enlisted for Company C nineteen Bertie County men, all of whom were eligible for Confederate conscription.[61] The division of allegiances of Bertie County citizens between the Confederacy and the Union was now becoming publicly evident.

On July 1 the provisions of the Confederate conscription law, enacted two and one-half months earlier, were enforced at Windsor when thirty-two Bertie County men were ordered into military service. The conscripts ranged in age from sixteen-year-old R. M. Hendricks to fifty-year-old William A. Adams—ages beyond the lawful range (eighteen to thirty-five years) for conscription. The men drafted on July 1 were sent to Murfreesboro, North Carolina, where they were eventually assigned to Company K, Thirty-third Regiment North Carolina Troops.[62]

The forced induction of Bertie County men into the Confederate army was, as Charles Smallwood termed it, a "bitter pill" for many local residents.[63] Opposition to mandatory Confederate service was be-

Cpl. Charles Freeman of Company C, First Regiment North Carolina Union Volunteers, was one of the first men in Bertie County to enlist in the Union army. He was mustered in as a private at Plymouth on July 23, 1862, at the age of eighteen, promoted to corporal on September 18, 1862, and present or accounted for until mustered out of service at New Bern on June 27, 1865. Photograph courtesy Delores Forehand.

ginning to develop in the county. The zeal with which Bertie residents had volunteered at the outbreak of war had waned. Arduous duty and the hardships of war and military life had become painful realities to the soldiers, the vast majority of whom were away from home and beloved family members for the first times in their lives. The war, which most residents of the county had desperately feared and sought to avoid, had not been a short one- or two-battle affair, as many citizens had expected. Volunteers were not coming forth in sufficient numbers to replenish the army's depleting ranks. As a result, the government turned to conscription as its only viable means of maintaining its army.

In Bertie County, certain military-age men, many who had maintained unionist views and sympathies, began leaving the county and entering the Union lines (primarily at Plymouth) to evade Confederate military service. The presence of Union forces at Plymouth offered those men an opportunity to avoid conscription. Federal military officers commonly referred to them as "conscription refugees."

While some Bertie County men immediately began seeking the Union gunboats and forces at Plymouth to avoid conscription, others remained at home but kept a watchful vigil for conscripting officers. Men began hiding in the woods, living in excavations and crudely constructed shelters to evade militia and conscription patrols. Relying on various means of communication—such as having family members hang a quilt in a window when it was safe to go to their houses—many men began living strained and tortuous lives in the woods and swamps. Hiding in the woods during the day and slipping out in nighttime darkness to obtain food and information from family members, friends, and Union sympathizers, numerous men were ardently determined to avoid Confederate military service. Bertie County men, who in their hearts remained loyal to the Union, began to suffer greatly for their sentiments while residing in a Confederate-controlled community.

The men hid in the woods singly, severally, and in small groups. Zadock Morris, a "Union man," took to the woods (and later joined the Union army) "because the rebels were going to carry him along with them."[64] Morris, Nazereth W. Parker, and Isaac Parker hid together and built a "shanty made of boards in the woods," which was "right comfortable . . . and kept the rain off." The three men would "sometimes steal out at night" and visit Union sympathizers, but because the risk of being seen or detained by Confederate authorities was quite great, they did not often venture out. The three men reportedly hid in the woods in this manner for approximately thirteen months. All eventually enlisted in the Union army.[65]

Some Bertie County men who were conscripted into the Confederate army served only briefly before returning to the county or joining the Union army. Years after the war John B. Harrell recalled: "I had been conscripted and carried into the C.S.A. [Confederate States Army]. . . . I served three days, was taken sick, got furloughed, got [the] furlough extended and before it ran out, I crossed at Eure's [a landing on Chowan River] and enlisted in the U.S. Army." Another county resident, Benjamin F. Jones, later stated that

I never was in the U.S. Army or C.S. Army or Navy. I expect if I ever was to be in army service it would have been U.S. Army service. I was a Union man and was opposed to the war. Notwithstanding, I was drafted in[to] the C.S. Army but never served. Did not have a gun or uniform at any time—no arms at all. I was at Murfreesboro, N.C. while in C.S. Army.

All of us who were there at Murfreesboro, N.C. were conscripts—forced there by C.S. Government officers. . . .

Orders came that we conscripts be let loose and then we be drafted. We were disbanded and I came back home and was drafted as others were. I just wouldn't go. I'd died before I would have gone. Others ran away to the Union Army before they would be drafted in[to] C.S.A.[66]

John R. Capps hid in the woods with a number of friends—Humphrey Keeter, Truston Castellow, Charles Mizell, Henry Mizell, Samuel Cobb, James Cullipher, Thomas J. Capehart, and Edwin

Hughes—who like himself were avoiding conscription. Once those men had been conscripted, they "took to the woods and canebrakes" to avoid the Rebel conscription officers.[67] Eventually, a substantial number of the conscription evaders would make their way to Plymouth and enlist in the Union army.

The presence of Union gunboats on the Chowan River not only provided a means of escape for conscription evaders but also exposed the area's most valuable agricultural product, cotton, to confiscation by Federal raiding parties. Planters stored thousands of pounds of the valuable commodity along the Chowan River and other tributaries in the northeastern sector of the state. To prevent Federal raiders from impounding it, Governor Clark directed the citizens to remove all cotton from within ten miles of the occupied waterways.

About the middle of June, Capt. William H. Cowles of Col. Laurence Baker's Ninth Regiment North Carolina State Troops (First Regiment North Carolina Cavalry) arrived at Colerain and found "2 or 3 lots of cotton" that had not been removed in accordance with the governor's directive. The captain had been sent to that section of the state "to burn cotton" and did so, destroying an estimated forty bales at Colerain. Soon afterward, the captain visited the plantation of Starkey Sharpe, a resident of nearby Harrellsville and a lieutenant in Hertford County's Sixth Regiment North Carolina Militia. There he similarly destroyed Sharpe's cotton.

On June 17 Sharpe, angered over the destruction, informed Governor Clark that cotton had been burned at Colerain and at his place and that he "was not aware that notice had been given to remove the cotton 10 miles from the water by the 6th of June." Sharpe asked the governor if he had given orders to burn cotton, specifically at Colerain, Harrellsville, Winton, Pitch Landing, and Murfreesboro—communities situated directly along the Chowan River and its connecting tributaries. Sharpe pointedly informed Clark that while Cowles had burned cotton found immediately along the Chowan River, he had failed to destroy larger quantities of the commodity found "not 5 or 6 miles from the water." Sharpe was incensed. He wrote: "My cotton was well secured in a thick pine thicket well sheltered with planks. I disliked much to have it burnt. I appealed to him [Cowles] not to burn my cotton—I would take it the next day from the water at any reasonable distance he might say." Sharpe further advised the governor that Cowles had burned a barn in the area that contained cotton. The enraged Sharpe disgustedly concluded that "this in Loyalty [is] worst than Yankees. . . . I scorn such contemptable treatment."[68]

The presence of Yankee forces in the immediate vicinity of Bertie County concerned the county men who were away in the Confederate army, separated from their families. Capt. Francis W. Bird (Company C, Eleventh Regiment North Carolina Troops), having learned that during their May 15 visit to Windsor, Flusser's marines had caused little harm, later wrote to his sister in Windsor: "I am glad our people were not treated as the captured often are. I think it is very probable you will be again visited soon."[69]

At a meeting of citizens of Bertie County that took place in Windsor on April 27, 1861, lawyer Francis Wilder Bird spoke out in behalf of North Carolina's secession from the Union. Bird subsequently served as a second lieutenant in the "Bertie Volunteers." As a captain, Bird in January 1862 organized a company of Bertie County men that subsequently became Company C, Eleventh Regiment North Carolina Troops. After having achieved the rank of lieutenant colonel of the Eleventh North Carolina, he was mortally wounded at Reams' Station, Virginia, on August 25, 1864. Engraving from Clark, *North Carolina Regiments*, 1: facing 583.

Sgt. William G. Parker of Bird's company was concerned for the safety and welfare of his wife, Emma, in case Union forces should occupy Bertie County. On June 16 she wrote and consoled him, advising him that as a combatant, she viewed his situation as worse than hers: "I do not know why you are so fearful about our county being taken by the Yanke[e]s. I think you [k]no[w] about them better than I do, but I fear your situation more than I do mine, but all I can do is put my trust in God."[70]

On July 9, 1862, citizens who resided near the Roanoke River in the south central sector of Bertie County were aroused in the early afternoon by musketry and cannon fire. Three Union gunboats—the *Commodore Perry*, the *Ceres*, and the *Shawsheen*—under the command of Lieutenant Flusser had advanced up the Roanoke River above Williamston. On board were Flusser's sailors and members of Captain

Hammell's company of the Ninth Regiment New York Infantry. About one o'clock in the afternoon, Confederate soldiers from Company B, Ninth Regiment North Carolina Troops (First Regiment North Carolina Cavalry) under the command of Capt. John H. Whitaker directed musket fire against the vessels from the woods on the Martin County side of the river. Flusser's and Hammell's men returned fire with small arms and cannons and "pushed on for Hamilton," a small Martin County town about twelve miles upriver from Williamston. For two hours, Flusser's gunboats were exposed to sniper fire from Confederates concealed in the woods as the vessels slowly steamed upstream.

About three o'clock the gunboats arrived off Hamilton, where approximately one hundred soldiers and sailors landed with one piece of field artillery. The Rebels who fired on the gunboats from the high banks of the river failed to confront the Federals once they landed. In the meantime, Flusser's men captured the Confederate steamer *Wilson* loaded with supplies for the Southern army. After remaining at Hamilton until late in the afternoon, the Federal troops again boarded the gunboats, took the *Wilson* in tow, and steamed downriver to Plymouth, shelling the woods along the riverbanks as they proceeded. The gunboats drew no Rebel fire on the return trip to Plymouth.[71]

In early August, Joseph B. Cherry, a Bertie County lawyer who had served as adjutant in the Eighth Regiment North Carolina State

Joseph B. Cherry, lawyer of Bertie, was another of the county's leading citizens to advocate North Carolina's secession from the Union as early as April 1861. Less than three weeks later he was appointed adjutant of the Eighth Regiment North Carolina State Troops. In early August 1862 Cherry organized a company of soldiers from Bertie County for cavalry service. That unit subsequently became Company F, Fifty-ninth Regiment North Carolina Troops (Fourth Regiment North Carolina Cavalry). Cherry served throughout the war until he was mortally wounded near Petersburg, Virginia, on April 1, 1865. Engraving from Clark, *North Carolina Regiments*, 3: facing 455.

Troops since May 1861, organized a company of soldiers from the county for cavalry service. At a time when conditions in the county were deteriorating, Federal forces were nearby, and many men were hiding in the woods to avoid military service, Cherry recruited 123 Bertie County men—substantially more than any other officer had enrolled previously. Cherry's success was directly attributable to the fact that the men enlisted under the "delusive promise" that they would not be sent out of the state. The empty promises enticed the conscription evaders, who assumed that they would be used as local defense troops, into enlisting.[72] Cherry, whom Confederate authorities had appointed a captain, formally organized his company at Windsor on August 9.[73] He and his men left the town on August 20 and traveled through Roxobel on their way to the camp of military instruction at Garysburg.[74]

As Cherry was organizing his company, a hard-drinking twenty-three-year-old Confederate deserter named John "Jack" Fairless was organizing a new company of North Carolina Union soldiers on the opposite side of the Chowan River. In early August, Fairless, a native of Gates County, took control of the elegant home of Dr. Richard Dillard Sr., an esteemed Chowan County secessionist leader. Dr. Dillard's estate, known as Wingfield, was situated directly on the eastern shore of the Chowan, a few miles upriver from Colerain. With the endorsement of Federal military authorities and the protection of Union gunboats, Fairless began assembling a company of Confederate deserters and conscription refugees, primarily from the non–slave-owning classes, which would become notorious for their renegade activities. Confederate military personnel and citizens in general scornfully referred to the men who served in Fairless's company, as well as those who served in other eastern North Carolina Union units, as "Buffaloes"; the term became synonymous with "thieves" and "outlaws."[75]

Fairless's company became Company E, First Regiment North Carolina Union Volunteers.[76] Citizens, particularly in Chowan County, in which the consequences of Fairless's soldiers' actions were more directly felt, came to despise his Wingfield contingent for its incessant pillaging and robbing. During August one Bertie County resident, twenty-four-year-old William E. Clark, crossed the Chowan River and enlisted in the "Wingfield Buffaloes."[77]

By August 1862, living conditions for Bertie County's poorer citizens had deteriorated to a point that created serious concerns for the county's civil authorities and leading citizens. On August 11, in an effort to alleviate some on the hardships on Bertie's residents, the county's magistrates ordered that the balance of the county's military fund (amount not disclosed) be turned over to the warden for the poor to assist the county's neediest residents. The magistrates further directed that pork and bacon, apparently owned by the county, be distributed to the wives of the county's Confederate soldiers. In addition, the officials ordered that a district patrol be instituted to guard the Chowan, Roanoke, and Cashie Rivers and that the patrol destroy all boats and "flats" found on those waterways.[78] The magistrates apparently were concerned that citizens and slaves might use the small vessels to flee from the county and trade with Union forces.

Charles Smallwood's private thoughts and laments likely conveyed the sentiments of many Bertie County residents. On July 31 he dejectedly recorded in his diary: "Where shall I be & what shall be the condition of the country on the 31st of July 1863? Shall we have peace or will the war continue? None but God can tell." Three weeks later he wrote: "12 months ago Hatteras was not taken[.] Hatteras, Roanoke Island, Newbern & near[ly] all of eastern NC is [now] in possession of the Federals & how much will be left not taken on the 22nd Aug 1863? God grant we may have peace." On August 27 he woefully penned: "No hope for peace."[79] Indeed, little hope for immediate peace then existed. Before the end would come, conditions would deteriorate further in Bertie County.

Notes

1. Sauers, "Laurels for Burnside," 14, 17, 19–20; Rush C. Hawkins, "Early Coast Operations in North Carolina," in *Battles and Leaders*, 1:640–645.

2. Sauers, "Laurels for Burnside," 17, 44; Hawkins, "Early Coast Operations," 645.

3. Bertie County Court Minutes, February 10, 1862.

4. Smallwood diary, February 10, 1862.

5. W. F. Lynch to S. R. Mallory, January 22, 1862, *Official Records . . . Armies*, ser. 1, 9:147.

6. Sauers, "Laurels for Burnside," 14, 17, 19–20; Hawkins, "Early Coast Operations."

7. Lt. A. Murray to Comdr. S. Rowan, February 12, 1862, *Official Records of the Union and Confederate Navies in the War of the Rebellion*, ser. 1, 6:637 (hereafter cited as *Official Records . . . Navies*).

8. L. M. Goldsborough to Hon. Gideon Welles, February 14, 1862, *Official Records . . . Navies*, ser. 1, 6:632; Kruman, *Parties and Politics*, appendix B. Following are the percentages of Union votes (where available) by county in the Albemarle Sound region for the February 1861 secessionist convention election: Pasquotank County, 79 percent;

Chowan County, 82 percent; Gates County, 70 percent; Bertie County, 82 percent; and Hertford County, 57 percent.

9. Smallwood diary, February 12, 1862.

10. Beth Gilbert Crabtree and James W. Patton, eds., *"Journal of a Secesh Lady"*: *The Diary of Catherine Ann Devereux Edmondston, 1860–1866* (Raleigh: North Carolina Division of Archives and History, 1979), 115–116.

11. Henry T. Clark to J. P. Benjamin, February 13, 1862, *Official Records . . . Armies*, ser. 1, 9:433.

12. Sauers, "Laurels for Burnside," 11.

13. D. M. Barringer to J. P. Benjamin, February 13, 1862, *Official Records . . . Armies*, ser. 1, 51, pt. 2:471–472.

14. Smallwood diary, February 15, 1862.

15. *Official Records . . . Navies*, ser. 1, 6:639–640.

16. S. C. Rowan to L. M. Goldsborough, February 22, 1862, *Official Records . . . Navies*, ser. 1, 6:654–655.

17. USS *Lockwood* logbook, entry for February 19, 1862, Records of the Bureau of Naval Personnel, Record Group 24, National Archives; Rowan to Goldsborough, February 22, 1862, *Official Records . . . Navies*, ser. 1, 6:654.

18. Hawkins, "Early Coast Operations," 646; Brig. Gen. A. E. Burnside to Adj. Gen. Lorenzo Thomas, February 23, 1862, and Col. Rush C. Hawkins to Brig. Gen. J. G. Parker, February 21, 1862, *Official Records . . . Armies*, ser. 1, 9:193–195.

19. Brig. Gen. R. C. Gatlin to Gov. Henry T. Clark, February 20, 1862, *Official Records . . . Armies*, ser. 1, 51, pt. 2:476; Thomas C. Parramore, "The Burning of Winton in 1862," *North Carolina Historical Review* 39 (January 1962): 22; Smallwood diary, February 15, 1862.

20. Rowan to Goldsborough, February 22, 1862, *Official Records . . . Navies*, ser. 1, 6:654; Hawkins to Parker, February 21, 1862, *Official Records . . . Armies*, ser. 1, 9:195; USS *Delaware* logbook, entry for February 19, 1862, Records of the Bureau of Naval Personnel, Record Group 24, National Archives.

21. Hawkins to Parker, February 21, 1862, *Official Records . . . Armies*, ser. 1, 9:195; Matthew John Graham, *The Ninth Regiment New York Volunteers (Hawkins' Zouaves)* (New York: E. P. Coby and Co., 1900), 160–162.

22. Graham, *The Ninth Regiment New York Volunteers*, 162.

23. Manarin and Jordan, *North Carolina Troops*, 2:98; Brig. Gen. R. C. Gatlin to Gen. S. Cooper, February 24, 1862, and Gatlin to Maj. Gen. J. G. Martin, February 21, 1862, *Official Records . . . Armies*, ser. 1, 51, pt. 2:478–479.

24. Col. S. B. Spruill to Brig. Gen. L. O'B. Branch, March ?, 1862, *Official Records . . . Armies*, ser. 1, 9:252; Manarin and Jordan, *North Carolina Troops*, 2:98.

25. Smallwood diary, March 15, 1862.

26. Smallwood diary, March 19, 1862.

27. Long, *The Civil War Day by Day*, 187; Barrett, *The Civil War in North Carolina*, 109.

28. Manarin and Jordan, *North Carolina Troops*, 1:371–372, 9:65.

29. Smallwood diary, February 28, 1862.

30. *North Carolina Public Laws, 1862–63*, 9–10.

31. General Orders No. 3, Executive Department of North Carolina, Adjutant General's Office (Militia), Raleigh, March 27, 1862, Civil War Collection, Military Collection, State Archives.

32. J. G. Martin to J. J. Rhodes, April 11, 1862, Adjutant General's Office (Militia) Letter Book, 1862–1864, State Archives (hereafter cited as AGO Letter Book [Militia]).

33. Compiled Service Records of North Carolina's Confederate Soldiers. The author reviewed all volumes of *North Carolina Troops* published to date in attempting to identify Bertie County Confederate soldiers.

34. Census data reveal that 877 free white men ages eighteen through thirty-five resided in Bertie County in 1860. Eighth Census, 1860: Bertie County, Population Schedule.

35. *Official Records . . . Armies*, ser. 4, 1:1095–1097.

36. William L. Shaw, *The Confederate Conscription and Exemption Acts* (Sacramento: California Civil War Centennial Commission, 1962), 374; *Official Records . . . Armies*, ser. 4, 1:1095–1097.

37. Smallwood diary, May 12, 1862.

38. Hal Bridges, *Lee's Maverick General: Daniel Harvey Hill* (New York: McGraw-Hill, 1961; Lincoln: University of Nebraska Press, 1991), 6–7, 178.

39. J. G. Martin to J. H. Bunch, April 26, 1862, AGO Letter Book (Militia).

40. Long, *The Civil War Day by Day*, 204.

41. Comdr. S. C. Rowan to Lt. S. P. Quackenbush, April 29, 1862, *Official Records . . . Navies*, ser. 1, 7:287–288.

42. Quackenbush to Rowan, May 3, 1862, *Official Records . . . Navies*, ser. 1, 7:305–306.

43. Compiled Service Records of North Carolina's Confederate Soldiers (Fifth Regiment N.C. State Troops); Manarin and Jordan, *North Carolina Troops*, 4:117. While Captain Garrett was a prisoner of war, the citizens of Bertie County elected him their state senator. On August 5 Federal authorities released Garrett from prison, and he immediately returned to his Bertie County home to allow his wounds to heal further before returning to his company. Garrett returned to his unit in September and, believing that his "usefulness would be greater" if he served in the Confederate army rather than in the North Carolina legislature, declined the senate seat in early October.

44. Lt. C. W. Flusser to Comdr. S. C. Rowan, May 18, 1862, *Official Records . . . Navies*, ser. 1, 7:383–384.

45. Flusser to Rowan, May 18, 1862, *Official Records . . . Navies*, ser. 1, 7:383–384; McCallum, *Martin County during the Civil War*, 96; USS *Commodore Perry* logbook, entry for May 14, 1862, Records of the Bureau of Naval Personnel, Record Group 24, National Archives (hereafter cited as USS *Commodore Perry* logbook).

46. Flusser to Rowan, May 18, 1862, *Official Records . . . Navies*, ser. 1, 7:383–384. Flusser reported that the cargo of the *Alice* included "[all] the church bells of Plymouth." It is possible, however—given that the *Alice* was loaded in Windsor—that one of the bells was from St. Thomas' Episcopal Church in Windsor. Rev. Cyrus Waters, rector of the church, was a vocal and staunch supporter of the Confederacy, and with his support the church donated its iron bell to the Southern government for use in making ammunition or cannons. Union forces arrested Waters when they visited Windsor on Janu-

ary 30, 1864. See *The Episcopal Church in Bertie County, 1701–1990: From Its Anglican Roots to the Twentieth Century* (Windsor: St. Thomas' Episcopal Church, n.d.), 46.

47. Flusser to Rowan, May 18, 1862, *Official Records . . . Navies*, ser. 1, 7:383–384; USS *Whitehead* logbook, entry for May 15, 1862, Records of the Bureau of Naval Personnel, Record Group 24, National Archives (hereafter cited as USS *Whitehead* logbook).

48. Flusser to Rowan, May 18, 1862, *Official Records . . . Navies*, ser. 1, 7:383–384.

49. Flusser to Rowan, May 18, 1862, *Official Records . . . Navies*, ser. 1, 7:383–384.

50. USS *Whitehead* logbook, entry for May 18, 1862; F. Roy Johnson, *Tales from Old Carolina* (Murfreesboro: Johnson Publishing Company, 1965), 231.

51. Comdr. S. C. Rowan to Adm. L. M. Goldsborough, May 17, 1862, *Official Records . . . Navies*, ser. 1, 7:374–375.

52. Flusser to "My Darling Mamma," December 3, 1863, Charles W. Flusser Papers, Navy Historical Foundation, Washington, D.C.; Charles W. Stewart, *Lion-Hearted Flusser* (Annapolis: United States Naval Institute, 1905), 19, 278, 281–282. Flusser's two brothers—Guy and Ottaker—served in the First Regiment Kentucky Cavalry and Fourth Regiment Texas Infantry respectively and were both killed during the war. Compiled Service Records of Confederate Soldiers Who Served in Organizations from Kentucky (microfilm, M319) and Compiled Service Records of Confederate Soldiers Who Served in Organizations from Texas (microfilm, M323), Record Group 94, National Archives.

53. Stewart, *Lion-Hearted Flusser*, 284–295.

54. Flusser to Rowan, May 19, 1862, *Official Records . . . Navies*, ser. 1, 7:391.

55. Barrett, *The Civil War in North Carolina*, 127.

56. USS *Whitehead* logbook, entry for June 2, 1862; USS *Whitehead* muster rolls, Records of the Bureau of Naval Personnel, Record Group 24, National Archives (hereafter cited as USS *Whitehead* muster roll, with appropriate date). Union gunboat crews were integrated with blacks and whites serving side by side, whereas blacks who later served in the Federal army were required to serve in segregated, all-black organizations commanded by white officers.

57. Smallwood diary, June 7, 1862.

58. Rowan to Adm. L. M. Goldsborough, June 12, 1862, *Official Records . . . Navies*, ser. 1, 7:476; Hawkins, "Early Coast Operations," 659. Hawkins recalled in his account that about one hundred men signed the enlistment roll during this visit.

59. Hawkins, "Early Coast Operations," 658–659.

60. Maj. Gen. A. E. Burnside to Hon. E. M. Stanton, May 5, 1862, *Official Records . . . Armies*, ser. 1, 9:385.

61. Compiled Service Records of North Carolina's Union Soldiers (First Regiment N.C. Union Volunteers).

62. Manarin and Jordan, *North Carolina Troops*, 9:235–244; Compiled Service Records of North Carolina's Confederate Soldiers (Thirty-third Regiment N.C. Troops).

63. Smallwood diary, July 8, 1862.

64. Eli B. Copeland, deposition dated February 5, 1897, Federal pension file of Zadock Morris (First Regiment N.C. Union Volunteers), Pension Case Files of the Bureau of Pensions and Veterans Administration, 1861–1942, Record Group 15, National Archives (hereafter cited as Federal pension file of Zadock Morris).

65. Nazereth W. Parker and Isaac Parker, depositions dated May 7, 1897, Federal pension file of Zadock Morris.

66. John B. Harrell, deposition dated February 4, 1897, and Benjamin F. Jones, deposition dated March 10, 1897, Federal pension file of Zadock Morris.

67. John R. Capps and Matilda Capps, depositions dated October 20, 1899, Federal pension file of John R. Capps (Second Regiment N.C. Union Volunteers), Pension Case Files of the Bureau of Pensions and Veterans Administration, 1861–1942, Record Group 15, National Archives (hereafter cited as Federal pension file of John R. Capps).

68. Starkey Sharpe to Henry T. Clark, June 17, 1862, Henry T. Clark, Governors Papers, State Archives.

69. F. W. Bird to "My Dear Sister" (Mary E. Winston), May 26, 1862, Robert W. Winston Papers, Southern Historical Collection, University of North Carolina Library, Chapel Hill (hereafter cited as Winston Papers).

70. Emma Parker to William G. Parker, June 16, 1862, William G. Parker Papers, Private Collections, State Archives (hereafter cited as Parker Papers).

71. Flusser to Rowan, July 11, 1862, *Official Records . . . Navies*, ser. 1, 7:556–557; Manarin and Jordan, *North Carolina Troops*, 2:2.

72. Manarin and Jordan, *North Carolina Troops*, 4:521, 2:309–315; Compiled Service Records of North Carolina's Confederate Soldiers (Fifty-ninth Regiment N.C. Troops [Fourth Regiment N.C. Cavalry]). See also Rep. Peyton Henry's remarks before the house of commons on December 12, 1863, published in the *Raleigh North Carolina Standard* on December 22, 1863.

73. Manarin and Jordan, *North Carolina Troops*, 2:309.

74. Smallwood diary, August 20, 1862.

75. Compiled Service Records of North Carolina's Union Soldiers (First Regiment N.C. Union Volunteers); William R. Trotter, *Ironclads and Columbiads: The Civil War in North Carolina—The Coast* (Winston Salem: John F. Blair, 1989), 214–217; Richard Dillard, *The Civil War in Chowan County, North Carolina* (Edenton: privately published, 1916), 13–14.

76. Compiled Service Records of North Carolina's Union Soldiers (First Regiment N.C. Union Volunteers).

77. Compiled Service Records of North Carolina's Union Soldiers (First Regiment N.C. Union Volunteers).

78. Bertie County Court Minutes, August 11, 1862.

79. Smallwood diary, July 31, August 21, 27, 1862.

CHAPTER 4

A Perilous and Painful Condition

Monday, September 15, was the scheduled first day of the fall 1862 session of Bertie County's superior court, and, as usual, a number of the county's leading citizens went to Windsor for the session. Judge Robert Strange French, who was to preside over the session, failed to arrive, however, so Sheriff A. H. Hassell briefly convened and then adjourned the court until the following day. The next morning, Sheriff Hassell again convened the court; but when he became satisfied "that Judge French would not attend . . . on account of [the] close proximity of the enemy," he discharged the jury and again adjourned court.[1]

Although the court session did not take place, a number of influential citizens of Bertie seized upon the occasion to discuss the deteriorating conditions within the county. The men were particularly concerned over the county's constant exposure to Federal gunboats and troops, the lack of Confederate soldiers to provide them protection, the thousands of slaves in the county for whom there was then an insufficient number of white men to control and oversee, and the conscription evaders lurking throughout the county. During the discussion, the participants decided that Lewis Thompson, the former Whig state senator, should visit Raleigh and meet directly with Gov. Zebulon Vance to seek immediate assistance from state and Confederate authorities. (Vance had been elected to the state's top office in August and had replaced Gov. Henry T. Clark on September 8.)

Thompson, for undisclosed reasons, was unable to visit the governor until about early October, so on September 18 John Pool—former state senator from Pasquotank County, unsuccessful candidate for governor in 1860, and an in-law of the influential Mebane family of Bertie County—wrote Vance a lengthy and detailed letter informing him of the dangerous conditions that existed in Bertie. Pool advised the governor that Federal gunboats were daily traversing the county's many waterways, along which lay the county's "most excellent farming lands," on which several thousand slaves resided. Pool also reminded Vance of the close proximity of the Federal military post at Plymouth to Bertie and the fact that no Confederate soldier was stationed in the county. According to Pool, "not the least show of protection" was being extended to Bertie County's citizens, who were "completely at the mercy" of the Federal forces. Pool further noted: "The people are, for the most part, loyal to the Confederacy & have acted with surprising prudence & faithfulness. But how long . . . is it prudent to Suffer these people to depend entirely upon the enemy for safety, & feel that they are neglected if not abandoned by their own Government?" Pool informed Vance that conscription efforts in the county had yielded few soldiers for the Confederate army and had instead driven "many, of not very reliable character" to the Federal forces at Plymouth. Pool believed that "many more" were ready to flee to Plymouth or the Federal gunboats if further execution of the conscription law were attempted. According to Pool, citizens of Bertie County loyal to the Confederacy had "more to dread" from the conscription "deserters" than from the "regular enemy."

Pool also wrote that "comparatively few slaves" had been lost but that it was with "great difficulty that the few [white] men left [in the county], unsupported by . . . military force," were able to maintain efficient police operations and prevent the additional flight of slaves. Pool felt that if the slave owners attempted to relocate their slaves farther away from the Union presence, "most of them would run off, at once—& any general attempt to move them would produce an almost universal stampede, resulting in the loss of the negroes, & endangering the lives of the few citizens."

But the "Southern men" of the county took "another view of the consequences" of removing slaves from the county. In Pool's words:

If the Slave holders, being men of means, fly, upon the approach of danger, & leave the poorer classes who are unable to move, & the families of soldiers in the Army, exposed not only to the enemy, but to the gangs of run away slaves, it will produce a state of things & of feeling much to be dreaded. It is not the duty of the influential slaveholder to remain & exert himself to preserve social order, & prevent an entire disruption of Society? It is hoped that the enemy will soon be driven away, & these people are bearing up under their troubles sustained by that hope—feeling that they have been & still are neglected—but yet willing to believe that the best has been done that circumstances would allow. Several months spent in this state of constant danger & anxiety has enabled the thinking men of this county to see what is necessary to be done, more clearly perhaps, than can be seen by those at a distance, even in authority, who must judge from reports only.

According to Pool, the citizens believed that the state and Confederate governments needed to take immediate actions to remedy the situation in the county. Pool advised the governor that several measures should be taken. First, a cavalry force was needed in the county. Pool specifically requested that two companies of the Nineteenth Regiment North Carolina Troops (Second Regiment North Carolina Cavalry)—Capt. John Randolph's company (H), which included Bertie County men, and Capt. Mills L. Eure's company (C)—be assigned to the county.[2] Pool wrote: "With this Cavalry to back them, the citizens left could preserve order, and prevent any great number of slaves from escaping, . . . & embolden the loyal citizens to speak & act with freedom & zeal. The loyal citizens of this county ought to have some support. The interest of the Confederacy in this section, requires it."

Second, Pool recommended to Vance that Pres. Jefferson Davis should exercise the discretion vested in him by the conscription act and exempt Bertie County from any further execution of the law. Pool noted: "There are not now enough men in the County for efficient police duty—& any attempt at executing the law, instead of getting soldiers for our Army, would send recruits to the enemy—for the correct minded men, subject to the law, have already gone to Camp. The substantial men of the county dread to see the others made their enemies. If the Conscript law is extended to 45 years, its execution would complete the ruin of the County."[3] Only nine days later, the Confederate government extended the conscription age limit to forty-five years. No executive action was taken to exempt Bertie County from that provision.[4]

Third, Pool warned Vance that no military orders requiring slaves to work on fortifications or serve in the army should be sent to Bertie County. Such orders, according to Pool, would "make the slaves run off & very few could be obtained under the order, for it would be idle to attempt to hunt negroes in this section" of the state. Pool offered an additional reason why slaves should not be ordered to work on Confederate fortifications: if the Confederates began rounding up slaves and taking them off, the Federals would have a "military excuse" to seize those who were left.

In concluding, Pool stated that he had written in accordance with the instructions of the "Bertie gentlemen" and that he also approved of their recommendations, believing that the proposed measures were the best actions that could be taken under the circumstances. He added: "If the Confederate authorities are not able to do something, it might be well to authorize the raising of a state force to operate in this section. . . . [S]omething ought to be done for this section of the State, at once."

Pool's correspondence conveyed an important message to Governor Vance: Bertie County's leading citizens now perceived that their county could no longer be depended upon to provide human resources to the Confederacy without dire repercussions within the county. The citizens could no longer significantly assist the Confederate military, but the county desperately needed that same military's support, assistance, and protection.

In less than two years, the sentiments of Bertie County's leading citizens had shifted dramatically. From December 1860 into the spring of 1861, the citizens ardently voiced their staunch support for the Union. In April and May 1861 the citizens just as vigorously called for North Carolina's withdrawal from the Union. Now, seventeen months into the war, the citizens felt that wartime demands upon the county should be relaxed.

Pool conveyed another serious concern of the leading citizens: that further enforcement of the conscription law might turn Bertie's less affluent citizens against its wealthier residents. In short, those individuals who were most likely to be forced into military service—the poorer class of citizens—had much less to gain economically from the war than the affluent landowners and slaveholders.

Sixteen months after Pool's letter, Vance urged President Davis to suspend the draft in the counties bordering Albemarle Sound. Davis interpreted the situation not as a political problem to be remedied but as a challenge, requiring the application of force to compel men to enter military service. Vance, however, refused to sanction such use of force against those in the eastern sector of the state who opposed conscription and the war.[5] In response to Pool's plea for cavalry troops, Vance in November 1862 recommended to the state legislature that a military force be sent to the northeastern part of the state. The legislature did not provide for such a force, however.[6]

Recognizing the defenseless state of the county, Col. Jonathan J. Rhodes, commander of the Bertie County militia, on October 7 wrote to North Carolina adjutant general James G. Martin regarding the creation of militia patrols in the county. Martin referred Rhodes's letter to Governor Vance, who authorized Rhodes to raise a patrol. On October 14 Martin wrote to Rhodes, advising him that Governor Vance "directs that you raise a patrol of 50 men not subject to the Conscription Act to be used for the protection of the county. The men will not be mounted as it is thought they will be of more service on foot."[7]

A foot patrol of Bertie County men not liable for Confederate conscription—that is, men who were over forty-five years of age and boys under the age of eighteen or persons who were exempted by special provisions of the conscription laws—was not the type of force John Pool and the leading citizens of the county desired. They had requested Governor Vance to dispatch to Bertie two companies of mounted soldiers, which would have numbered about 150 to 200 men. A fifty-man patrol, primarily composed of relatively old men, was of little military consequence to the Union army's forces at Plymouth or the gunboats that cruised the area waterways. The patrol, armed with personal weapons such as shotguns and muskets, could not have prevented the landing of even a token force of Union soldiers and marines supported by gunboat artillery. Possibly the best service such a patrol might have provided would have included enforcement of martial law and limited protection for the general citizenry against runaway slaves and troublesome whites.

The urgent need for some form of resident military force prompted citizens of the upper Albemarle Sound region to meet in Halifax County on October 25. At the meeting, citizens from Bertie, Martin, Halifax, and Northampton Counties decided that "local defense" companies were needed to afford some protection for residents. They "ordered the printing and distribution of an act authorizing the formation of companies for local defense."[8] It is unclear whether a company of "local defense" was ever organized in Bertie County.

The war, which had been ongoing for one and one-half years, was beginning to extract a heavy psychological toll on the citizens. Concerns over welfare for oneself and family members at home and in the Confederate army, exposure to Union raids, the presence of runaway slaves and unruly whites, and daily strife in providing basic needs were wearing down the stamina of Bertie County citizens. Confederate forces were not achieving victories on the battlefield as frequently as they had been able to do during the early months of the conflict. The war had reached an important turning point for the Confederacy: Gen. Robert E. Lee's army had crossed into Maryland in September and had been stopped by Gen. George B. McClellan's Union forces at the small town of Sharpsburg, Maryland, on Antietam Creek on September 17. In that battle—the war's bloodiest single-day encounter—Lee's forces had suffered an appalling number of casualties.[9] Upon learning that Lee's army had been roughly handled at Sharpsburg, Charles Smallwood wondered "When will this state of affairs end?"[10] Surely many Bertie County citizens pondered the same agonizing question.

One wealthy Bertie County planter, John B. Griffin of the Woodville area, became despondent over the conditions within the Confederacy and the county. The fifty-five-year-old Griffin was one of the county's most affluent residents. He owned 2,531 acres of land valued at $27,000 and was the fourteenth largest landowner in the county. He owned sixty-eight slaves, making him the twenty-second largest slave owner in Bertie. The total value of his personal property was approximately $61,000. Griffin financially supported the Confederate and North Carolina governments' war efforts by purchasing bonds and notes. By early November 1862 he held $5,000 in Confederate securities, $2,500 in North Carolina bonds, and $1,650 in Confederate currency.[11] But Griffin apparently could no longer withstand the stress posed by deteriorating conditions in the Confederacy. On November 14, 1862, he committed suicide by shooting himself, reportedly "on acc[oun]t of the troubles of the country."[12] He left a wife and five children, whose ages ranged from five to sixteen years.[13]

In October, Bertie native Joseph O. Cherry traveled throughout the county recruiting men for a company he was organizing. Cherry's company, once organized, was to serve in a partisan ranger regiment Maj. Samuel J. Wheeler intended to raise. During the four-week period from October 20 to November 15, Cherry, who had been commissioned a captain, enlisted thirty-eight Bertie County men for the proposed company. A dozen of those men, however, after enlisting, decided not to serve in the company and promptly deserted or failed to appear at the first company muster.[14] During November and early December four of Cherry's recruits—Doctrin E. Todd, Augustus White, William H. Butler, and William J. Pugh—slipped out of Bertie County and enlisted in the First Regiment North Carolina Union Volunteers at Plymouth.[15]

Some men, believing they were going to be conscripted, enlisted in Cherry's company but subsequently deserted. The actions of twenty-one-year-old William J. Pugh reflect the indecisiveness other military-age males likely experienced when confronted with the specter of forced induction into the Confederate army. Pugh, believing he "might be pressed into the rebel army," went to Windsor, where Cherry was recruiting, took the Oath of Allegiance to the Confederate States of America, and enlisted on October 30, 1862. After Pugh signed up, Cherry allowed him to go home "to get ready to join the command." While at home, Pugh reconsidered his decision to serve in the Confederate army, changed his mind, and decided to flee to the Union forces at Plymouth. He hired an unidentified man to take him to Plymouth, where he enlisted as a private in Company C, First Regiment North Carolina Union Volunteers, on November 21, 1862—only twenty-two days after taking the Confederate oath and enlisting in Captain Cherry's company.[16]

While Captain Cherry was obviously disappointed at enlisting men who would not serve, Wheeler was unable to obtain a sufficient number of companies to constitute a regiment. He succeeded in obtaining only four companies and therefore organized a battalion instead of a regiment. Wheeler's organization became the Twelfth Battalion North Carolina Cavalry. Cherry's company, while awaiting the anticipated completion of the regiment, operated in the Hertford County area, performing picket, scouting, and courier duty.[17]

By the end of November 1862, approximately 750 Bertie County men had enlisted or been conscripted into Confederate service. At that time the statutory conscription ages ranged from eighteen to forty-five years. (In 1860 about 1,180 white men aged sixteen to forty-three were reported to be residing in the county; those men would have been approximately eighteen to forty-five years old—legal conscription ages—by November 1862.) Thus, more than 60 percent of the county's conscription-age males had entered Confederate service by late 1862.[18]

By the fall of 1862 another serious problem—speculation in goods and commodities—had arisen in North Carolina. Shortages in essential products and goods necessary for maintaining the citizens' lives had become acute. Scarcity of goods, high prices, and the Union blockade of the state's coastal waterways had political as well as military repercussions. Individuals who owned desperately needed goods and commodities began to hoard the items and await anticipated increases in prices. Governor Vance believed that such speculation in the necessities of life had become an organized business immensely profitable to the speculators and equally devastating to the poor citizens, causing unnecessary suffering for the state's citizens.

On November 26, 1862, the governor issued a proclamation intended "to stop, if possible, the wicked system of speculation which is blighting the land." Four days earlier the state legislature had issued a joint resolution addressing the speculation problem and authorizing

Vance to implement an embargo upon exports from the state. Vance's proclamation forbade all private citizens, for a period of thirty days, to carry from or export out of the state any salt, bacon, pork, beef, corn-meal, flour, potatoes, shoes, leather, hides, cotton cloth and yarn, or woolen cloth. Vance directed that colonels of the militia enforce the proclamation.[19] Speculation apparently had become a serious problem in Bertie County, which was a rich agricultural resource. During the 1859 growing season Bertie farmers and planters produced hundreds of thousands of bushels of corn, beans, peas, potatoes, and other agricul-tural commodities and owned tens of thousands of livestock animals.[20]

On December 12 Adjutant General Martin directed Colonel Rhodes of the Bertie County militia to communicate with Col. John Bowen Odom of the Northampton County militia to prevent specu-lators from violating the governor's proclamation. Martin further di-rected Colonel Rhodes to "seize all pork and beef and other articles prohibited by the proclamation from being carried out of the state and that articles so seized shall be turned over to the state . . . especially pork and beef." Martin advised Rhodes that if he needed assistance in carrying out the directive and enforcing the governor's proclamation, he was to request such assistance from Brig. Gen. Beverly H. Robert-son, cavalry commander at Garysburg.[21]

Throughout the summer and fall, Bertie County men made their way to the Union forces at Plymouth and Wingfield, where they en-listed in the First Regiment North Carolina Union Volunteers. By the end of 1862 more than forty Bertie men had enlisted in that regiment. Five men (William E. Clark, Mathias Harrell, William Council Liv-ermon, Gabriel T. Morris, and Whitman Harrell) enlisted in Jack Fair-less's notorious Buffalo company at Wingfield.[22]

Throughout the fall and into the winter months, Federal gunboats under the command of Lt. Comdr. Charles W. Flusser remained active, defending Plymouth and patrolling Albemarle Sound, the Chowan and Roanoke Rivers, and other area waterways. Generally, multiple num-bers of gunboats were present at any time, enforcing President Lincoln's blockade on the waterways at the upper end of Albemarle Sound. On January 5, 1863, 2d Lt. Daniel W. Lewis of Company D, Fifty-ninth Regiment North Carolina Troops (Fourth Regiment North Carolina Cavalry), commander of the Rebel pickets on the Chowan River, dis-patched to Col. Dennis D. Ferebee, his regimental commander, a message indicating that thirteen Union gunboats had appeared in the Chowan River at Colerain. Lewis further reported that "12,000 Yan-kee troops in the counties of Gates and Chowan [were] on their way to re-enforce General [John G.] Foster at New Berne." Lewis mentioned the widespread belief that the gunboats were "going to take on the 12,000 Yankee troops at Holly['s] Wharf, or Dillard's Farm [Wingfield]." Lewis greatly exaggerated the number of gunboats and Federal soldiers in the area. Upon receiving Lewis's dispatch on January 7, Maj. Gen. Samuel G. French, commander of the Confederate Department of North Carolina, dismissed the report, noting "doubts about the correctness of the information."[23]

No Union naval or army forces in the numbers reported by Lewis were present in the Chowan River in early January; nevertheless, to the lieutenant and other Confederate officers and authorities in northeastern North Carolina, the Union soldiers at Wingfield had become an intense concern. From the time John Fairless established Wingfield as headquarters for Company E, First Regiment North Carolina Union Volunteers, in early August, the Buffaloes there had become an intolerable nuisance to the Confederate authorities and secessionist citizens of Chowan County. The group pillaged, plundered, and destroyed properties in the area while "decoying" runaway slaves from Bertie, Chowan, Perquimans, and Hertford Counties.[24]

Under Fairless's leadership, Company E exhibited little military discipline and order. Even Union military leaders in the area held the Wingfield Buffaloes in low regard. In a September 19, 1862, report to Comdr. Henry K. Davenport, Flusser referred to Fairless's contingent as "our home guard thieves," even though Flusser had only the day before dispatched troops under the command of Acting Lt. Thomas J. Woodward, commander of the gunboat *Shawsheen*, to Edenton to confront a thirty-man force that intended to attack Fairless's company.[25]

After successfully thwarting the planned attack, Woodward proceeded to Wingfield, where he was appalled at the sorrowful military scene he encountered. Of the sixty-three recruits that had enlisted in the company, only twenty were present—"the others had gone to their homes or elsewhere, as they chose." Woodward found Lieutenant Fairless "in a state of intoxication, threatening to shoot some of the remaining men, and conducting himself in a most disgraceful manner." Woodward reported to Flusser that Fairless "has no control over his men, and [by] the manner in which he conducts himself he is doing much injury to the cause of the U.S. Government." Woodward learned that some of the men who had left camp had taken their military weapons with them and that members of the company had smuggled ammunition out of the camp and sold it to local citizens for liquor. Woodward seized the remaining arms he found and took them aboard his gunboat for safekeeping. He reported that Fairless's men "say they will serve under him no longer. They are now left in charge of a man they call lieutenant, with no clothing, no rations; [and] are dependent on the county for subsistence."[26]

Just over a month after Woodward's visit to Wingfield, Fairless's hell-bent attitude and propensity to drink brought his life to a sudden and violent end. On October 20 a drunken Fairless took eight men from his company and "went out on a reconnaissance," during which he became involved in a heated dispute with Pvt. James Wallace. Wallace, a deserter from Company C, Nineteenth Regiment North Carolina Troops (Second Regiment North Carolina Cavalry), had enlisted only seventeen days previously. During the dispute, Fairless shot Wallace, wounding him in the leg. Before the impaired Fairless could fire a second time, Private Wallace "shot him dead."[27]

William Council Livermon, a Bertie County native and member of Fairless's company, later provided an account of the shooting to a Federal official. Livermon recalled: "Mr. Fairless was in one of his drinking sprees [when] he took a Squad of men From the Company. Said he was going out to fight the Rebs. After Getting about 3 miles from Camp at a Place cauld Byrums Store . . . Fairless got in a Dispute with one of his men Name[d] Wallis. He Shooth Wallis in the Thy. Wallis retirn[ed] the fire Shoothin with his musket Killing Fairless Instantly."[28]

With Fairless's death, command of the Wingfield Buffaloes fell to 1st Lt. Joseph W. Etheridge, a resident of Roanoke Island.[29] The Wingfield Buffaloes had established their notoriety, and local officials and citizens desperately wanted them eradicated. On November 17 a hand-picked Confederate force under Capt. Ned Small of Edenton crossed the Chowan River at Harrellsville, just north of Bertie County, intending to attack Wingfield. The following day, local guerrillas joined Small, and the combined force attacked the Buffalo camp but was repelled—primarily because of artillery fire from the gunboat *Shawsheen*. Small's force attacked a second time in the early evening hours of November 19 but was again driven from the scene by a cannonade from two Union gunboats, the *Shawsheen* and the *Lockwood*. On November 19 Woodward informed Flusser that Small's troops "have not effected their object in capturing the home guard or destroying the headquarters."[30]

For the next several months, the Wingfield Buffaloes remained at the Dillard estate, where they were active "in capturing and destroying goods on their way to rebeldom." Finally, in early February 1863,

Confederate authorities decided that a determined effort should be made to remove the Union contingent at Wingfield. Maj. Gen. D. H. Hill, commander of Confederate forces in North Carolina, ordered that the Chowan County fortification be destroyed "without fail." On February 11, 1863, Companies B, E, and F of the Forty-second Regiment North Carolina Troops were detached as a special battalion under the command of Lt. Col. John E. Brown and ordered to attack the Union encampment at Wingfield. Brown's force departed Weldon on the eleventh and marched to Merry Hill, Bertie County, where it arrived on the fifteenth. Brown established his camp at Merry Hill; stationed pickets along the Chowan River at Harrellsville, Colerain, and other points almost to Plymouth; and began making arrangements for his attack.[31]

Within two weeks, Brown had formulated his assault plan. On the night of February 28 he and his battalion crossed the Chowan River in small rowboats, landed in Chowan County about fifteen miles south of Wingfield, and marched through the night to a point near the Buffalo encampment. The distance to Wingfield proved to be farther than Brown had planned, so at dawn he halted his weary troops and concealed them in the woods, where they spent the day observing the Union soldiers.

Throughout the day, the Buffaloes languished around camp and engaged in target practice with small arms. Late in the afternoon, some of the men began leaving the camp, apparently intending to visit their homes. Brown's pickets captured several of the soldiers, but in the process one Union soldier spied some of Brown's men and hurried back to the camp, sounding the alarm. The *Underwriter*, a Union gunboat, immediately began shelling Brown's position. With his plan foiled, Brown withdrew and retired back across the river to his camp at Merry Hill, arriving there on March 2.[32]

Back at his camp, Brown began planning another expedition to Wingfield. At 4:30 in the afternoon on March 22, Brown's force left camp, crossed the Chowan River, and marched through the night to Wingfield. At daybreak Brown's battalion fired on the Buffalo pickets, forcing them to withdraw inside the fortification's breastworks. This time no artillery shells landed from a guardian gunboat. Fortunately for Brown and his men, the gunboat had been dispatched elsewhere.

Brown's men succeeded in driving most of the Union soldiers from the fortification, but approximately twenty Buffaloes took refuge in a blockhouse, from which Brown's men, lacking artillery, could not dislodge them. The Confederates began to destroy the buildings and quartermaster and commissary stores. Three of Flusser's gunboats, having been alerted to the attack, then steamed back to Wingfield and forced Brown to withdraw. Brown's men had heavily damaged the Buffalo camp; but after the Confederates withdrew, the Union soldiers returned.[33]

Brown's soldiers began retracing their trek to Wingfield, attempting to reach their rowboats and return across the river to their Bertie County sanctuary without being seen or attacked by the Union gunboats then patrolling the river. Brown split his force into two detachments, retaining command of one and placing the other under the command of 1st Lt. William J. Ellis. Ellis's detachment crossed the river safely without being fired upon by the gunboats, but Brown's group was not so fortunate. The gunboat *Underwriter* blocked Brown's intended crossing point at Rockyhock Creek. Federal authorities dispatched two hundred Federal cavalrymen from Gatesville to pursue Brown. In the meantime, the gunboat lobbed artillery shells at the Rebels' suspected position while Federal sailors found and confiscated Brown's boats.

Marines landed from Federal gunboats in the area, placing Brown's detachment in a precarious predicament. Brown's men, seemingly trapped by those vessels, marines, and approaching cavalry, faced a difficult challenge: they would have to fight their way through superior forces. Brown formed his men into battle ranks and charged the Union adversaries, who were concealed about 150 yards away. The gallant charge, accompanied by the terrifying "Rebel yell," unnerved the Federal troops, who wildly fired a musketry volley over the heads of the attacking Rebels. The startled Federal troops then fell back into the swamp.[34]

Lieutenant Ellis formed a relief expedition to attempt to bring his commanding officer to safety. During the night of March 24, Ellis's men succeeded in ferrying Lieutenant Colonel Brown and his men across the Chowan River. Three days later Gen. D. H. Hill wrote to Col. George C. Gibbs of the Forty-Second Regiment North Carolina Troops and informed him that Confederate scouts reported that a Federal advance was to made upon Hamilton. To meet the expected advance, Brown's battalion departed Bertie County and marched to Fort Branch on the Roanoke River near Hamilton.[35]

In mid-April, Confederate authorities dispatched the Forty-first Regiment North Carolina Troops (Third Regiment North Carolina Cavalry) to attack Wingfield. In the meantime, however, Col. Josiah Picket, commander of Union army forces at Plymouth, had concluded that there was little benefit in maintaining the Wingfield garrison. He ordered that the location be abandoned and that the facilities, rifle pits, and houses be destroyed. On April 17 most of the members of Company E, First Regiment North Carolina Union Volunteers, departed Wingfield and boarded a Federal steamer for Plymouth. A few hours later the North Carolina cavalry sent to attack the camp arrived and found a note tacked to the side of one of the undestroyed blockhouses. The note read: "A leetle too late."[36]

Throughout 1862 Flusser's gunboats routinely patrolled the waterways of the upper Albemarle Sound, curtailing the movement of Confederate goods and stores and rescuing runaway slaves and white refugees. Mindful that Confederate civil authorities controlled Bertie County, Flusser stationed the gunboat *Henry Brinker* at the mouth of the Cashie River in September to break up contraband trade with Windsor.[37] Windsor had become a depot for gathering goods and commodities for the Confederate government, and Flusser intended to prevent the movement of such items over the waterways.

While Confederate authorities officially governed Bertie County, some county residents realized that they could benefit economically by trading with the Union forces—the forces that had blockaded the area waterways. The extent of such trade between residents of Bertie and Federal troops and authorities cannot be determined from extant records. The problem was of such concern, however, that on February 23, 1863, North Carolina adjutant general James G. Martin advised Col. Jonathan J. Rhodes of the Bertie County militia that "Those persons who trade with the enemy should be arrested and punished by civil authority for violation of the state law."[38]

Upon occupying Plymouth in the spring of 1862, Lieutenant Flusser quickly began developing intelligence on the topography of the area and the attitudes and dispositions of the people. Flusser possessed a penchant for gathering information from available sources, discounting misinformation intended to mislead him, and utilizing reliable information to the benefit of the Union military. Using "good" cigars and whiskey as media of exchange, Flusser often "bought" information from area residents. Bertie County citizens, including William Hyman (owner of Hyman's Ferry, located a few miles up the Roanoke River from Plymouth) and a certain Mr. Bell, regularly provided Southern newspapers and information to Flusser and his subordinate officers.[39] Flusser developed a thorough knowledge of the geography and topography of the Albemarle Sound region; that knowledge, together with

By late December 1863 additional Bertie County men endeavored to assist the Union military in raising and supplying the Second Regiment North Carolina Union Volunteers. William G. Coggin, a thirty-two-year-old resident of the county, desired to become a sutler for the regiment. In such capacity, he would procure supplies, goods, and stores for sale to members of the regiment. Capts. Calvin Hoggard and Littleton Johnson recommended Coggin to Capt. Charles H. Foster. On January 4, 1864, Coggin wrote to Foster, requesting appointment as sutler and stating that he had done as much for the new regiment as any person by obtaining recruits. Unknown to Coggin, Foster had issued orders the week before authorizing him to be named sutler.[34] By January 12 Coggin had accumulated "three or four hundred dollars" worth of goods at Plymouth and promised Foster that he would raise money for the regiment and its members' families. He also promised to help Captains Hoggard and Johnson recruit in Bertie County.[35]

In late December 1863 Captain Foster had authorized Jonathan T. Mizell to raise a company of soldiers for the Second Regiment North Carolina Union Volunteers.[36] Mizell, Bertie County's first Union army officer and former commander of Company C, First Regiment North Carolina Union Volunteers, had resigned on November 24, 1863, after serving more than fifteen months. He was officially discharged on December 11, 1863.[37] Captain Foster now sought his assistance. On December 26 Foster issued special orders authorizing another resident of Bertie County—a Mr. Morris—to assist Lt. DeForest Masters in raising a company of soldiers.[38] Extant records fail to identify Morris fully or to shed any light on his effectiveness in assisting Masters.

By the middle of January 1864, Capt. Byron B. Bower and his company of Georgia cavalry had begun thoroughly frustrating Capt. Calvin Hoggard's efforts to recruit men for the Union army in Bertie County. On January 14 Hoggard informed Capt. Charles H. Foster that his recruiting efforts had not been as successful as they would have been had he been able to go into Bertie. Hoggard noted, however, that he hoped to enter the county shortly and to be able to obtain a "pretty number" of recruits.[39] The contest of wills between Bower and Hoggard was intensifying.

Between January 14 and 29, Hoggard slipped into Bertie County to recruit for his regiment. His effort was largely unsuccessful, however. Captain Bower's Georgia cavalry "was so thick" that Hoggard "could do but little" recruiting. Hoggard did capture one Georgia cavalryman, as well as that soldier's horse and arms, but his excursion generally failed to yield its anticipated results.[40]

The exact date Hoggard entered Bertie County is not evident from available records, but he may have made the trip on January 20, during the evening hours of which a Federal expedition departed Plymouth and proceeded toward the small village of Harrellsville. Gen. Henry W. Wessells had received reports that the Confederate government had accumulated "a considerable quantity of stores" at Harrellsville. Wessells directed Lt. Col. Wilson C. Maxwell of the 103d Regiment Pennsylvania Infantry to organize a detachment of soldiers and proceed to Harrellsville and "capture and destroy the property." Gunboats transporting the Federal force arrived off Harrellsville at about four o'clock in the afternoon of the twenty-first, and troops immediately landed. The Federal raiders soon found the goods destined for the Confederate government stored at John H. Garrett's farm. The troops set fire to Garrett's buildings, which held "a large quantity of meat salted for the Confederate Govt."

As the Federals destroyed the stores, Capt. Langley Tayloe's company (E) of the Sixty-eighth Regiment North Carolina Troops attacked, and a spirited and brisk engagement ensued. Despite the intervention of Tayloe's soldiers, the Union troops successfully destroyed between 150,000 and 200,000 pounds of pork, 270 barrels of salt, 10,000 pounds of tobacco, 32 barrels of beef, and other stores. They also captured a number of prisoners (including Garrett, who was sent to New Bern and jailed for several months), horses, and mules.[41] During the engagement, one Federal soldier and one Confederate soldier were killed. Two Confederate soldiers were wounded, including Pvt. Drew Peele of Bertie County, a member of Captain Tayloe's company.[42]

Six days later, Maxwell was given the responsibility of leading a similar raid. On January 26 General Wessells dispatched Maxwell with a force of infantry to Mars Hill, a small crossroads community in northern Bertie County about ten miles from Harrellsville. Wessells had learned that the North Carolina government had accumulated a substantial quantity of stores and goods at Mars Hill.

Maxwell's force departed Plymouth aboard gunboats on the afternoon of the twenty-sixth and proceeded to Colerain. According to an unidentified Bertie County citizen's account, "about 9 p.m., several Yankee gunboats came very unexpectedly up the Chowan river, and landed 500 men at Mr. Etheridge's near Coleraine. They marched at once to Mars Hill." Concealed by the nighttime darkness, Buffaloes led Maxwell's soldiers to the small community, marching primarily on secondary routes and avoiding the main roads. The North Carolina government had accumulated an estimated 200,000 pounds of pork at Mars

Hill. On the night of January 26 a twenty-one-man detachment from Capt. Jesse G. Holliday's company of the Fifteenth Battalion North Carolina Cavalry guarded the pork. In the predawn hours of the twenty-seventh, Maxwell's vastly superior force totally surprised and routed Holliday's troopers. After the Confederates fled, the Federals burned the pork.

After completing their destructive work at Mars Hill, the Union soldiers marched back to Colerain, confiscating livestock, rescuing slaves, and capturing a number of citizens along the way. According to a citizen's account, the Yankees also vandalized homes, destroyed personal property, treated females insultingly, and attempted to "produce a state of starvation" by destroying a gristmill and the grain stored in it as they marched back toward the Chowan River and the waiting gunboats.[43] The expedition proved to be the most destructive undertaken by Federal forces in the county during the war.

At Colerain a small band of Confederate soldiers from Bethlehem, Hertford County, having been alerted to the raid, attacked Maxwell's force before it could reboard the gunboats. The Confederates, members of the Sixty-eighth Regiment North Carolina Troops, along with some cavalry troopers, "vigorously" attacked the Federals at the home of William Etheridge, wounding one Pennsylvania soldier, Pvt. Lemuel Slagle, who was shot through the lungs, and capturing another, Pvt. John Maynard. The Confederates also had several men captured, including Pvts. David C. Askew and William W. Morris, both Bertie County residents.[44]

The clerk for the 103d Regiment Pennsylvania Infantry recorded in the regimental records the following description of the Harrellsville and Mars Hill raids:

On the 20 of January 1864, an expedition was sent out to Harrellsville, N.C. under Lt. Col W. C. Maxwell to destroy stores which had been collected by the enemy; a great quantity of pork was destroyed, about 125,000 pounds, a number of wagons, carts, horse, mules and oxen captured, also eleven bales of cotton, the enemy was driven off.

On the 26th an expedition for a similar purpose was sent out under the same officers, the enemy rates the loss in pork this time at about 200,000 pounds, many horses with cavalry equipments, mules, wagons, carts, & etc., were taken, and considerable property of the enemy destroyed. This in Bertie County; both expeditions immensely successful with no loss of our side, but one man wounded and one man missing.[45]

The large loss of state-owned pork at Mars Hill greatly irritated Governor Vance. Col. James W. Hinton, commander of the Sixty-eighth Regiment North Carolina Troops, was responsible for providing protection and monitoring Federal military activity in Hertford and Bertie Counties. Vance, upon learning of the destructive Federal raid in the Bertie County community, sought to charge Hinton with "official negligence in relation to the destruction of the meat belonging to the State." On February 4, 1864, Colonel Hinton, upon learning that charges might be pressed against him and that Maj. John Devereux, principal quartermaster commissary officer in the North Carolina Adjutant General's Office, had been sent to "look into the matter & ascertain who was to blame," wrote to the governor to explain how the Union forces had been able to destroy the pork. From Murfreesboro, Hinton wrote:

Not knowing the representations that may have been made to Maj. Devereaux I feel it due to myself to make a plain statement of facts & then ask you to decide whether any blame can justly be attached to me.

At the time the meat was burned I had two companies of infantry stationed about four miles from where the meat was stored. The balance of my infantry command which consisted of detachments of companies then being brought across the Chowan & numbering less than 200 men were encamped about two miles from this place. [Lt. Col. James M.] Wynn's Cavalry Battalion [Fifteenth Battalion North Carolina Cavalry] was also stationed here doing picket & courier service in conjunction with [Colonel Joel R.] Griffin's [Sixty-second Regiment Georgia] Cavalry as low as Harrellsville. I had also three pieces of artillery stationed here.

I received a dispatch from Edenton Monday night [January 25] stating that the enemy would in the course of four or five days attempt to burn Mizzell's meat. As soon as I received the dispatch I sent Captain [Jesse G.] Holliday's company of cavalry below with orders to prep all the team that could possibly be obtained and have Mizzell's meat moved at once. The next morning I started below with all the force I had—Artillery, Cavalry & Infantry. Before I had gotten four miles from Murfreesboro I received a dispatch that the meat had already been burned. When I arrived at Bethlehem about four miles from the place where Mizzell's meat was stored I learned these facts: Holliday with his Cavalry company reached the place where the meat was stored 9 o'clock at night. At three o'clock of the same night the enemy 600 strong came upon him by superior force drove him back & burned the meat. Having Buffaloes with them familiar with the whole country they were enabled to march the entire distance from their gunboats without touching the main roads.

I knew not until the day before the burning that there was any considerable amount of meat there. If I had, knowing my inability to protect it I should have . . . had it removed.

It is as much as I can do, with the small force at my command, to protect the meat interest at this point, & if I divide the force neither will be protected. It is fifty-two miles from this place to the mouth of the Chowan & the enemy can land at almost any point they may want to land at. You will readily see that it is actually impossible for me to protect so long a line with so small a force.[46]

The lack of adequate Confederate forces in Bertie County had cost the state government a valuable and badly needed commodity. Almost seventeen months had passed since John Pool had written Governor Vance, urgently requesting that two cavalry companies be assigned to the county. Whether two such companies, in addition to Captain Bower's company of Georgia cavalry, could have prevented the Mars Hill raid is subject to speculation; however, the number of Confederate troops in the area was clearly inadequate to provide even basic protection for the populace and the crucial Confederate and state stores.

At Plymouth on the evening of January 29, a large congregation, which included Gen. Henry W. Wessells and Lt. Comdr. Charles W. Flusser, attended a vocal and instrumental concert in the Methodist church performed by "amateurs" for the benefit of the North Carolina Union soldiers and their families. During the performance, Wessells and Flusser abruptly left the church by climbing out a window. Shortly thereafter the regimental adjutants were summoned, and more officers quickly departed. By then the remaining members of the audience realized that "something was up." The "something" was an immediate joint army-navy raid on Windsor.[47]

On January 29 Col. Joel R. Griffin, commander of the Sixty-second Regiment Georgia Cavalry, had arrived in Windsor and was visiting his troopers stationed there. At that time the regimental contingent included Captain Bower's company (B), Capt. Rhodes T. Duval's company (D), and an artillery detachment from Company H. Griffin, whose regimental headquarters were at Franklin, Virginia, periodically visited his picket stations and outposts scattered in southeastern Virginia and eastern North Carolina. Wessells's and Flusser's hasty departure from the concert at Plymouth possibly indicated that they had been unexpectedly informed of Griffin's presence at Windsor and that they wanted to send an armed expedition immediately to the town.

As the concert was taking place in Plymouth, members of the Sixty-second Regiment Georgia Cavalry were enjoying a "serenade" in Windsor. Confederate military musicians provided the music, and citizens of Windsor probably attended. The festivities continued until about midnight, during which those in attendance had "quite a merry time."[48]

About eight o'clock in the evening, the Union troops at Plymouth began preparing for the expedition as details of soldiers from the various

The commander of Union army forces at Plymouth was Brig. Gen. Henry Walton Wessells, under whom Capts. Littleton Johnson's and Calvin Hoggard's companies served and fought during the Battle of Plymouth. Wessells often cooperated with his naval counterpart at Plymouth, Lt. Comdr. Charles W. Flusser, in conducting joint raids and expeditions against Southern "targets" in Bertie County and other locales in the Albemarle region. Photograph from Luther S. Dickey, *History of the Eighty-fifth Regiment Pennsylvania Volunteer Infantry, 1861–1865* (New York: J. C. and W. E. Powers, 1915), facing 224.

regiments organized and received supplies. Wessells designated Lt. Col. Samuel Tolles of the Fifteenth Regiment Connecticut Infantry to lead the army contingent and cooperate with Flusser. The assembled force totaled almost four hundred men, including soldiers from Tolles's regiment, the Sixteenth Regiment Connecticut Infantry, the Second Regiment North Carolina Union Volunteers, the Eighty-fifth Regiment New York Infantry, and the 101st and 103d Regiments Pennsylvania Infantry. Marines and sailors from Flusser's gunboat squadron, along with several pieces of artillery, augmented the force.

In order to surprise and surround the Georgia cavalry, Flusser—who would accompany the expedition—planned a multipronged advance on Windsor that would utilize gunboats and a troop transport. Under the cover of the predawn darkness, soldiers and marines aboard the army transport steamer *Massasoit* were to disembark at Cedar Landing on the Roanoke River and march toward the town, approaching from the south. As that contingent progressed, other soldiers aboard gunboats in the Cashie River were to land several miles downriver from the town and march to the Windsor bridge across the Cashie; still others were to move around behind Windsor and establish an ambush at Hoggard's Mill bridge, approximately one-half mile north of the town. The fourth "prong" of the raid would consist of gunboats that would ascend the Cashie River and land troops directly at the town. Inasmuch as the Cashie runs immediately along the east side of Windsor, Flusser apparently anticipated that the attack would push the Georgia cavalry west and north of the town.

About eleven o'clock that night, preparations for the expedition had been completed, and the Federal troops boarded the transport *Massasoit* and the gunboats *Bombshell* and *Whitehead*. Shortly before midnight the Federal vessels steamed away from Plymouth—the *Massasoit* ascending the Roanoke and the *Bombshell* and the *Whitehead* simultaneously descending the river. The two latter vessels then entered the Cashie River—a waterway with which the crews of both vessels had become familiar during the previous months' operations.[49]

In the early morning hours of January 30, the *Massasoit* anchored off Cedar Landing about eight miles from Windsor and discharged approximately three hundred infantrymen, sailors, and marines, including Lieutenant Commander Flusser, who immediately began marching toward Windsor. At two o'clock in the morning, the *Bombshell* and the *Whitehead* anchored in the Cashie River off Joseph Cooper's landing, about seven miles from Windsor, and discharged a detachment of about ninety soldiers, including Capt. Calvin Hoggard and at least thirty Buffaloes, as well as John A. Reed, a Pennsylvanian who recently had been appointed a lieutenant in Hoggard's regiment. Confederate pickets observed the Union landing, and a courier was dispatched to Windsor to advise Colonel Griffin and Captain Bower that the "Yankees were landing." The courier arrived at the Georgia cavalry camp about 3:00 A.M. and duly advised the Confederate officers of the activity down the river, but Griffin and Bower made no effort to confront the Federals who landed at Cooper's or to ascertain their intentions.[50]

Capt. Calvin Hoggard, intimately familiar with the roads, paths, and topography of his home county, led the detachment, which landed at Cooper's by way of the countryside, passing within less than a mile of the "Windsor" bridge over the Cashie River. Once the detachment reached the road that connected Windsor and Edenhouse, a group of sixty-one soldiers under the command of Lt. DeForest Masters moved toward the Windsor bridge (immediately east of the town), while Hoggard led the remaining men, numbering about thirty, toward the Hoggard's Mill bridge. Hoggard's men reached the bridge at daybreak and fired on the Confederate sentry stationed there. The sentry promptly fled, and Hoggard's men quickly dismantled timbers from the bridge and hastily used them to construct breastworks. Hoggard and his Buffaloes then concealed themselves and awaited the attack on Windsor by their Union comrades. Hoggard's orders were to "hold the bridge" during the forthcoming engagement.

The sounds of Hoggard's men firing on the sentry at the bridge alerted the Georgia cavalrymen in their camps at Windsor. Within a few minutes the troopers, "saddled up" and pulling one light artillery piece, galloped off toward the bridge, at which they arrived "in 15 minutes." At the bridge, Hoggard's men fired on the Georgians from behind the assembled breastworks on the opposite bank.

The Georgians attempted to make a stand, limbered up their single artillery piece, and hastily fired one round at Hoggard's position, "but to no effect." The Confederates turned their mounts away from the bridge and started back toward their camps, but, to their "astonishment and surprise," before they had gone two hundred yards they heard what Marcene Bower, Capt. Byron Bower's brother, later characterized as "the yell of 1,500 Yankees."[51] The Georgians had run headlong into the Union soldiers and marines who had marched through the darkness from Cedar Landing. No Confederate pickets had reported a Yankee troop landing during the night on the Roanoke River, and the Georgia cavalrymen were caught off guard. On the other hand, the Federals had no cavalry, and even though they forced the outnumbered Rebel troopers to flee to the west of Windsor, they could not adequately pursue the horsemen. Lt. John A. Reed noted that the Rebels "turned and ran like sheep."[52]

From the vicinity of Hoggard's Mill bridge, the Union soldiers briefly pursued the fleeing Rebels. The Union troops captured two Georgians, as well as the soldiers' horses. The Georgians cut across fields, passing by a schoolhouse to the west of town. Lieutenant Commander Flusser's artillerists "practiced with their howitzers for a while, shelling the country in the direction the rebels had gone." Lieutenant Reed, later commenting on the conduct of Captain Hoggard's Buffaloes, noted that the men had "done well."[53]

As the Union contingent from the Roanoke River had approached Windsor, a detachment of soldiers under the command of Capt. John Donaghy of the 103d Regiment Pennsylvania Infantry was dispatched to the left (west of town) "at double quick" to come in on the Georgians' flank. Before that detachment reached its designated position, the Georgia cavalry had "skedaddled." From a distance, Donaghy's men saw some of the "mounted rebels fleeing across a field." The overly eager Federals, desiring to "get a pop at the rebs," began firing without orders, endangering an unseen line of Union skirmishers in their front. "Some vigorous language" from Captain Donaghy, as well as several blows with the flat of his sword, prompted the soldiers to cease their senseless firing.[54]

The *Whitehead* and the *Bombshell*, which had remained anchored in the Cashie River until seven o'clock in the morning of January 30, arrived off Windsor about midmorning. There additional Union soldiers landed, and the two vessels turned around in the river and awaited the return of the troops.[55]

The conquering Union troops destroyed the Georgians' camps and confiscated various items left behind by the fleeing cavalrymen, including several boxes of ammunition, musical instruments, clothing, cooking utensils, and saddlebags. The Union soldiers "had exciting times in breaking up the rebel cavalry camps."[56] Captain Bower's company clerk entered in the company's muster roll the following description of the surprise attack by the Federals: "This company was surrounded in camp at Windsor, NC on the night of the 30th Jany, 1864 by 1200 of the enemy, coming up in four different directions; were not taken by surprise but forced to cut [our] way out through the enemy, losing two men & killing seven of enemy besides wounded many others. The enemy were accompanied by Gun Boats which landed five co's at Windsor and on Roanoke River."[57] The clerk overestimated the number of Federal troops involved in the action, as well as the number of casualties inflicted upon those men.

The Federal troops occupied Windsor for several hours after the engagement, during which time they captured five secessionist citizens—Rev. Cyrus Waters, Dr. Turner Wilson, Lorenzo Webb (the town banker), Thomas Skirven, and James L. Mitchell. In the early afternoon Captain Hoggard's Buffaloes, having passed through the streets of Windsor, boarded the *Whitehead* with the citizen prisoners. The secessionist citizens of Windsor surely looked upon Hoggard and his men with great disdain as they passed through the town, proudly glowing in their accomplishment of the day. About two o'clock in the afternoon, the *Whitehead* and the *Bombshell* steamed away from Windsor. The troops that had marched from Cedar Landing retraced their route to the waiting *Massasoit*.[58]

The Federal forces safely returned to Plymouth during the evening of January 30, having been gone for about twenty-four hours. The Federal soldiers placed the citizen prisoners, along with a number of captured Confederate soldiers, in the custody of the provost marshal at Plymouth. The citizen prisoners were sent to New Bern, held for a short time, and then released. Wessells and Flusser apparently never brought any specific charges against the captured Windsor men.

On January 31 Colonel Griffin had reached Jackson, Northampton County, where he telegraphed Confederate authorities in Rich-

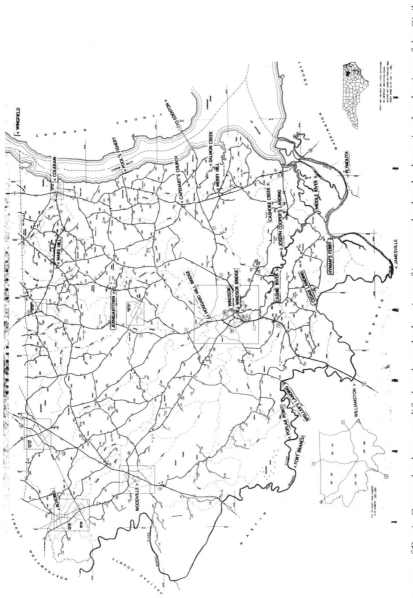

This modern map of Bertie County has been modified to show the locations of important landmarks that existed at the time of the Civil War. Map supplied by the author.

mond: "Yesterday morning with [a] force of 200 men and [a] mountain rifled piece, after fight of two hours with 1,200 of enemy and three pieces of artillery, [Yankees] were driven from Windsor, NC to their boats. We lost 6 men, enemy not known."[59] Like Captain Bower's company clerk, Griffin greatly exaggerated the results of the confrontation and the size of the Union forces.

Flusser, after receiving a copy of Griffin's report, which had been published in a Raleigh newspaper, wrote to his superior officer, Rear Adm. Samuel P. Lee, commander of the North Atlantic Blockading Squadron, that the report was "false from beginning to conclusion. I planned the affair, and we would have captured the entire party had we been ten minutes earlier. . . . We marched about 16 miles. There was no fight, and nothing worth reporting. The rebels ran. I fired three or four times at them at long range. We held the town of Windsor several hours, and marched back . . . to our boats without a single shot from the enemy."[60]

Maj. Gen. John J. Peck, commander of the Union army forces at New Bern, was so pleased with the results of the expedition to Windsor that on February 23 he issued orders officially congratulating General Wessells's men. The orders announced "with satisfaction the success of an expedition sent to Windsor by General H. W. Wessells . . . which resulted in breaking up the cantonment of a company of Georgia cavalry."[61]

Colonel Griffin, having come so close to being captured, primarily blamed the attack on the unionist citizens in Bertie County. On February 4 Griffin sent Governor Vance a "plain statement of the actual state of affairs at present in Bertie County." Writing from his headquarters at Franklin, Virginia, Griffin informed Vance that most of Bertie County's citizens were now taking a stand against the Confederacy and that numerous Buffaloes had taken to the swamps. Griffin wrote:

I have recently returned from Windsor, Bertie Co. where I had a little affair with [the] enemy who advanced upon the town a force of 1200 men in three different directions, for the purpose of capturing our little force (100 men) at that point. . . .

While a portion of the co[unty] is loyal, it is nevertheless evident as (I have seen with my own eyes) that the majority [of] the people proper are taking [a] position against us. Old and young, rich and poor, educated and ignorant are alike bound to Lincoln, and those that remain true are the exception. Their swamps are full of armed Buffaloes and deserters. Their homes open wide their doors with ready hospitality to receive and entertain Yankee soldiers and Yankee spies.

They seek in Plymouth Yankee papers of protection and have on their persons papers and permits to trade. . . .

The enemy has in his service organized companies from this county, and trusts not without reason to the friendly feeling and active cooperation of those at home. As evidence of this, a detachment of 250 men who took part in the late expedition against Windsor . . . marched through the country . . . subsisted and concealed by their Bertie friends and simultaneously with advance of main bodies appeared at bridges 2 miles in rear of town on [the] Coldrain [sic] road. Their approach was only known at camp from reports of one of Capt Bowers scouts, the entire population religiously preserving their secret.

When my scouts go through this country as Confederates they are fired upon by these people. When they [im]personate Yankees as they have done recently in several instances, they are trusted, all their wants are supplied, and when they represent themselves cut off and in danger of capture by Rebels, horses and arms are given them.

The loyal people of this section are overpowered. They dare not take bold ground. [F]ive of the best and most loyal citizens of Windsor were carried off last Saturday. . . . My statements are not exaggerated. They can be proven.[62]

The Federal raid on the Georgia cavalry, in which Captain Hoggard conspicuously participated, intensified the personal animosity between him and Capt. Byron Bower. Hoggard had allegedly proclaimed that he would capture Buffalo-persecuting Bower or lose his life trying. Likewise, Bower desperately wanted to apprehend the "Chieftain of the N.C. Buffalo Band," who was the "instigator and leader of the party that attempted to surprise [Bower]" at Windsor on January 30.[63] Bower's chance came on the night of February 12—less than two weeks after the Federal raid on Windsor.

Bower learned that Hoggard would visit his wife at their home on that night. Bower dismounted about seventy-five men of his command and proceeded cautiously to Hoggard's residence, arriving there unobserved. The Georgians surrounded the house and knocked on the door. A woman inside the house inquired who was outside. "Friends," came the response from a Georgian, who requested "an interview" with Captain Hoggard. In a few minutes the door opened, and "the renowned Buffalo confronted twenty-five [as] daring looking rebels as ever drew Yankee blood." Hoggard, attired in his Union uniform complete with captain's bars and finding resistance to be in vain, instantly surrendered.[64]

Captain Bower and his men escorted "the renegade and Buffalo Captain" to their camp. Since Hoggard's capture "was an affair of considerable importance," Bower detained Hoggard "for public gaze" at the camp for a day. He then assigned a detail of six soldiers to escort Hoggard to Brig. Gen. Matt W. Ransom's headquarters at Weldon. During the trip the guards stopped at night to rest at an undisclosed location and placed Hoggard in a room. Four of the Confederate guards fell asleep, and the other two, carelessly tending to their assigned duties, allowed Hoggard to escape to "Yankeeland." A greatly antagonized Captain Bower blamed his troopers for "carelessly & stupidly" letting Hoggard escape.[65]

Several days after Hoggard's escape, Lanthan Bower, Captain Bower's brother and a member of the captain's company, wrote to his parents that he "never was scared in my life as I was when I heard the guard say [Hoggard] had made his escape." Another brother, Marcene Bower, wrote home that he "never hated anything more in [his] life than Captain Hoggard's escape."[66]

Following the escape, Captain Bower, who had retained Hoggard's army coat and boots, returned them to the Buffalo officer as a gentlemanly gesture. Hoggard responded with a letter to Bower thanking him "kindly" for returning the items and the "treatment he received while a prisoner." Bower, impressed by the letter, sent it to the *Petersburg Express* for publication, noting that it was "a perfect gem of its kind."[67] Such were the sentiments at times during this war of Americans against Americans or, in this case, Southerners against Southerners.

In Bertie County the divisiveness among certain residents had became more aggravated. Charles H. Stevenson, a thirty-two-year-old county resident, had fled to Plymouth and left his wife in Bertie. Mrs. Stevenson was residing at "the Reddick Place" when, on an undisclosed date, ten Bertie County secessionists (Thomas Heckstall and his brother, John W. Heckstall, Whit Swain, George Mardre, Thomas Gilliam, Bill Rascoe, John Vick, Augustus Thompson, Robert Miller, and Alfred Smithwick) visited the property, looking for her husband. The men reportedly "laid around the house all night, with the speculation of catching [Charles Stevenson] going to or coming from the House." Stevenson did not appear, however.

Stevenson, who later learned that the Heckstalls and others had waited for him, fired off an angry letter to Thomas Heckstall in which he threatened to influence Union military authorities to establish a headquarters in Windsor. Stevenson was aware of other activities in which those men had engaged to further the Southern cause—activities such as attempting to capture Bertie County men who had fled to Plymouth when they returned home to visit their families and rounding up conscripts. In a bluffing vein, he wrote that the Federal authorities

assure me, that you all will not be forgotten, when they visit Bertie, which will not be long. First, we intend to make Windsor Headquarters soon, and then somebody else's house will be watched. The Yankees know what sort of lies you told Bowers

[Captain Bower] upon certain men in Bertie while you had him stationed at your house drinking in Brandy, who went to Plymouth and who sold cotton to the Yankees. We know you have tried to blow hot and cold both, but we understand you, and will take the Secesh out of you old fellow and John Hexstall. We will remember his smartness for telling Bowers when to go below Windsor and catch the fellows that had gone over to see their families. Besides he has been active . . . in carrying conscripts to Raleigh. . . . I want you to see all the fellows that you carried down to Reddick's with you and tell them to get themselves in readiness by the time we come over and get up all of their negroes' clothes and have them ready as we intend to take them all off [along] with you.[68]

Captain Bower's cavalrymen had indeed been busy rounding up unionist citizens and confiscating their horses. On March 16, 1864, Bower wrote to his father: "[W]e have caught a great many Buffaloes . . . and have a picket fight now and then. . . . Every man in the company is now mounted—the deficiency made up by taking Buffalo horses."[69] Bower also described to his father "a remarkable incident" in which he had been a primary party only a few nights previously. While "hunting Buffaloes," he had unexpectedly encountered a "negro Yankee deserter" whom he had previously captured but who had escaped. Bower found the black man in a house, surrounded it with his troopers, and concealed himself at the door. As the unfortunate man opened the door, Bower placed his pistol against the man's chest, "fired and stepped back for him to fall dead." But to the captain's astonishment, "after falling nearly to the ground," the man "recovered and run off and made his escape." Bower referred to him as "a lucky nigger."

During the winter of 1864 Bertie County authorities and Captain Bower continued to attempt to conscript men for Confederate service, but with the same dismal results that had been achieved ever since the conscription law was enacted. Finally, on February 16, 1864, William N. H. Smith, the Confederate congressman in whose district Bertie County was situated, wrote to James A. Seddon, the Confederate secretary of war, and suggested—as John Pool had done previously—that the execution of the conscript law should be suspended in the county. Smith declared: "It is impracticable to enforce the conscript law in that county fully, and when an attempt has been made it has resulted in securing but few men for the service, while many have escaped to places beyond the reach of our authority; some have joined the enemy, and returned only to ravage and plunder." Smith felt that "sound policy, as well as a proper regard to the true and faithful people" of Bertie County, required a suspension of the draft. On February 18 Seddon referred Smith's appeal to Pres. Jefferson Davis, who in turn referred it to Gen. Braxton Bragg for his advice. Bragg tersely noted: "I have never known any good to result from a suspension of our laws in disaffected districts." President Davis disapproved Congressman Smith's suggestion.[70]

By March 1864 life in Bertie County had become depressingly predictable for the remaining residents. Union gunboats controlled the area waterways and periodically landed troops for small raids. One such raid occurred on March 12, when gunboats landed troops at Colerain to engage in a raid on stored tobacco and cotton. Two days later, Federal troops operating at an undisclosed location in the county captured and carried to Plymouth eight or nine Rebel prisoners.[71] On March 20 Lt. Edgar York and ten soldiers from Capt. Calvin Hoggard's company landed at the mouth of the Cashie River, hoping to rescue Confederate deserters. Finding no deserters at the landing point, York led his detachment about three miles into the county and captured five soldiers, three horses, and related equipment.[72]

In mid-March, Jonathan White, another Bertie County Confederate deserter who had fled to Plymouth and taken the Oath of Allegiance to the United States, offered Charles H. Foster assistance in recruiting for the Second Regiment North Carolina Union Volunteers. On March 15 Foster authorized White to recruit for the regiment, with the understanding that White's success would be "properly rewarded."[73]

By early April 1864 a substantial contingent of Bertie County citizens, white and black, was living within the Union lines across the Roanoke River at Plymouth. More than one hundred Bertie County whites were serving in the Union army at that location.[74] The Union military was caring for and supporting many men, women, and children—dozens of whom were relatives of the Bertie County Buffaloes. The people in its care felt relatively safe and secure at Plymouth. For almost two years the Union military had occupied the town and had strenuously endeavored to make it resilient to Confederate attack. But by early April the safety and security enjoyed by the refugees appeared to be in jeopardy: Confederate forces would soon attack Plymouth.

For about a year the Confederates had been constructing an ironclad gunboat at Edwards Ferry in Halifax County. For months, rumors had reached General Wessells and Lieutenant Commander Flusser that the ironclad, a ram named the *Albemarle*, was virtually completed and ready for service. The two commanders were gravely concerned about the potentially formidable weapon and had expressed their concerns to superior officers. Federal military leaders had considered the propriety

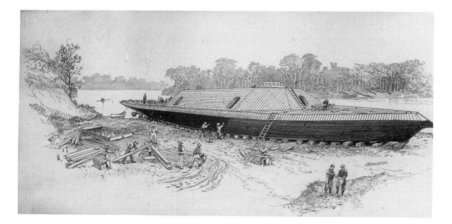

General Wessells and Lieutenant Commander Flusser were aware of rumors that the Confederate War Department was constructing an ironclad gunboat known as the *Albemarle* at Edwards Ferry in Halifax County. The two officers, gravely concerned about the threat that such a vessel might represent, expressed their fears to superior officers. This engraving shows the ram under construction. Engraving from the files of the Division of Archives and History.

of raiding Edwards Ferry and destroying the ram, but nothing had been undertaken.

As early as mid-August 1863, Maj. Gen. John J. Peck, commander of the Eighteenth Army Corps (North Carolina), had suggested to his superior, Maj. Gen. John G. Foster, commander of the Department of Virginia and North Carolina, that a raid be undertaken to destroy the *Albemarle* in its stocks. Peck, aware that the Confederates had constructed and armed Fort Branch at Rainbow Bluff near Hamilton to prevent Union gunboats from ascending the river, suggested an overland expedition through Bertie County. He felt that eight hundred to one thousand "good cavalry" would be sufficient for the raid. He presented his plan to Foster; the plan recommended that the cavalry land "6 or 8 miles above Plymouth" and move toward Edwards Ferry on a less traveled road from Windsor to Roxobel. Peck also suggested that a simultaneous demonstration from Norfolk via Winton toward Weldon would draw the Confederates' attention away from Edwards Ferry and "materially enhance the chance of success." In late August Foster rejected Peck's plan, noting that "our force will not permit the proposed movement at present."[75] The Union military undertook no efforts to destroy the Confederate ram during its construction.

In early April, Wessells and Flusser received from Bertie County sources information that Confederate forces were massing and would attack Plymouth. On April 6 Flusser received from an unidentified person in Bertie County a letter that advised him "to prepare for an attack, as one will soon be made by land and water." One week later Wessells received from residents of Bertie and Hertford Counties information that a large Rebel force had assembled up the Roanoke River and, accompanied by the ram *Albemarle*, would attack Plymouth "this week."[76]

Confederate infantry, artillery, and cavalry led by a young North Carolinian, Brig. Gen. Robert F. Hoke, reached Plymouth about four o'clock in the afternoon of April 17 and attacked and laid siege to the town and the twenty-eight hundred troops stationed there. The ram *Albemarle*, under the command of Capt. James W. Cooke, arrived and joined the action in the early morning hours of April 19, sinking the Union gunboat *Southfield*. Lt. Comdr. Charles W. Flusser was killed shortly after the *Albemarle* engaged the Federal gunboats and forced them to withdraw to Albemarle Sound.

Sunrise on the nineteenth found the Union forces at Plymouth virtually surrounded by the Confederates. Captain Hoggard's and Johnson's Bertie County Buffaloes were caught in an extremely perilous position. A substantial number of them were Confederate deserters and were well aware that Generals Hoke and George E. Pickett, commander of the Confederate Department of Virginia and North Carolina, had executed twenty-two members of the Second Regiment North Carolina Union Volunteers at Kinston two months previously for being Confederate deserters. Essentially all of the other Buffaloes had fled to Plymouth to escape Confederate conscription and desperately feared being captured by the Rebels. During the battle the army transport *Massasoit* made two trips from Plymouth to Roanoke Island, transporting to safety women, children, and other noncombatants, including an undetermined number of Bertie County citizens.[77]

By the morning of the twentieth it was clearly evident that the Union forces could not hold out much longer against General Hoke's Confederates. With surrender imminent, Captains Hoggard and Johnson ordered their men to escape the best way they could. A substantial number of Bertie County men, including Hoggard and Johnson, escaped by swimming the Roanoke River and hiding and wading in the area swamps until they reached the safety of their homes or were picked up by Union gunboats. Many of the men who reached their homes were again forced to hide in the woods and swamps, just as they had done previously to avoid conscription officers.[78]

General Wessells surrendered his command to General Hoke about eleven o'clock in the morning of April 20. Within a few days the Union prisoners, including a substantial number of Bertie County Buffaloes, were marched to Tarboro and then transported by train to the Confederate prison at Andersonville, Georgia. There the majority of the Buffaloes, including at least twenty-one Bertie County men, would perish.[79]

A large number of captured Federal soldiers confined at the notorious Confederate prison at Andersonville, Georgia, died from disease and were interred in shallow graves. At least twenty-one Bertie County Buffaloes died at Andersonville, and all except one (Pvt. John Augustus Stone of Company F, Second Regiment North Carolina Volunteers) were buried under assumed names or as unknown soldiers. The North Carolina Union soldiers captured at Plymouth assumed the names of Northern soldiers or others in an attempt to disguise their Southern identities. Many took the bogus names to their prisoner-of-war graves. Photograph courtesy National Archives, Washington, D.C.

For days after the battle, Union gunboats operating in the upper end of Albemarle Sound and the Cashie River rescued Union soldiers and refugees, white and black, who had escaped from Plymouth. On April 21 the *Whitehead* picked up thirty Federal soldiers on the Cashie.[80]

During the battle, the Forty-ninth Regiment North Carolina Troops had occupied the eastern section of Bertie County along the Chowan River, serving as guards to protect General Hoke's flank in case Union forces had ventured down the Chowan from the Norfolk area. On April 27 officers of that regiment, aware that Union soldiers had escaped into Bertie County, sent Companies A, C, and G to Cashoke Creek and the Cashie River to search for the "enemy or hiding places for deserters, tories or negroes." They found none. The following day those companies rendezvoused with the rest of the regiment at Merry Hill. On the thirtieth the regiment left the Chowan River area and marched across Bertie County, passing through Windsor and Indian Woods on its way toward Martin County.[81]

Plymouth, now occupied and controlled by Confederate troops, was no longer a refuge for runaway slaves and white refugees from Bertie County. Unionist citizens from the Albemarle area, including those from Bertie, were imprisoned in Plymouth during the summer of 1864.[82] The loss of Plymouth effectively terminated the enlistment of Bertie County white men in the Union army. Only five county men enlisted in the First and Second Regiments North Carolina Union Volunteers throughout the remainder of the war.[83]

The *Albemarle*, from its strategic position at Plymouth, now controlled navigation on the Roanoke River. Confederate authorities had hoped to use the *Albemarle* and another ironclad being constructed on the Neuse River to attack and drive the Union naval forces from the North Carolina sounds, but their plan never materialized. After the Confederates captured Plymouth, Union naval leaders immediately positioned a number of gunboats at the upper end of Albemarle Sound to watch for and attack the vessel if it ventured out of the Roanoke River. On May 5 at about one o'clock in the afternoon, Captain Cooke led the *Albemarle*, accompanied by a smaller steamer, the *Cotton Plant*, and the gunboat *Bombshell*, which the Confederates had sunk during the battle of Plymouth and subsequently raised and repaired, out of the Roanoke River and into Albemarle Sound. The Union gunboat *Ceres* and several other vessels were steaming toward the mouth of the Roanoke when their crews spotted the Confederate ships. The Union vessels reversed course and began proceeding down the sound, away from the *Albemarle* and its companion ships. The Confederate vessels pursued the Union gunboats for more than a dozen miles.

About two o'clock in the afternoon, the Union vessels encountered the remainder of the Federal fleet coming up the sound from the direction of Roanoke Island and immediately rendezvoused with the warships. The Federal fleet then consisted of seven gunboats (the *Ceres*, the *Mattabessett*, the *Sassacus*, the *Wyalusing*, the *Miami*, the *Commodore Hull*, and the *Whitehead*) under the command of Comdr. Melanchton Smith. The Union gunboats immediately formed into a "line of battle" and proceeded toward the three Confederate vessels.

At 4:40 P.M. the engagement, commonly called the Battle of Batchelor's Bay, began. Within twenty minutes the *Bombshell* surrendered to the *Sassacus*, and shortly thereafter the *Cotton Plant* escaped from the scene of the engagement and steamed back up the Roanoke River. The *Albemarle* was now alone in a one-sided confrontation with the Federal fleet. For almost three hours the ironclad battled the Union gunboats. During the engagement the *Sassacus* rammed the *Albemarle*, severely shaking it and demoralizing some of its crew, but with little other effect. According to Gilbert Elliott, builder of the *Albemarle*, the *Sassacus* "struck the *Albemarle* squarely just abaft her starboard beam,

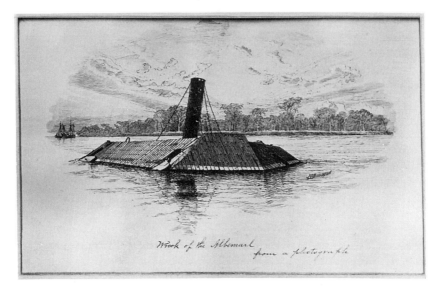

Wreck of the Albemarle from a photograph

On the afternoon and evening of May 5, 1864, in a naval engagement known as the Battle of Batchelor's Bay, a fleet of seven Union gunboats under the command of Comdr. Melanchton Smith engaged the Confederate ram *Albemarle*, which was accompanied by a gunboat, which soon surrendered, and a steamer, which quickly departed the battle scene. For nearly three hours the *Albemarle* sustained a ramming and withering gunfire from the Union vessels and finally withdrew to Plymouth in the gathering darkness. Thereafter, the vessel never represented a threat to Union shipping. Engraving from the files of the Division of Archives and History.

causing every timber in the vicinity of the blow to groan, though none gave way. The pressure from the revolving wheel of the *Sassacus* was so great it forced the after deck of the ram several feet below the surface of the water, and created an impression on board that she was about to sink."[84]

The Federal gunboats, mounting fifty-five guns, fired away continuously at the *Albemarle*, riddling its smokestack to the point that it would not draw properly. About 7:30 p.m., with darkness fast approaching, the gunboats ceased firing, and the *Albemarle* limped back to Plymouth under steam power generated by burning bacon and lard. The vessel would never again venture that far from Plymouth.[85]

Late May found a number of the Bertie County Buffaloes who had evaded the Confederates at the fall of Plymouth attempting to make their way back to their regiment. On May 24 Lt. Col. Walter S. Poor, who in early April had succeeded Charles H. Foster as commander of the Second Regiment North Carolina Union Volunteers, reported to Capt. John A. Judson, assistant adjutant general at New Bern, that he had received information that there were twenty or more men in Bertie County who had "escaped massacre at Plymouth awaiting an opportunity to come inside [the Union] lines." Poor advised Judson that Capt. Littleton Johnson, the Confederate army deserter and commander of Company B, had several men in his company—obviously Bertie County residents—who were well acquainted with the whereabouts of the soldiers and could conduct them to safety. Most of the Bertie County Buffaloes who escaped from Plymouth eventually made their way back to the regiment.[86]

By the spring of 1864 economic conditions in Bertie County had deteriorated to the point that starvation seemed a real possibility to some residents. The Confederate government, desperate for goods and stores to maintain and supply its depleted army, was impressing corn and meat in the county. Prices for once-plentiful commodities and foodstuffs had become exorbitant: flour, $450 per barrel; coffee, $13 per pound; "black cotton" or cotton yarn, $100 per bushel; and corn, $75 to $100 per barrel "if it could be found."

Charles Smallwood, who earlier in the war had dutifully recorded daily entries in his diary but now could hardly endure to put pen to paper, wrote in seeming desperation during May 1864: "What we are to do or how to keep from starvation I do not know. . . . Who can stand it? How long—how long shall these things last?"[87] Unfortunately for Bertie County citizens and those of the American nation, almost another year.

Notes

1. Compiled Service Records of North Carolina's Confederate Soldiers.

2. Thomas J. Stafford to "Dear Mother & sisters," August 8, 1863, Thomas Stafford Letters, Port o' Plymouth Museum, Plymouth. Most of the forty-seven Bertie County Confederate army deserters enlisted in the First and Second Regiments N.C. Union Volunteers. One man enlisted in the 104th Regiment Pennsylvania Infantry, one entered the United States Navy, and seven joined the First Regiment U.S. Volunteer Infantry.

Regarding the latter category of Federal enlistees, in January 1864 the Federal government began offering Confederate prisoners of war an opportunity to gain their freedom if they agreed to enlist in the Union army. Thousands of such prisoners, a sufficient number to organize six regiments, accepted the Federal offer. The men who joined those organizations, the First through Sixth Regiments U.S. Volunteer Infantry, became known as "Galvanized Yankees." Seven Bertie County men (John Ryan Belch, James H. Casper, Joseph J. Farmer, John T. Harris, James Ervine Hughes, John H. Parker, and John Stone), Confederate soldiers imprisoned at Point Lookout, Maryland, took the Oath of Allegiance to the United States and enlisted in the First Regiment U.S. Volunteer Infantry during January and February 1864.

The First Regiment U.S. Volunteer Infantry quietly organized at Point Lookout in March 1864 under the oversight of Maj. Gen. Benjamin F. Butler, under whose command (Department of Virginia and North Carolina) the prison was located. In late 1863 Butler had earnestly lobbied the War Department to authorize the enlistment of Confederate prisoners in the Union army. President Lincoln and Secretary of War Edwin Stanton supported the organization of the regiment at Point Lookout. Lt. Gen. Ulysses S. Grant, commander of all Union armies, had strongly opposed enlisting Confederate prisoners in the Union army and refused to use the Galvanized Yankees for any functions other than minor guard duties. About 40 percent of the members were North Carolinians.

General Grant did not desire to have the Galvanized Yankees face their former Southern comrades in battle and possibly become prisoners of war. On August 9, 1864, he informed the War Department that he was ordering the First Regiment U.S. Volunteer Infantry to the northwestern frontier. "It is not right," he explained, "to expose them where, to be taken prisoners, they must surely suffer as deserters." From that date until the end of the war, Grant was firmly opposed to using former Confederates against Confederates. On the northwestern frontier, the Galvanized Yankees faced a new adversary, the plains Indians. The First Regiment was dispatched to Minnesota and Missouri River forts. See Compiled Service Records of North Carolina's Union Soldiers (First and Second Regiments N.C. Union Volunteers) and Compiled Service Records of United States Volunteer Infantry (First Regiment). A comprehensive study of desertion during the Civil War is Ella Lonn, *Desertion During the Civil War* (New York: Century Company, 1928). Causes of Confederate desertion are covered in chapter 1 of that work. For a thorough study of the Galvanized Yankees, see Dee Alexander Brown, *The Galvanized Yankees* (Urbana: University of Illinois Press, 1963).

3. Muster roll dated April 30, 1864, for Company E, Sixty-eighth Regiment N.C. Troops, entry 63, Civil War Collection, Military Collection, State Archives.

4. Muster roll dated April 30, 1864, for Company F, Sixty-eighth Regiment N.C. Troops, entry 63, Civil War Collection, Military Collection, State Archives; J. W. Evans, "Sixty-eighth Regiment," in Clark, *North Carolina Regiments*, 3:713.

5. John Pool to Gov. Z. B. Vance, December 29, 1863, Zebulon B. Vance Papers, Private Collections, State Archives.

6. Compiled Service Records of North Carolina's Confederate Soldiers (service record of John T. Mebane, Sixty-eighth Regiment N.C. Troops).

7. Littleton Johnson to Capt. Charles H. Foster, October 16, 1863, Compiled Service Records of North Carolina's Union Soldiers (service record of Capt. Littleton Johnson, Second Regiment N.C. Union Volunteers); Compiled Service Records of North Carolina's Confederate Soldiers (service record of Littleton Johnson, Thirty-second Regiment N.C. Troops); Norman C. Delaney, "Charles Henry Foster and the Unionists of Eastern North Carolina," *North Carolina Historical Review* 37 (July 1960): 348–349.

8. Compiled Service Records of North Carolina's Union Soldiers.

9. Memorandum from the U.S. Navy Bureau of Navigation to the Bureau of Pensions, September 11, 1896, Federal pension file of Isham Lyers (U.S. Navy); David Thompson, affidavit dated July 5, 1889, Federal pension file of Asa Sanderlin (U.S. Navy). Both documents from Pension Case Files of the Bureau of Pensions and Veterans Administration, 1861–1942, Record Group 15, National Archives.

10. C. C. Barnacastle to Capt. C. H. Foster, November 14, 1863, Compiled Service Records of North Carolina's Union Soldiers (service record of C. C. Barnacastle, Second Regiment N.C. Union Volunteers).

11. Barnacastle to Foster, November 16, 1863, Compiled Service Records of North Carolina's Union Soldiers (service record of C. C. Barnacastle, Second Regiment N.C. Union Volunteers).

12. Barnacastle to Foster, November 17, 1863, Compiled Service Records of North Carolina's Union Soldiers (service record of C. C. Barnacastle, Second Regiment N.C. Union Volunteers).

13. Barnacastle to Foster, November 21, 1863, Compiled Service Records of North Carolina's Union Soldiers (service record of C. C. Barnacastle, Second Regiment N.C. Union Volunteers).

14. Foster to Maj. Gen. J. J. Peck, December 7, 1863, Letter, Indorsement and Order Book, Second Regiment N.C. Union Volunteers, Record Group 94, National Archives; Compiled Service Records of North Carolina's Union Soldiers (service record of C. C. Barnacastle, Second Regiment N.C. Union Volunteers).

15. Bertie County 1860 Tax Lists; Eighth Census, 1860: Bertie County, Population and Slave Schedules; Bertie County Marriage Certificates, Register of Deeds Office, Windsor. Calvin Hoggard married Margaret A. Smithwick on December 23, 1858.

16. Bertie County Confederate Tax Census.

17. John R. Capps, deposition dated October 20, 1899, Federal pension file of John R. Capps, Second Regiment N.C. Union Volunteers, Pension Case Files of the Bureau of Pensions and Veterans Administration, 1861–1942, Record Group 15, National Archives.

18. Compiled Service Records of North Carolina's Union Soldiers (service record of Capt. Calvin Hoggard, Second Regiment N.C. Union Volunteers).

19. Calvin Hoggard to Capt. C. H. Foster, December 15, 1863, Second Regiment N.C. Union Volunteers Regimental Papers, Record Group 94, National Archives; Hog-

gard to Foster, January 15, 1864, Compiled Service Records of North Carolina's Union Soldiers (service record of Calvin Hoggard, Second Regiment N.C. Union Volunteers).

20. Lewis Bond to Gov. Z. B. Vance (with accompanying statements by B. B. Russell, Robert Brown, and William P. Mitchell), December 5, 1863, Zebulon B. Vance, Governors Papers, State Archives.

21. Elizabeth Jernigan, affidavit dated February 15, 1889, Federal pension file of William Jernigan (Second Regiment N.C. Union Volunteers), Pension Case Files of the Bureau of Pensions and Veterans Administration, 1861–1942, Record Group 15, National Archives.

22. Martha White, affidavit dated June 21, 1884, Federal pension file of Augustus White (First Regiment N.C. Union Volunteers); Duncan L. Cale, deposition dated September 4, 1869, Federal pension file of Zediciah Mizell (First Regiment N.C. Union Volunteers); and James R. Byrd, affidavit dated March 4, 1891, Federal pension file for James R. Byrd (Second Regiment N.C. Union Volunteers). All documents from Pension Case Files of the Bureau of Pensions and Veterans Administration, 1861–1942, Record Group 15, National Archives.

23. Typescript of Will E. Dunn to "Sister," December 13, 1863, William E. Dunn Letters, Port o' Plymouth Museum, Plymouth.

24. USS *Whitehead* logbook, entries for October 20, 23, November 26, December 1, 2, 4, 12, 22, 23, 1863.

25. USS *Miami* logbook, entries for December 7, 8, 1863, Records of the Bureau of Naval Personnel, Record Group 24, National Archives (hereafter cited as USS *Miami* logbook); USS *Miami* muster roll dated December 31, 1863, Records of the Bureau of Naval Personnel, Record Group 24, National Archives.

26. USS *Whitehead* logbook, entries for December 12, 22, 1863.

27. USS *Whitehead* logbook, entry for January 6, 1864.

28. An act by the North Carolina General Assembly abolished the militia and created the home guard in July 1863. The militia had lost much of its manpower to the Confederate war effort. The home guard was generally comprised of all able-bodied men between the ages of eighteen and fifty. The Thirty-first Battalion North Carolina Home Guard appears to have been organized in Bertie County, although no rolls of officers and men are known to have survived.

29. B. B. Bower to "Pa," December 10, 1863, Bower letters.

30. B. B. Bower to "Pa," December 10, 1863, and B. B. Bower to Capt. John J. Pegram, December 29, 1863, Bower letters.

31. Bertie County Court Minutes, November 1863 session and December 5, 1863 "special called session"; James H. Ward to Gov. Z. B. Vance, December 29, 1863, Zebulon B. Vance, Governors Papers, State Archives.

32. *Raleigh North Carolina Standard*, December 22, 1863.

33. Compiled Service Records of USCT (Thirty-seventh Regiment); Dyer, *A Compendium of the War of the Rebellion*, 200. The Third North Carolina Colored Infantry was later redesignated the Thirty-seventh Regiment U.S. Colored Troops.

34. Coggin to [Lt.] Col. C. H. Foster, January 4, 1864, Calvin Hoggard and Littleton Johnson to Foster, January 6, 1864, and Special Orders No. 79, December 27, 1863, Second Regiment N.C. Union Volunteers Regimental Papers, Record Group 94, National Archives.

35. Coggin to Foster, January 12, 1864, Second Regiment N.C. Union Volunteers Regimental Papers, Record Group 94, National Archives.

36. Special Orders No. 81, December 28, 1863, Second Regiment N.C. Union Volunteers Regimental Papers, Record Group 94, National Archives.

37. Compiled Service Records of North Carolina's Union Soldiers (service record of 1st Lt. Jonathan T. Mizell, First Regiment N.C. Union Volunteers).

38. Special Orders No. 78, December 26, 1863, Second Regiment N.C. Union Volunteers Regimental Papers, Record Group 94, National Archives. The author has been unable to ascertain the identity of "Mr. Morris." Morris was a fairly common name in Bertie County. For example, more than two dozen Morris men of military age resided in the county during the war. See Eighth Census, 1860: Bertie County, Population Schedule.

39. Capt. Calvin Hoggard to [Lt.] Col. C. H. Foster, January 14, 1864, Second Regiment N.C. Union Volunteers Regimental Papers, Record Group 94, National Archives.

40. Hoggard to Foster, January 29, 1864, Second Regiment N.C. Union Volunteers Regimental Papers, Record Group 94, National Archives.

41. Brig. Gen. I. N. Palmer to Maj. R. S. Davis, January 29, 1864, *Official Records . . . Armies*, ser. 1, 33:23; John H. Garrett to Gov. Z. B. Vance, June 15, 1864, Zebulon B. Vance, Governors Papers, State Archives.

42. Muster roll dated April 30, 1864, for Company E, Sixty-eighth Regiment N.C. Troops, entry 63, Civil War Collection, Military Collection, State Archives.

43. Brig. Gen. I. N. Palmer to Maj. R. S. Davis, January 29, 1864, *Official Records . . . Armies*, ser. 1, 33:23–24; Manarin and Jordan, *North Carolina Troops*, 2:643; excerpt from an article containing a letter dated January 30, 1864, from an unidentified Bertie County citizen to the *Petersburg* (Virginia) *Express*, contained in the Bower letters.

In addition to capturing a number of citizens, the Federal troops appear to have seized three Bertie County members of the Sixty-eighth Regiment North Carolina Troops. Those men were William H. Freeman, L. Hoggard, and James T. Williams. See Compiled Service Records of North Carolina's Confederate Soldiers (Sixty-eighth Regiment N.C. Troops) and muster roll dated April 30, 1864, for Company E, Sixty-eighth Regiment N.C. Troops, entry 63, Civil War Collection, Military Collection, State Archives.

44. Muster roll dated April 30, 1864, for Company E, Sixty-eighth Regiment N.C. Troops, entry 63, Civil War Collection, Military Collection, State Archives.

45. Records of Movements, Union, 103d Regiment Pennsylvania Infantry.

46. Col. J. W. Hinton to Gov. Zebulon Vance, February 4, 1864, Zebulon B. Vance, Governors Papers, State Archives.

47. John Donaghy, *Army Experience of Capt. John Donaghy, 103d Penn'a Vols., 1861–1864* (Deland, Fla.: E. O. Printing Co., 1926), 142.

48. Marcene Bower to "Pa," February 6, 1864, Bower letters.

49. Brig. Gen. I. N. Palmer to Maj. R. S. Davis, January 29, 1864, *Official Records . . . Armies*, ser. 1, 33:24, 106; USS *Miami* and USS *Whitehead* logbooks, entries for January 29, 1864; Diary of Samuel J. Gibson, January 29, 1864, Manuscripts Division, Library of Congress (hereafter cited as Gibson diary).

50. USS *Whitehead* logbook, entry for January 30, 1864; Lt. John A. Reed to Capt. C. H. Foster, January 30, 1864, Compiled Service Records of Pennsylvania's Union Soldiers (service record of John A. Reed, 101st Regiment Pennsylvania Infantry, hereafter cited as Reed to Foster, January 30, 1864); Marcene Bower to "Pa," February 6, 1864, Bower letters.

51. Marcene Bower to "Pa," February 6, 1864, Bower Letters.

52. Reed to Foster, January 30, 1864; Marcene Bower to "Pa," February 6, 1864, Bower letters.

53. Donaghy, *Army Experience*, 143; Reed to Foster, January 30, 1864.

54. Donaghy, *Army Experience*, 142–143.

55. USS *Whitehead* logbook, entry for January 30, 1864.

56. B. F. Blakeslee, *History of the Sixteenth Connecticut Volunteers* (Hartford, Conn.: Case, Lockwood and Brainard Co., 1875), 49.

57. Records of Movements, Confederate, Sixty-second Georgia Cavalry.

58. USS *Whitehead* logbook, entry for January 30, 1864; Cyrus Waters to P. H. Winston, July 8, 1864, P. H. Winston Papers, Private Collections, State Archives; Gibson diary, January 30, 1864; Crabtree and Patton, *"Journal of a Secesh Lady,"* 518; Connaritsa Baptist Church Records, June 1864, North Carolina Baptist Historical Collection, Wake Forest University, Winston Salem. J. L. Mitchell, church clerk, made this entry in the church's daybook: "Owing to my having been taken off by the Yankies in January [1864], and not having the Church books for several meetings, after my return, I was unable to record the proceedings of March, April and May."

59. Report of Col. J. R. Griffin, January 31, 1864, *Official Records . . . Armies*, ser. 1, 33:107.

60. Lt. Comdr C. W. Flusser to Acting Rear Adm. S. P. Lee, February 20, 1864, *Official Records . . . Navies*, ser. 1, 9:423–424.

61. *Official Records . . . Armies*, ser. 1, 33:106.

62. Col. Joel R. Griffin to Gov. Zebulon Vance, February 4, 1864, Zebulon B. Vance, Governors Papers, State Archives.

63. B. B. Bower to "Ma," February 22, 1864, Bower letters.

64. Lanthan Bower to "Pa & Ma," February 26, 1864, and undated article titled "Capture of a Notorious Buffalo," Bower letters.

65. B. B. Bower to "Ma," February 22, 1864, Bower letters.

66. Lanthan Bower to "Pa & Ma," February 26, 1864, and Marcene Bower to "Pa & Ma," February 27, 1864, Bower letters.

67. B. B. Bower to "Pa," March 16, 1864, Bower letters.

68. Charles H. Stevenson Jr. to Tom Heckstall (undated), Thomas Heckstall Papers, Private Collections, State Archives.

69. B. B. Bower to "Pa," March 16, 1864, Bower letters.

70. W. N. H. Smith to Hon. James A. Seddon, February 16, 1864, *Official Records . . . Armies*, ser. 1, 33:821–822.

71. Gibson diary, March 12, 14, 1864.

72. Capt. Calvin Hoggard to [Lt.] Col. C. H. Foster, March 20, 1864, Second Regiment N.C. Union Volunteers Regimental Papers, Record Group 94, National Archives.

73. Lt. DeForest Masters to C. H. Foster, March 14, 1864, and Special Orders No. 64, March 15, 1864, Second Regiment N.C. Union Volunteers Regimental Papers, Record Group 94, National Archives.

74. Compiled Service Records of North Carolina's Union Soldiers (Second Regiment N.C. Union Volunteers).

75. Maj. Gen. J. J. Peck to Maj. Gen. J. G. Foster, August 17, 1863, *Official Records . . . Armies*, ser. 1, 29, pt. 2:63–64; Lt. C. W. Flusser to Acting Rear Adm. S. P. Lee, August 21, 1863, *Official Records . . . Navies*, ser. 1, 9:175.

76. Lt. Comdr. C. W. Flusser to Acting Rear Adm. S. P. Lee, April 6, 1864, and Brig. Gen. H. W. Wessells to Captain J. A. Judson, AAG, District of North Carolina, April 13, 1864, *Official Records . . . Navies*, ser. 1, 9:586–587, 628–629.

77. USS *Miami* logbook, entry for April 18, 1864; J. W. Merrill, comp., *Records of the 24th Independent Battery, N.Y. Light Artillery, U.S.V.* (New York: Ladies Cemetery Association of Perry N.Y., 1870), 213; Gilbert Elliott, "The Ram 'Albemarle': Her Construction and Service," in Clark, *North Carolina Regiments*, 5:315.

78. One hundred five Bertie County men—twenty-six who were Confederate army deserters—were serving in Companies B and E, Second Regiment N.C. Union Volunteers, when Hoke's Confederate force attacked. George Morris, affidavit dated December 9, 1892, Federal pension file of Kenneth Butler; John Butler, affidavit dated July 9, 1889, Federal pension file of John Butler; Emeline Byrd, affidavit dated June 9, 1890, Federal pension file of James Byrd; Doctrin Williams, deposition dated March 15, 1890, Federal pension file of Laton Gardner; Timothy Hoggard, deposition dated September 8, 1890, Federal pension file of Calvin Hoggard; William L. Mitchell, affidavit dated November 28, 1889, Federal pension file of Worley T. Hoggard; Elizabeth E. Mitchell, widow's declaration for pension dated October 1, 1883, Federal pension file of James H. Mitchell; and James Corbit, affidavit dated January 2, 1892, Federal pension file of William Henry Myers. (The foregoing pension files are those of former members of the Second Regiment N.C. Union Volunteers, and all are found in the Pension Case Files of the Bureau of Pensions and Veterans Administration, 1861–1942, Record Group 15, National Archives.)

79. Federal pension files of Bertie County members of the Second Regiment N.C. Union Volunteers, Pension Case Files of the Bureau of Pensions and Veterans Administration, 1861–1942, Record Group 15, National Archives; Compiled Service Records of North Carolina Union Soldiers (Second Regiment N.C. Union Volunteers).

The North Carolinians who were captured at Plymouth and died at Andersonville are not shown on the prison's death rolls as members of their regiment. When it became evident that Wessells would be compelled to surrender to Hoke, at least some of the Buffaloes who were unable to escape from Plymouth transformed themselves into members of various Northern units. The number of such transmogrifications is uncertain, but sufficient evidence exists to demonstrate that a number of the North Carolinians "assumed the roles" of Northerners.

80. USS *Whitehead* logbook, entry for April 21, 1864.

81. T. H. Pearce, ed., *Diary of Captain Henry A. Chambers* (Wendell: Broadfoot Publishing Co., 1983), 190–193; Manarin and Jordan, *North Carolina Troops*, 12:13.

82. Handwritten listing, "Prisoners Confined in Military Prison Plymouth, N.C.," June 24, 1864, September 9, 1864, in Thomas Merrill Pittman Collection, Private Collections, State Archives.

83. Compiled Service Records of North Carolina Union Soldiers (First and Second Regiments N.C. Union Volunteers).

84. Elliott, "The Ram 'Albemarle,' " in Clark, *North Carolina Regiments*, 5:321–322; USS *Ceres* and USS *Mattabessett* logbooks, entries for May 5, 1864, Records of the Bureau of Naval Personnel, Record Group 24, National Archives (hereafter cited as USS *Ceres* and USS *Mattabessett* logbooks); USS *Miami* and USS *Whitehead* logbooks, entries for May 5, 1864; Edgar Holden, "The Albemarle and the Sassacus," in *Battles and Leaders*, 4:628–633.

85. Elliott, "The Ram 'Albemarle,' " in Clark, *North Carolina Regiments*, 5:321–322; Holden, "The Albemarle and the Sassacus," in *Battles and Leaders*, 4:628–633; USS *Ceres*, USS *Mattabessett*, and USS *Miami* logbooks, entries for May 5, 1864.

86. Lt. Col. Walter S. Poor to Capt. J. A. Judson, May 24, 1864, Letter, Indorsement and Order Book Second Regiment N.C. Union Volunteers, Record Group 94, National Archives.

87. Smallwood diary, May 1864 (no specific date recorded).

CHAPTER 6

The Final Year of War

After Confederate forces captured Plymouth in April 1864, Federal raids and recruiting efforts in Bertie County subsided drastically. No longer were there substantial numbers of Union soldiers along the county's southern border conveniently able to raid the county or to provide protection to citizen refugees, conscription evaders, and runaway slaves. The nearest concentration of Union soldiers was now at Roanoke Island, about sixty miles away via Albemarle Sound.

With Plymouth and the entire Roanoke River back under Confederate control, Federal military commanders in eastern North Carolina concentrated on devising ways to destroy the dreaded ram *Albemarle*. The Union navy, ever vigilant for the reappearance of the ironclad, stationed a substantial number of gunboats in Albemarle Sound. On any given day, multiple numbers of those vessels were in evidence at the upper end of the sound, picketing near the mouths of the Roanoke and Cashie Rivers. The Union navy could not afford to allow the *Albemarle* to roam the Albemarle Sound and wreak havoc on its wooden gunboat fleet.

Within a few weeks after the Confederates captured Plymouth, Federal naval authorities began dispatching reconnaissance teams to the town to ascertain the condition and position of the *Albemarle*. Those teams commonly landed from gunboats or launches on the Cashie and Middle Rivers or near the mouth of the Roanoke River on the opposite (north) bank from Plymouth and slipped through the swamps until within sight of the town.

On May 12, one week after the Battle of Batchelor's Bay, Acting Ensign John R. Peacock and a small crew ascended the Middle River about six miles and crossed the island formed by the Middle and Roanoke Rivers. The trek across the swampy, one-mile-wide island was difficult and fatiguing and took four hours. Arriving opposite Plymouth about five o'clock in the afternoon, the Federal sailors observed the *Albemarle* lying at a wharf near the lower end of town. Peacock, viewing the vessel from a distance of about two hundred yards, could see no significant damage to the exterior iron armor of the ram, even though Union gunboat artillery had heavily battered it for almost three hours only a week earlier.[1]

On May 17 Capt. Melanchton Smith, now the Union navy's senior officer in the North Carolina sounds, sent another reconnaissance team to observe the *Albemarle*, which then lay at anchor in the river off Plymouth.[2] The following day an armed boat crew from the Federal gunboat *Ceres* ascended the Cashie River, reconnoitering the area and looking for Rebel picket boats.[3]

On the morning of May 24 the Federal gunboat *Whitehead* was stationed near the mouth of the Roanoke River when its crew observed a small boat coming down the river with the *Albemarle* following closely. The crew of the *Whitehead* immediately dropped anchor, brought the gunboat's one-hundred-pound Parrot rifle to bear on the *Albemarle*, and fired a shell at the ram. The shell missed its target, striking the water near the ram's stern. Without firing a shot, the *Albemarle* reversed direction and returned to Plymouth.[4]

In the early afternoon of the following day, five volunteers—John W. Lloyd, Charles Baldwin, Alexander Crawford, John Laverty, and Benjamin Lloyd—from the Federal gunboat *Wyalusing* left on an expedition intended to destroy the ram. Carrying two torpedoes (in essence, waterborne mines), each loaded with one hundred pounds of gunpowder, the men ascended the Middle River in a dinghy, landed, and transported the explosive devices across the island on a stretcher. Upon reaching the Roanoke River, Charles Baldwin and John W. Lloyd swam across the river with a line and towed the torpedoes across. The men intended to float the devices down the river with the current, guiding them with the line and exploding them under the *Albemarle*. Baldwin and Lloyd successfully rigged the torpedoes so that they floated toward the ram, getting ever closer with the moving water. If the torpedoes reached the *Albemarle* and exploded as planned, the two sailors would surely be instant heroes in Federal military circles.

The daring effort did not succeed, however. Confederate pickets positioned in the vicinity of the ironclad spotted Baldwin and fired at him before he could carry out the demolition. According to a Union navy report, "Everything . . . worked favorably from the time of starting until the torpedoes were within a few yards of the ram, when Baldwin was discovered and hailed by a sentry on the wharf. Two shots were then fired and a volley of musketry followed, which induced John W. Lloyd . . . to cut the guiding line, throw away the coil, and swim the river again." Baldwin did not follow. Lloyd joined Laverty and Benjamin Lloyd, and the three men returned across the island to the *Wyalusing*. Baldwin, who had come so tantalizingly close to sinking the ironclad, returned to his home vessel with Crawford on the morning of May 27. Both men had endured a rainy night in the swamps of the Roanoke River and had been absent about thirty-eight hours. Capt. Melanchton Smith later wrote to Acting Rear Adm. Samuel P. Lee: "I can not too highly commend this party for their courage, zeal, and unwearied exertion in carrying out a project that had for sometime been under consideration." Having failed to destroy the *Albemarle*, the Union navy soon thereafter placed torpedoes in the Roanoke River, near its mouth, in hopes of sinking or heavily damaging the ram if it again ventured that far down the river.[5]

During May and June, Bertie County Union soldiers who had eluded the Confederates at Plymouth in April made their way to the Union gunboats at the upper end of Albemarle Sound. Some of the Bertie County Buffaloes remained concealed in the woods near their homes from six to eight weeks before they were able to slip out of the county, avoiding contact with the county's home guard and Capt. Byron B. Bower's cavalry. One of those men was Capt. Calvin Hoggard.

Hoggard, like a number of other Bertie County Buffaloes, escaped at Plymouth by swimming the Roanoke River and wading more than a mile through the Roanoke and Cashie River swamps to "get over in Bertie County" to his home. Near the end of May, Hoggard began making his way back toward the Union gunboats in the area, it being his "first opportunity" to make the attempt.[6] About five o'clock in the morning of May 31 the crew of the gunboat *Whitehead*, which was stationed in Albemarle Sound at the mouth of the Cashie River, sighted two men in a canoe silently gliding down the river. Captain Hoggard and an otherwise unidentified Buffalo soldier were in the canoe, having slipped out of Bertie County. The *Whitehead* took Hoggard and his companion aboard; the two men had spent six weeks in Bertie County without being captured by the Confederates.[7]

By early June 1864 Captain Bower's Georgia cavalry company was the only Confederate army unit remaining in Bertie County. Capt. John T. Mebane's company had withdrawn from the county in late January and marched to Jackson, Northampton County, where it joined other companies from northeastern North Carolina to form the Sixty-eighth North Carolina.[8] But Captain Bower's company was soon withdrawn from the area and transferred to the Petersburg vicinity. In Virginia, Lt. Gen. Ulysses S. Grant's Federal army had relentlessly attacked and confronted Gen. Robert E. Lee's Army of Northern Virginia for weeks. Lee had steadily fallen back toward Petersburg and in the face of an aggressive adversary needed all the armed men he could gather from Virginia and North Carolina. Bower's company departed Bertie County in June, although the exact date of its departure is not known. Bower's military records reveal that during the middle of the month he was still in the county collecting tax-in-kind goods from citizens. By the end of June, Bower's company, along with the rest of the Sixty-second Regiment Georgia Cavalry, had arrived in the Petersburg area and joined Lee's army.[9]

The summer of 1864—the fourth summer of the war—produced little change in conditions in Bertie County. Union gunboats continued to patrol and control area waterways other than the Roanoke River, and citizens still fled to the gunboats, seeking to enter Union lines. During late July "many men" from the upper Albemarle Sound area whom Confederate authorities had attempted to conscript were reported along the banks of the Chowan River "looking for a chance to escape" into Union lines.[10]

On July 28 Union naval commander William H. Macomb dispatched a gunboat expedition up the Chowan River to Manning's Landing in Gates County. The following day two of the vessels that comprised the expedition—the gunboat *Whitehead* and the army transport steamer *Thomas Collyer*—arrived at Colerain in the early morning and landed troops. During the day, the Federals engaged a detachment of Confederate soldiers in an inconsequential "little fight" at the town. The Federal troops remained in the area all day, finally reboarding their vessels and steaming away about 7:30 in the evening.[11]

The *Whitehead* proceeded only a short distance from Colerain when crewmen discovered that one of their own, Seaman John Keeney, had been left ashore. The gunboat immediately reversed its course and steamed back to the town, where a crew went ashore and searched for Keeney. The searchers failed to find their comrade, who was subsequently suspected of having deserted.[12]

In September 1864 Federal naval authorities were extremely anxious about conditions at the upper end of Albemarle Sound. The authorities decided that the ram *Albemarle* had to be captured or destroyed. Adm. Samuel P. Lee, commander of the North Atlantic Blockading Squadron, approached Lt. William B. Cushing and requested him to devise a plan to capture or destroy the vessel. During the war Cushing had developed a reputation for daring exploits, having commanded successful raids in the North Carolina sounds, southeastern Virginia, and the Wilmington area. Lee surmised that Cushing was a most capable officer for the mission.

Cushing initially considered two alternatives for destroying the *Albemarle* but settled on using a small steam-propelled launch armed with a howitzer and torpedo to rush the ram and explode the torpedo beneath it. A second boat would stand by to defend the launch and renew the attack if the first one failed. Admiral Lee believed that the plan was sound and directed Cushing to present it to navy officials in Washington, D.C. While the officials were skeptical that the plan would succeed, Gustavus V. Fox, assistant secretary of the navy, approved it and authorized Cushing to purchase and outfit the suitable vessels.

Cushing traveled to New York and for several weeks selected his boats and outfitted them with the necessary armaments and accouterments. Twelve-pound howitzers and fourteen-foot booms rigged for torpedoes were affixed to the bow of each vessel. After the vessels were readied, Cushing started southward but lost one boat before reaching Norfolk. Taking the other boat through the Chesapeake and Albemarle Canal, he reached the Federal fleet in the upper end of Albemarle Sound about October 24 or 25 and obtained seven volunteers to accompany him on the mission. On the night of October 26 Cushing and his volunteers entered the Roanoke River but had the misfortune of running aground and were forced to return to the Federal fleet.

The following night Cushing and his team cautiously entered the Roanoke River a second time. The night was "dark and stormy," and it was "raining heavily at times." Cushing and his men proceeded quietly up the river in the launch—its engine covered with tarpaulins to prevent the light of its fires from being seen and to deaden its sound—staying close to the right (north) bank and almost under the overhanging trees and towing another small vessel, which carried a crew assigned to capture Confederate pickets stationed aboard the wreck of the *Southfield*. After a cautious run of several miles, Cushing's boats passed within thirty feet of the wreck and, astonishingly, were not detected by the pickets. "Luckily, they [the pickets] were asleep or did not see" the Federal sailors as they passed by. Cushing, therefore, did not attempt to board the wreck and capture the Confederates but stealthily continued toward the *Albemarle*, which was moored at the Plymouth wharf and encircled by a boom of cypress logs for protection. Cushing, believing that he and his men would be detected if they continued to approach the ram, decided to land and dash suddenly aboard the ironclad from shore. Before he and his men could carry out that maneuver, however, Confederate sentries observed his vessels and opened a "brisk" fire from the shore and the deck of the *Albemarle*.

"The situation had changed in an instant," and there was now no time for indecisiveness. Cushing "in a loud tone of voice" ordered the launch's engineers to steam "ahead fast!" toward the ram. The momentum of the vessel carried it across the boom of logs and close enough to the ram that Cushing excitedly ordered the torpedo boom lowered until the forward motion of the launch carried the device under the overhang of the *Albemarle*. Cushing seized the torpedo's detaching line and, after waiting momentarily to allow the device to rise up to the hull of the ram, grasped the detonating line, exploding the torpedo at the same time a round of canister from a cannon on the ram blew the bottom out of the launch. The torpedo opened a hole in the hull of the *Albemarle* "big enough to drive a wagon in," causing it to settle quickly to the bottom of the river.

On the night of October 27, 1864, Lt. William B. Cushing led a team of volunteer officers and men that stealthily ascended the Roanoke River for eight miles and miraculously sank the Confederate ram *Albemarle* at its wharf in Plymouth. Cushing's feat led directly to the Union navy's recapture of Plymouth several days later. Photograph from the files of the Division of Archives and History.

Cushing ordered his men to save themselves and, discarding his sword, revolver, shoes, and coat, swam away from the chaotic scene. Cushing and one of his men escaped; two of his men drowned, and the five others were captured. Cushing reached the gunboat *Valley City* about midnight on the twenty-eighth, at which time he learned that he had been presumed killed during the attack on the *Albemarle*.[13] Regarding Cushing's feat, Capt. Alexander F. Warley, commander of the *Albemarle* on the fateful night it was destroyed, later wrote: "a more gallant thing was not done during the war."[14] For his exploit, Cushing received the congratulations of the Navy Department and the thanks of the United States Congress and was promoted to the rank of lieutenant commander.

With the *Albemarle* resting on the bottom of the Roanoke River, the Federal navy quickly moved to retake Plymouth. On October 29 Comdr. William H. Macomb started up the river with his fleet but, upon arriving at the wreck of the *Southfield*, discovered that the Confederates had effectively blockaded the channel by sinking schooners. On the following day, Macomb, having ascertained from a reconnaissance by the *Valley City* that Plymouth could be approached by steaming up the Middle River and entering the Roanoke River above the town, sent his fleet by that route. As his gunboats passed on the far side of the island formed by the two rivers, they lobbed artillery shells across the island into the town. Before nightfall the Federal fleet (consisting of the gunboats *Commodore Hull*, *Whitehead*, *Tacony*, *Shamrock*, *Otsego*, *Wyalusing*, *Chicopee*, *Valley City*, and two tugs) was safely in the Roanoke River above Plymouth, where it anchored for the night.

At 9:30 in the morning of the thirty-first, Macomb formed his vessels into a line of battle and slowly proceeded toward Plymouth. Confederate batteries opened fire on Macomb's gunboats as soon as they came within range, but after about an hour the Southerners, exposed to "grape and canister . . . poured in very heavily from the ships," gave up the fight and abandoned Plymouth. After six and one-half months, the town was once again under Federal control. Union soldiers reoccupied the village shortly thereafter.[15]

With Plymouth back under Union military domination, Bertie County's exposure to Federal raiding parties again increased. During the first half of November, Federal troops visited George W. Capehart's plantation on Salmon Creek several times. On November 15 Capehart's plantation overseer wrote to Capehart (who had relocated to the Piedmont area of North Carolina) that the hogs were "very wild," having been "run so much by the Yankees." The overseer advised

Capehart that the Yankees had threatened to "destroy the place" if "a single piece of property" was moved from the plantation. During the previous week, a Union crew had come up the creek to the plantation to determine if any property had been moved. Moreover, Negroes residing on the plantation were informing the Union troops of activities in the area. Capehart's overseer observed: "You can't move anything secretly for the negroes will tell them [the Yankees] everything."[16]

Since its completion in early 1863, Fort Branch, the Confederate bastion situated at Rainbow Bluff immediately across the Roanoke River from Bertie County, had effectively sealed the upper end of the waterway from Union gunboat traffic. By early December 1864, Federal navy and army authorities had decided to send a joint expedition to the bluff to capture the fort. Gunboats under the command of Commander Macomb were to move on Fort Branch in conjunction with an army force from Brig. Gen. Innis Palmer's eastern North Carolina command, led by Col. Jones Frankle, commander at Plymouth.[17]

On December 9 Macomb ascended the Roanoke River with the *Wyalusing* (Macomb's flagship), the *Otsego*, the *Valley City*, and two tugs—the *Belle* and the *Bazely*. Upon reaching Jamesville, the *Otsego* and the *Bazely* struck torpedoes and immediately sank. The cooperating soldiers were to meet the gunboats at Jamesville, but they failed to arrive. Macomb, without the accompanying army force, decided to proceed up the river on the eleventh.

Confederate troops had placed dozens of torpedoes in the river; therefore, Macomb's vessels exercised extreme caution in proceeding, and boat crews meticulously dragged the waterway for the "infernal" explosive devices. By December 13 the naval vessels had progressed only as far as Cedar Landing, along the Bertie County shoreline. There one hundred soldiers landed from the *Ceres*, which had departed Plymouth the day before, and reconnoitered the area. Federal military authorities had contemplated marching a force through Bertie County and moving on Edwards Ferry, where the Confederates were rumored to have begun constructing another ironclad gunboat.[18] No such endeavor was undertaken, however. The gunboats remained at Cedar Landing until the seventeenth, allowing the boats to drag the river for torpedoes.

By December 18 the expedition had progressed up the river past Williamston. In the late afternoon of that day the *Chicopee*, which like the *Ceres* had followed Macomb's fleet up the river, anchored off Speller's Landing in Bertie County. There an armed party went ashore and arrested the property's owner, Thomas Speller Sr., for disloyalty to the

Union and to prevent him from giving the Confederates information concerning movements by Union forces.[19] (Speller, one of Bertie County's more affluent citizens, had three sons—James, Hugh, and Charles—who were soldiers in the Confederate army.[20]) Federal records do not reveal how long Speller was detained, but he may have been held until about December 23, the date on which the Union expedition up the Roanoke River was terminated.

At about five o'clock in the afternoon on December 20, small boats from the *Chicopee*, the *Valley City*, and the *Wyalusing* were near Poplar Point, several miles downriver from Rainbow Bluff, dragging the river for torpedoes in advance of the gunboats, when Confederate riflemen opened fire on the vessels from both sides of the river. The gunboats retaliated with musketry and artillery fire, gradually falling back down the river until the exchange ceased, primarily because of darkness. The following day Commander Macomb deployed skirmishers to clear the banks of the Southerners, and the gunboats again attempted to ascend the river. As soon as the vessels began moving, the Confederates fired on them with muskets. Macomb's gunboats pressed forward but, upon rounding Poplar Point, "received four shots from a battery but a few hundred yards off." Three of the four shells slammed into the *Valley City*, killing one sailor and wounding three others, including thirteen-year-old John Wood of Bertie County.[21]

Wood, the child of a former slave, had been rescued by Union troops during a raid on John Pool's fishery on May 12, 1863. He enlisted in the Union navy and by December 1864 was rated as a first-class boy. He died two days after being wounded and became Bertie County's youngest battle casualty of the war.[22]

The Union gunboats again attempted to ascend the river on December 22 but, as on the two previous days, came under heavy Confederate musketry and artillery fire. By that time Commander Macomb had apparently become thoroughly frustrated with the expedition. He had lost two vessels, and the soldiers who were to cooperate with his force had failed to rendezvous with the fleet. For almost two weeks his gunboats had slowly progressed up the river, meticulously dragging for torpedoes and finding as many as forty in some bends of the waterway. Confederates concealed in the woods along the riverbanks now fired upon his vessels, making it impossible for his men to drag the river effectively. Having obviously concluded that the expedition could not succeed, Macomb abandoned the operation on December 23 and ordered his gunboats to return to Plymouth, where they arrived on the twenty-eighth.[23]

Union army forces under the command of Colonel Frankle did advance on the Hamilton/Rainbow Bluff area while Commander Macomb's fleet was between Jamesville and Cedar Landing. At Butler's Bridge, two miles from Hamilton, on December 12, the Union soldiers encountered a Confederate contingent composed of detachments of the Seventieth Regiment North Carolina Troops (First Regiment North Carolina Junior Reserves), the Sixty-fifth Regiment North Carolina Troops (Sixth Regiment North Carolina Cavalry), Capt. Edgar J. Lee's Alabama battery, and the Sixty-eighth Regiment North Carolina Troops. The Federals, while capturing a number of Rebel soldiers, were unable to dislodge the Southerners and fell back toward Williamston. Eight days after the encounter, Brig. Gen. Edward A. Wild, who accompanied Colonel Frankle's force on the expedition, informed Union army officials that "we failed to surprise the enemy on Rainbow Bluff. They were re-enforced . . . from Weldon. The navy could not help us on account of the multitude of torpedoes [in the river]."[24]

On New Year's Day, 1865, Commander Macomb ascended the Cashie River to ascertain if a suitable landing site could be found for an overland raid to Edwards Ferry. Union military leaders at Plymouth continued to hear rumors that the Confederates, having achieved a degree of success with the ram *Albemarle*, were constructing another such vessel up the Roanoke River. Colonel Frankle was seriously concerned by the rumors and wanted to send a force to Edwards Ferry immediately to destroy any vessel being built there. He felt confident that by sending an expedition through Bertie County, he could achieve his objective. Writing from Plymouth on January 5, he advised General Palmer's assistant adjutant general:

If I can be provided with a sufficient number of transports to convey my forces to Windsor, I am satisfied that I can easily effect a landing at or near that place and march thence to Edwards Ferry and destroy the ram there. I am satisfied that this can be done from the fact that the enemy's force in that vicinity comprise only the 67th & 68th NC with the 1st and 10th Junior Reserves. As the ram is on this side of the river, they will not be likely to expect a movement on the Bertie side. And even should they discover the movement, they could hardly cross a force sufficient to oppose my progress. . . . If the expedition through Bertie to Edwards Ferry be thought advisable, I would like to set about it at once that its object may be accomplished much easier now than at any future time.[25]

Within a few days the assistant adjutant general advised Colonel Frankle that "it was not the wish" of General Palmer that the proposed expedition be attempted. Therefore, no raid was made upon Edwards Ferry at that time.

Before the end of the month, however, Frankle initiated an expedition intended to destroy the putative ram. During the night of January 20 and the following morning, Union gunboats and steamers transported detachments of soldiers from the Second Regiment Massachusetts Heavy Artillery and the Third Regiment New York Artillery from Plymouth to Colerain for a raid on Edwards Ferry. Frankle intended to march his force across Bertie County to the reported ram construction site in Halifax County. Shortly after arriving off Colerain, one of the Federal steamers, the *Allison*, struck cypress stumps near the shore and sank. The sinking forced Frankle to change his plans abruptly and keep his force in the immediate area of Colerain to protect the stricken vessel and the naval personnel attempting to raise it.

For the next two weeks, Union gunboats and steamers arrived at Colerain, bringing troops and firepower to assist and protect the expeditionary forces. Onshore, the army expedition became a "cotton and tobacco raid" upon certain influential Colerain men who strongly supported the Confederacy. While at Colerain, Frankle's force "captured" 50 bales of cotton, 23 boxes of tobacco, 180 bales of tobacco, and various other items belonging to Joseph H. Etheridge (an affluent secessionist planter), Maj. John Wilson (of the Bertie County home guard), and J. Stevenson Jr.

During their stay at Colerain, a few of the Union soldiers became intoxicated and ventured outside established lines, committing various depredations such as killing livestock and poultry that belonged to Joseph H. Etheridge. Colonel Frankle, upon arriving on the scene and being informed by Etheridge of the soldiers' acts, had the men arrested and charged with being outside the established lines. According to Frankle, none of Etheridge's missing property was found in the men's possession. Therefore, they were not charged with committing the depredations. Stolen property of other area citizens was found in the possession of certain soldiers, however. Frankle later reported that articles "of complaining citizens were at once restored, and the men in whose possession such articles were found were summarily punished."

Frankle's men also confiscated mules and "teams" belonging to Etheridge's brother-in-law, Col. Samuel B. Spruill, the former Whig state senator and former commander of the Nineteenth Regiment North Carolina Troops (Second Regiment North Carolina Cavalry). Frankle refused to return Spruill's property because his actions and "sentiments were actively on behalf of the South." Frankle, in a relenting gesture, granted Colonel Spruill "his release from arrest" after Spruill was detained by a Union army captain at the scene.[26]

On January 27 and 28 a detachment of the Fifteenth Battalion North Carolina Cavalry captured two members of the Second Regiment Massachusetts Heavy Artillery in the Colerain area.[27] About January 31 Confederate authorities dispatched a detachment of the Thirteenth Battalion North Carolina Light Artillery and a regiment of North Carolina Junior Reserves to "drive off" the Union forces at Colerain.[28] On February 2 Union pickets near Colerain reported that Confederate troops were near and advancing toward the town. The gunboat *Valley City* began lobbing artillery shells "with an elevation from 1000 to 2000 yards" across the town in the direction of the approaching North Carolina troops. During the day, a detachment of the Twelfth Regiment New York Cavalry skirmished with the approaching Confederates and, in conjunction with the shelling from the *Valley City*, prevented them from reaching Colerain.[29] Two days later, on February 4, the Union forces finally raised the *Allison*. Late in the day the soldiers boarded the Federal vessels and departed Colerain, the expedition having "never marched a foot" from that village during the two weeks.[30]

By January 1865 some of the Bertie County citizens who had fled to the Union lines and were now back at Plymouth with the reoccupying Federal forces began venturing back into their home areas. On January 8 the Federal Provost Marshal's Office at Plymouth began issuing passes for persons to travel through the Union lines established about the town. During the remainder of the month, twenty-nine individuals obtained passes to go into Bertie County. Apparently, Confederate control within the county had deteriorated to the point that at least some of the citizen refugees felt they could return home without suffering severe consequences.

In February the number of persons receiving passes at Plymouth to go into Bertie County more than doubled from the previous month, further indicating that citizens were becoming more willing to travel back into the county. The Provost Marshal's Office granted such passes to sixty-five people during February.[31]

By February 1865 the Confederacy was gasping its last breaths; the war was quickly coming to a conclusion, although Confederate leaders continued to take measures to extend the life of their government. The Confederate government had become so desperate for manpower to replenish its depleted and still shrinking army that the Southern Congress was genuinely considering conscripting blacks for military service. On February 20 the Confederate House of Representatives, after long debate, authorized the use of slaves as soldiers. The following day a dispirited Pres. Jefferson Davis wrote to an Alabama newspaper editor: "It is now becoming daily more evident . . . that we are reduced to choosing whether the negroes shall fight for us or against us."[32]

In Bertie County and the surrounding area, news that the Confederate government was considering the use of blacks in its army generated great consternation among the remaining slaves. Many of the slaves who had remained on the plantations throughout the war now decided that the time had come to flee the county to avoid Confederate conscription. The slaves had labored under bondage all of their lives, but they would not now be forced to fight for the Confederacy.

Hundreds of slaves from Bertie and other counties fled to Plymouth seeking Federal protection. According to a Halifax planter's wife, all of her plantation neighbors had lost slaves. On February 19 nearly one hundred Halifax County slaves—men, women, and children—reportedly crossed into Bertie County "on their way to the Yankee lines" at Plymouth.[33]

On February 20 Commander Macomb reported to Rear Adm. David D. Porter, commander of the North Atlantic Blockading Squadron:

Since the rebel Congress has decided to draft the negroes into their Army, the contrabands have been pouring into our lines at such a rate that there will be very few left to cultivate crops next year.

I received information yesterday that a number of negroes ran away from their masters, [and] were waiting a short distance up the [Roanoke] river for a chance to reach Plymouth. I sent up six boats from this ship [the *Shamrock*] and the *Mattabessett* and brought them off. There were about 120 or 130 of them.[34]

On February 28 the North Carolina Adjutant General's Office, in an effort to prevent or at least discourage slaves in the Albemarle region west of the Chowan River from escaping to Federal forces, ordered Capt. David C. Clark of the state home guard to raise a "volunteer company" of men "to operate in . . . Bertie, Northampton, Halifax & Edgecome [counties]."[35]

With the rampant exodus of slaves from area plantations, opportunistic Northern recruiters at Plymouth attempted to exploit the situation by hastily enlisting large numbers of soldiers. The recruiters sent out other blacks from Plymouth to assist the fleeing slaves in reaching the town so that they might be persuaded to join the Union army. On February 26 Colonel Frankle advised his superiors at Beaufort of the practice and stated that he was sending 250 black recruits to Roanoke Island because he did not have sufficient rations to feed them.[36]

Bertie County slaves, like others from nearby counties, enlisted in the Union army in substantial numbers at Plymouth during February. During the one-week period from February 17 through 23, 119 Bertie County blacks enlisted in the Fourteenth Regiment United States Colored Heavy Artillery.[37] When faced with fighting for or against President Davis's Confederacy, there was but one logical and ethical choice for Bertie County slaves—against.

Not every African American from Bertie County who saw military service during the Civil War served in the Union army or navy. At the age of twelve, Benjamin Gray "enlisted" for service as a powder boy aboard the Confederate ram *Albemarle*. His principal duty was carrying bags of gunpowder from the vessel's below-deck magazine to the gun deck above. Later in Gray's life the state of North Carolina granted him a pension for his Confederate service. Photograph courtesy Harry L. Thompson.

Despite the worsening condition of the Southern armies, North Carolina legislators opposed the arming of slaves on the Confederacy's behalf. In February the state's house of commons passed a resolution protesting "the arming of slaves by the Confederate government, in any emergency that can possibly arise."[38] On March 13 the Confederate Congress, after much debate, finally sent to President Davis a bill calling for the use of Negroes in the Confederate army. The president signed the measure into law, but it was too late to be of any real value.[39]

On February 21 the gunboat *Valley City* departed Plymouth and began descending the Roanoke River. About midday it picked up Daniel Capehart, a runaway slave from either Cullen Capehart's or George W. Capehart's plantation. The slave apparently recommended to the gunboat's commander that a raid should be undertaken up

Salmon Creek to the "Capehart Plantation." At 2:10 that afternoon the *Valley City* anchored in the creek and sent two armed boat crews up the creek to Capehart's. Shortly after five o'clock another boat crew landed, and within two hours the crews began bringing furniture and other goods from the Capehart plantation to the gunboat. The crewmen also took custody of thirteen black men, women, and children.

The *Valley City* remained in Salmon Creek during the night. At about ten o'clock its sailors captured an "open boat" loaded with salt, beef tallow, and lard. Three men—John Duquid, Samuel Melson, and William R. Melson—were captured with the vessel.[40] The Union sailors learned that William R. Melson was a private in Company G, Seventeenth Regiment North Carolina Troops, and was on a furlough. They transferred him to the Provost Marshal's Office at Plymouth, which in turn sent him to the prisoner-of-war camp at Point Lookout, Maryland.[41] At eleven o'clock two more armed crews went ashore from the *Valley City*. Those crews returned to the gunboat about midnight with six more slaves who had been gathered from the area. Finally, at about sunrise on the following morning, the *Valley City* steamed out of Salmon Creek, its crew having completed a successful night of raiding.[42]

By March 8 Maj. Gen. William Tecumseh Sherman's army, which for months had been devastatingly raiding Georgia and South Carolina, entered North Carolina. Union forces in the Albemarle Sound area were alerted to be ready to assist Sherman in whatever manner was requested.[43] After almost four years, the war was now rapidly coming to a close.

In the upper Albemarle Sound area, Confederate civil and military authority had disintegrated to the point that armed "bushwhackers," primarily Confederate deserters, began preying on the local populace. As early as December 1864 "prowling bands of guerrillas" were reported to "continually infest" Bertie and Hertford Counties and were "a source of considerable anxiety" to the residents. In early February the North Carolina Adjutant General's Office "called up" several battalions of the North Carolina home guard, including Bertie County's Thirty-first Battalion, to arrest "deserters, Buffaloes & others commiting crimes" in Bertie and Hertford Counties.[44] About March 15 Col. Jones Frankle at Plymouth learned that in Bertie County a band of bushwhackers was "infesting the county near Windsor, pillaging and killing" and generally creating mayhem. The reports that reached Frankle indicated that the number of bushwhackers involved was variously estimated from twenty to forty. Even though Bertie County had officially remained within Confederate lines throughout the war, Frankle informed Union army officials at Beaufort that he might be able to go into the county and capture the bushwhackers.[45] Indeed, the county had furnished a considerable number of men for the Union military services and in many aspects was friendly and loyal toward Federal troops. Nevertheless, Frankle did not undertake such an expedition. It is unclear whether his superiors directed him not to go into the county or if he personally decided against the humanitarian raid.

Across the Chowan River from Bertie County, bushwhackers had likewise preyed upon and robbed citizens near Edenton in February. There the citizens took it upon themselves to eradicate the villains. Armed citizens "pursued the scoundrels," capturing four of the perpetrators. The citizens, having endured almost four years of intolerable hardships as a result of the war, had no mercy for the bushwhackers. The citizens of Edenton "summarily executed" the four men. The following morning the bodies of nine additional bushwhackers were found on a road near the town, apparently having been executed by vigilante citizens. Men of "influence" in Edenton then appealed to Colonel Frankle for Federal military protection from the pillagers and robbers.[46]

In the early morning hours of March 24, the Union gunboats *Ceres* and *Wyalusing* entered Salmon Creek and proceeded to "Capehart's Farm," where they anchored off a landing at nine o'clock. While for all practical purposes the outcome of the war was readily apparent, the Union navy was about to engage in one more raid against several of Bertie County's prominent secessionist citizens. The sailors first raided the Capehart plantation (either Cullen or George Capehart's). For about an hour, "all hands" loaded a schooner with corn. Then, at ten o'clock, the Federals proceeded up the creek to William T. Sutton's plantation, where they arrived two hours later. During most of the afternoon the Federal raiders loaded Sutton's corn; at about 4:30 they departed with their bounty and an undetermined number of slaves.[47]

The raid had been highly successful for the Union sailors, but they had been unable to carry off all of the goods they found. The following morning the *Ceres*, accompanied by a schooner, again ascended Salmon Creek to Capehart's landing. Once again sailors landed and confiscated more corn found on the plantation. At eleven o'clock the gunboat took the loaded schooner in tow and began proceeding down the creek, heading for Plymouth with the confiscated corn.[48]

On Palm Sunday, April 9, Gen. Robert E. Lee surrendered the Army of Northern Virginia to Gen. Ulysses S. Grant at the little village of Appomattox Court House, Virginia.[49] After four years of excruciatingly arduous service, the principal army of the Confederacy had been compelled to surrender to Grant's overwhelmingly larger force. At Appomattox Court House on that day, only nineteen Bertie County soldiers—out of hundreds who had served in the Army of Northern Virginia—were present.[50] Although other Confederate forces were still active and carrying on the war effort, the surrender of Lee's army essentially meant the death of the Confederacy.

The following night Union commanders at Plymouth "plainly heard" thunderous explosions from up the Roanoke River, although they did not know the cause of the explosions. No Federal troops were known to be operating upriver, so an engagement between Confederate and Union forces could be ruled out as an explanation. On April 12 Confederate army deserters arriving in Plymouth informed Union military leaders that the Confederates had "blown up" Fort Branch and abandoned it on the night of the tenth, destroying ordnance, pitching armaments down the bluff into the Roanoke River, and withdrawing toward Weldon. Colonel Frankle immediately relayed that important information to his superiors at North Carolina Union headquarters in New Bern.

During the night of the eleventh, thirteen Confederate deserters from the "Halifax Navy Yard" up the Roanoke River arrived in Plymouth. The men advised Frankle that the Confederates had burned most of the vessels being constructed at Halifax, including a ram, and also reported that a ram under construction at Edwards Ferry had also been destroyed.[51]

News of Lee's surrender and the abandonment of Fort Branch spurred Bertie County citizens in Plymouth to begin returning home immediately. Although General Sherman was still pressing Gen. Joseph E. Johnston's forces in the Piedmont region of North Carolina, the citizens knew that for all practical considerations the war was over. During the nine-day period from April 11 through 19, the Federal Provost Marshal's Office at Plymouth issued nearly one hundred passes to enter Bertie County. On the twentieth that office rescinded the requirement that citizens venturing outside the Union lines at Plymouth needed passes.[52]

On April 26 Johnston surrendered to Sherman near Durham.[53] Two days later the members of Johnston's army were paroled. Only twenty-one Bertie County men were present at that time.[54] The conflict was over, and citizens who had fled from Bertie could now go home. The county's few Confederate soldiers who had been with their units at the final surrenders began returning home. The conscription evaders could now come out of hiding. After four long years of war and strife, the people of Bertie County could now mend the divisions that had separated them during the war and try to put their lives and community back together. It was also springtime—planting time for the upcoming agricultural season—and a time for the people to return to their peaceful way of life before the war.

In May 1865 several Federal gunboats ascended the Roanoke River on one final expedition, primarily searching for Confederate vessels. During the expedition, Union sailors confiscated several small vessels and various other items.[55] By early June the Union gunboats had concluded their mission and began departing the area for Northern ports and deactivation.

The Union military would maintain a presence in eastern North Carolina, overseeing police activity and other official acts such as elections.[56] During May, Colonel Frankle began overseeing the organization of local police forces in the counties situated in the Albemarle Sound area. On May 23 he reported to his superiors that he had not yet received from Bertie County a list of names for the county's local police force.

In a May 29 proclamation Andrew Johnson, who had become president of the United States after the assassination of Lincoln in April, granted amnesty and pardons to all persons (with a few exceptions) who directly or indirectly participated in the rebellion. The proclamation further required that such persons recite a prescribed Oath of Amnesty, pledging themselves "henceforth" to support, protect, and defend the Constitution of the United States. Johnson's proclamation restored to the citizens of the former Confederate States of America all property rights, except as to slaves and in certain special cases. Johnson also appointed provisional governors in the Southern states. In a separate proclamation, the president appointed William H. Holden provisional governor of North Carolina.[57]

On June 27 Bertie County's white Union soldiers (i.e., the Buffaloes) were mustered out of service at New Bern. On that date only 108 of the 204 Bertie County men who had enlisted in the First and Second Regiments North Carolina Union Volunteers were still serving in the Union army.[58] By the end of June and early July those men began returning to the county. On July 1, 1865, eighteen prominent Bertie County citizens assembled at the courthouse in Windsor to take the

Oath of Amnesty to the provisional government of North Carolina in order to be commissioned as justices of the peace.

At the Bertie County courthouse in Windsor on July 1, Lewis T. Bond, a county justice of the peace, "produced authority from the provisional governor" to administer the prescribed oath to the prospective justices. Bond then administered the oath to John T. Bond, William K. Folk, Joseph W. Beasley, Abner A. White, George W. Cobb, William T. Bond, James S. Perry, William J. Mitchell, Thomas W. Thompson, William Gray, Lewis Bond, Joseph B. Nichols, David E. Tayloe, George Bishop, William A. Pugh, William P. Mitchell, William H. Pierce, and George W. McGlaughon. After reciting the oath, the men "proceeded to organize and hold a special court for the transaction of county business."[59]

During the war Bertie County became a divided community in a divided nation. The conflict divided and alienated the county's citizens, producing allegiances to both the Federal and Confederate governments. More than 860 county men served in the Confederate army or as officers in the county's militia/home guard. Sixty-two of those men "switched" sides and also served in the Union military forces. Except for John R. Capps, who earlier in the war had hidden in the woods to avoid Confederate military service, all of those men served first in Confederate units, then went over to the Union military forces. Capps served in the Second Regiment North Carolina Union Volunteers, escaped at the Battle of Plymouth, and later enlisted in the Sixty-eighth Regiment North Carolina Troops. In all, 620 Bertie County men, white and black, served in the Union army or navy; of that number, 222 men were white, while 398—predominantly runaway slaves— were black. The county had significantly contributed its human resources to the military forces of the North and the South.

The war had cost the lives of more than three hundred Bertie County men in the Confederate and Union militaries. Sixty Bertie men (of whom fifty were Confederate soldiers) were killed in battle, several men died accidentally or were killed by fellow soldiers, 59 died in Federal and Confederate prisons, and 181 died of disease. In addition to the deaths, 19 men (14 Buffaloes) were last reported as missing in action and/or captured. Those men probably perished as well, most likely as prisoners of war.

The county's citizens also contributed, voluntarily and involuntarily, other resources—particularly agricultural commodities and livestock—to both war efforts. The citizens, who resided immediately west of the Chowan River, the unofficial line of demarcation between

Federal-controlled and Confederate-controlled territories, traded with both sides while trying to avoid being detected by the opposite side. Confederate and Federal soldiers confiscated commodities, equipment, implements, and farm animals in the county. For the most part, Federal raids into Bertie were aimed at the county's more affluent supporters of the Confederacy—men such as John Pool, Cullen and George W. Capehart, Joseph H. Etheridge, and Samuel B. Spruill. Confederate soldiers persecuted and harassed the families of Buffaloes, stealing and confiscating goods and animals, and also gathered commodities and supplies from the populace in general under the guise of the "tax-in-kind" law. Citizens of Bertie County were sources of military and other intelligence to both sides. They suffered for their allegiances, regardless of which government they supported.

For the most part, Bertie County's white servicemen (Confederate and Union) returned home after the war. In contrast, a substantial number of the county's black servicemen, after being discharged from the Federal army or navy, did not return to the county but instead relocated to other areas of the country to start new lives. Those men apparently felt that it was better for them to live outside Bertie rather than return to the county and live among the whites for whom many of them had been slaves.

From the secession crisis in the spring of 1860 until the return of the county government to the ideals and auspices of the Federal government in the summer of 1865, the Civil War and the events that led up to it tore at the fabric of life and social order in Bertie County. By the summer of 1865 the citizens were long ready to put the conflict behind them and mend the divisions that had permeated their community. The time had come to return to their fields and other livelihoods and once again enjoy the peace and serenity of their rural environs. The time had come to begin healing the wounds of war.

Notes

1. Capt. Melanchton Smith to Acting Rear Adm. S. P. Lee, May 12, 1864, *Official Records . . . Navies*, ser. 1, 10:49–50.

2. Smith to Lee, May 20, 1864, *Official Records . . . Navies*, ser. 1, 10:73.

3. USS *Ceres* logbook, entry for May 18, 1864.

4. USS *Whitehead* logbook, entry for May 24, 1864; Smith to Lee, May 24, 1864, *Official Records . . . Navies*, ser. 1, 10:86.

5. Smith to Lee, May 30, 1864, Acting Vol. Lt. James M. Williams to Capt. M. Smith, June 8, 1864, *Official Records . . . Navies*, ser. 1, 10:95, 135–136.

6. Timothy Hoggard, deposition dated September 8, 1890, Federal pension file of Calvin Hoggard (Second Regiment N.C. Union Volunteers).

7. USS *Whitehead* logbook, entry for May 31, 1864.

8. Special Orders No.— (unnumbered copy), January 20, 1864, Records of the Adjutant General's Office, State Archives.

9. Compiled Service Records of Confederate Soldiers Who Served in Organizations from the State of Georgia (service record of Capt. Byron B. Bower, Sixty-second Regiment Georgia Cavalry), Record Group 109, National Archives; *Official Records . . . Armies*, ser. 1, 36, pt. 2:669, pt. 3:892–893.

10. Brig. Gen. I. N. Palmer to Comdr. W. H. Macomb, July 26, 1864, *Official Records . . . Armies*, ser. 1, 40, pt. 3:501.

11. Brig. Gen. Innis N. Palmer to Maj. Gen. B. F. Butler, July 31, 1864, *Official Records . . . Armies*, ser. 1, 40, pt. 1:821–822.

12. USS *Whitehead* logbook, entry for July 29, 1864; USS *Whitehead* muster roll, September 30, 1864, Record Group 24, National Archives.

13. W. B. Cushing, "The Destruction of the Albemarle," in *Battles and Leaders*, 4:634–640; undated account of the sinking of the *Albemarle* by Francis E. Swan in the Papers of Dudley W. Knox, Manuscripts Division, Library of Congress.

14. A. P. Marley, "Note on the Destruction of the Albemarle," in *Battles and Leaders*, 4:642.

15. Comdr. W. H. Macomb to Rear Adm. D. D. Porter, November 1, 1864, *Official Records . . . Navies*, ser. 1, 11:12–15.

16. A. Smith to George W. Capehart, November 15, 1864, Capehart Family Papers, Southern Historical Collection, University of North Carolina Library, Chapel Hill.

17. Maj. Gen. B. F. Butler to Brig. Gen. I. N. Palmer, November 30, 1864, Rear Adm. David D. Porter to Comdr. W. H. Macomb, December 1, 1864, *Official Records . . . Navies*, ser. 1, 11:114–115.

18. Comdr. W. H. Macomb to Rear Adm. D. D. Porter, December 11, 13, 1864, *Official Records . . . Navies*, ser. 1, 11:160–162, 164; USS *Ceres* logbook, entries for December 13–14, 1864.

19. USS *Chicopee* logbook, December 18, 1864, Records of the Bureau of Naval Personnel, Record Group 24, National Archives; Lt. Comdr. Earl English to Comdr. W. H. Macomb, January 31, 1865, *Official Records . . . Navies*, ser. 1, 11:175.

20. Thomas H. Speller's sons and their Confederate units (as of December 1864) were: Charles B., Fifty-ninth Regiment N.C. Troops (Fourth Regiment N.C. Cavalry); Hugh H., Thirty-second Regiment N.C. Troops; and James J., CSA Conscription Bureau.

21. USS *Valley City* logbook, entry for December 20–21, 1864; Acting Master John A. J. Brooks to Comdr. W. H. Macomb, December 21, 1864, English to Macomb, January 31, 1865, and Macomb to Rear Adm. David D. Porter, December 30, 1864, *Official Records . . . Navies*, ser. 1, 11:168–169, 175, 178.

22. USS *Valley City* logbook, entries for May 12, 1863, and December 20, 22, 1864.

23. Macomb to Porter, December 30, 1864, *Official Records . . . Navies*, ser. 1, 11:180–181.

24. Philip Shiman, *Fort Branch and the Defense of the Roanoke Valley, 1862–1865* (N.p.: Fort Branch Battlefield Commission, c. 1990), 73–76; Brig. Gen. E. A. Wild to Brig. Gen. I. N. Palmer, December 20, 1864, *Official Records . . . Armies*, ser. 1, 42, pt. 3:1050.

25. Col. J. Frankle to Capt. J. A. Judson, January 5, 1865, U.S. Forces at Plymouth, N.C., Department of Virginia and North Carolina, Letters Sent (January-May 1865), Records of the United States Army Continental Commands, Record Group 393, National Archives.

26. Frankle to Judson, February 8, 1865, U.S. Forces at Plymouth, N.C., Department of Virginia and North Carolina, Letters Sent (January-May 1865), Records of the United States Army Continental Commands, Record Group 393, National Archives.

27. Compiled Service Records of Union Soldiers Who Served in Organizations from the State of Massachusetts (service records of Pvts. Edward Walsh and Patrick Butler, Second Regiment Massachusetts Heavy Artillery), Record Group 94, National Archives.

28. Manarin and Jordan, *North Carolina Troops*, 2:551; Records of Movements, Confederate, Thirteenth Battalion N.C. Cavalry.

29. USS *Valley City* logbook, entry for February 2, 1865; Frederick Phisterer, *New York in the Rebellion*, 5 vols. (Albany: Weed, Parsons and Co., 1890), 1:271.

30. USS *Valley City* logbook, entry for February 4, 1865.

31. U.S. Forces at Plymouth, N.C., Department of Virginia and North Carolina, Record of Passes Issued by the Union Provost Marshal, Plymouth, N.C., 1865, Records of the United States Army Continental Commands, Record Group 393, National Archives.

32. Long, *The Civil War Day by Day*, 641–642.

33. Crabtree and Patton, *"Journal of a Secesh Lady,"* 670.

34. Comdr. W. H. Macomb to Rear Adm. David D. Porter, February 20, 1865, *Official Records . . . Navies*, ser. 1, 12:44.

35. Stephen E. Bradley Jr., *North Carolina Confederate Militia and Home Guard Records*, Volume 2: *Militia Letter Book 1864–1865 and Home Guard Orders* (Virginia Beach: privately printed, 1995), 64 (hereafter cited as Bradley, *Militia and Home Guard Records*).

36. Col. Jones Frankle to Capt. J. A. Judson, February 26, 1865, U.S. Forces at Plymouth, N.C., Department of Virginia and North Carolina, Letters Sent (January-May 1865), Records of the United States Army Continental Commands, Record Group 393, National Archives.

37. Compiled Service Records of USCT (Fourteenth Regiment U.S. Colored Heavy Artillery).

38. "Resolution Against the Policy of Arming Slaves" by the North Carolina House of Representatives, March 4, 1865, Library of Congress.

39. Long, *The Civil War Day by Day*, 651.

40. USS *Valley City* logbook, entry for February 21, 1865.

41. Manarin and Jordan, *North Carolina Troops*, 6:259.

42. USS *Valley City* logbook, entry for February 22, 1865.

43. Barrett, *Civil War Battleground*, 88; Rear Adm. David D. Porter to Comdr. W. H. Macomb, March 28, 1865, *Official Records . . . Navies*, ser. 1, 12:87.

44. Bradley, *Militia and Home Guard Records*, 2:63. Bertie County's Thirty-first Battalion was to "confine itself in the main to Bertie Co[unty]," while the Sixty-first and Seventy-first Battalions were to operate in Hertford County and upper Bertie.

45. Col. Jones Frankle to E. T. Parkinson, Assistant Adjutant General, March 15, 1865, U.S. Forces at Plymouth, N.C., Department of Virginia and North Carolina, Letters Sent (January-May 1865), Records of the United States Army Continental Commands, Record Group 393, National Archives.

46. Frankle to Judson, February 18, 1865, U.S. Forces at Plymouth, N.C., Department of Virginia and North Carolina, Letters Sent (January-May 1865), Records of the United States Army Continental Commands, Record Group 393, National Archives.

47. USS *Ceres* logbook, entry for March 24, 1865.

48. USS *Ceres* logbook, entry for March 25, 1865.

49. Long, *The Civil War Day by Day*, 670.

50. Compiled Service Records of North Carolina's Confederate Soldiers (First, Fifth, Eleventh, Thirty-second, and Thirty-third Regiments N.C. State Troops and the CSA Medical Corps).

51. Col. Jones Frankle to Capt. J. A. Judson, April 12, 1865, U.S. Forces at Plymouth, N.C., Department of Virginia and North Carolina, Letters Sent (January-May 1865), Records of the United States Army Continental Commands, Record Group 393, National Archives.

52. U.S. Forces at Plymouth, N.C., Department of Virginia and North Carolina, Record of Passes Issued by the Union Provost Marshal, Plymouth, N.C., 1865, Records of the United States Army Continental Commands, Record Group 393, National Archives.

53. Long, *The Civil War Day by Day*, 682.

54. Compiled Service Records of North Carolina's Confederate Soldiers (Third Battalion N.C. Light Artillery, Nineteenth Regiment N.C. Troops [Third Regiment N.C. Cavalry], and Fifty-ninth Regiment N.C. Troops [Fourth Regiment N.C. Cavalry]).

55. Comdr. W. H. Macomb to Hon. Gideon Welles, Sec. of Navy, May 22, 1865, *Official Records . . . Navies*, ser. 1, 12:148–152.

56. Col. Jones Frankle to Capt. J. A. Judson, May 23, 1865, U.S. Forces at Plymouth, N.C., Department of Virginia and North Carolina, Letters Sent (January-May 1865), Records of the United States Army Continental Commands, Record Group 393, National Archives.

57. Long, *The Civil War Day by Day*, 690–691.

58. Compiled Service Records of North Carolina's Union Soldiers (First and Second Regiments N.C. Union Volunteers).

59. Bertie County Court Minutes, July 1, 1865.

APPENDIX 1

Bertie County Confederate Servicemen[1]

**FIRST REGIMENT NORTH
CAROLINA INFANTRY**
(six months service)

Company L: The "Bertie Volunteers"
Jacocks, Jesse Copeland, captain
Bird, Francis Wilder, second lieutenant
Speller, James J., third lieutenant
Sutton, Stark Armstead, first lieutenant
Askew, Aaron O., private
Askew, Benjamin F., private
Askew, William L., private
Askew, William W., private
Best, James J., private
Burden, James M., private
Butler, George W., private
Butler, Leven E., private
Butler, William H., private
Capehart, James W., private
Carter, Joseph B., private
Carter, Robert E., corporal
Conner, James Richard, private
Cooper, Thomas Watson, corporal
Craig, Clingman, private
Crichlow, John, private
DeBow, James N., private
Dudley, John T., private
Ellison, Thomas J., private
Farmer, Joseph J., private
Gaskins, William T., private
Gilliam, John H., private
Gilliam, William H., private
Gray, William L., private
Green, John W., private
Hardy, John H., private
Harmon, Enoch, private
Harrell, Asa T., private
Harrell, George B., private
Harrell, Hiram P., private
Hawkins, William H., private
Hoggard, Thomas W., private
Johnson, Henry L., private
Jordan, James B., sergeant

Jordan, Jesse N., private
McGlaughon, John R., private
Mardre, William B., private
Miller, Robert B., private
Miller, William C., private
Mitchell, Franklin V., private
Mitchell, Jeremiah P., private
Mitchell, John H., private
Mitchell, Joseph S., private
Mitchell, Thomas H., private
Mitchell, Thomas J., private
Mitchell, William J., private
Morris, Calvin J., private
Morris, Frederick, private
Morris, James D., private
Myers, Nathan, private
Myers, Samuel Lafayette, private
Myers, Thomas L., private
Nixon, John E., private
Outlaw, David C., private
Outlaw, Edward Ralph, corporal
Outlaw, Joseph S., private
Owens, Richard, private
Parker, Thomas H., private
Peele, Thomas H., private
Peele, William E., private
Phelps, William Thomas, private
Powell, William W., private
Rascoe, Peter, private
Rawls, James R., private
Rayner, James T., private
Rice, Napoleon B., private
Robbins, Henry T., private
Roundtree, Jackson, sergeant
Ruffin, Thomas, sergeant
Skiles, Henry, private
Skirven, George F., first sergeant
Speller, Hugh Hyman, private
Sutton, John M., private
Sutton, Louis B., private
Swain, Whitmell W., corporal
Tayloe, Francis Marion, private
Thomas, John, private

Thomas, Joseph T., private
Thompson, David, private
Thompson, Thomas W., private
Todd, William H., private
Watford, David A., private
Watford, Joseph J., private
White, John H., private
White, Rensellar C., private
Whyte, Solomon H., private
Wilkins, Walter W., sergeant
Williams, James Marshall, private
Williford, Joseph A., private
Williford, Richard H., private
Woodburn, Lucius L., private
Woodman, Arthur, private

Company M
Hodder, James O., private

FIRST REGIMENT NORTH CAROLINA STATE TROOPS

Company A
Smith, Henry, private
Wiggins, James M., corporal

Company F
Blackstone, William R., private
Copeland, Joshua F., private
Dunning, James W., private
Dunning, Joseph J., private
Dunning, William J., private
Earley, James H., private
Powell, James R., private
Tyler, Lucius A., private

THIRD BATTALION NORTH CAROLINA LIGHT ARTILLERY

Company A
Britt, William G., private
Butterton, James H., private
Cofield, David J., private
Cofield, Thomas B., private
Harrell, James J., private
Mardre, Thomas A., private
Newbern, William T., private
Oder, Nathaniel L., private
Phelps, John Washington, corporal
Phelps, John William, private
Phelps, William Thomas, private
Ruffin, Thomas, private
Simmons, Bartholomew H., private
Smithwick, William Hyman, private

Williams, Charles H., private
Williford, Joseph N., private

Company B
Gaskins, David J., second lieutenant
Alexander, Thomas B., artificer
Barrow, Thomas A., private
Boswell, Thomas J., private
Burkett, James H., private
Butler, Thaddeus W., private
Cale, William H., private
Cullipher, John C., private
Dunning, William C., blacksmith
Farmer, James W., private
Fraim, John G., sergeant
Gaskins, John S., sergeant
Goff, Thomas G., private
Harmon, Abram T., private
Henry, Robert M., private
Jilcott, George H., private
Lassiter, John, private
Madison, James M., private
Miller, West, private
Miller, William R. C., private
Mizell, George, private
Mizell, Jonathan, private
Mizell, William, private
Nixon, James A., private
Nixon, John E., private
Nowell, Josiah, private
Only, William D., private
Outlaw, John L., private
Peele, William E., private
Perry, Jarvis B., private
Perry, Josiah, private
Perry, William, private
Powell, John R., sergeant
Raby, Cader Monroe, private
Shoulars, George J., private
Steely, Lafayette, private
Terry, William Thomas, private
Tyler, Lucius A., private
White, James R., private
Williams, James L., private
Worley, Robert D., private

Company C
Sutton, John M., captain
Fraim, John G., second lieutenant
Powell, John R., first lieutenant
Barrett, James B., private
Barrow, Thomas A., private

Brewer, Lewis T., private
Britt, William G., private
Butterton, James H., corporal
Capehart, James W., sergeant
Cofield, David J., private
Cofield, Thomas B., private
Conner, Andrew J., private
Dunning, William C., sergeant
Earley, Abner W., private
Earley, Moses C., private
Farmer, James W., private
Freeman, William J., private
Harmon, Abram T., private
Harrell, Abner, private
Jenkins, Charles T., private
Jenkins, James E., private
Jilcott, George H., private
Lassiter, John, private
Livermon, James Hartwell, Jr., private
Mardre, Thomas A., private
Newbern, William T., private
Newsome, Junius G., private
Oder, Nathaniel L., private
Oder, William A., private
Outlaw, John L., private
Outlaw, John S., private
Peele, Joseph J., private
Peele, William E., private
Phelps, John Washington, corporal
Phelps, John William, private
Phelps, William Thomas, private
Ruffin, Thomas, private
Shoulars, Cullen C., private
Shoulars, George J., sergeant
Simmons, Bartholomew H., private
Smithwick, William Hyman, sergeant
Terry, William Thomas, private
Tyler, Lucius A., private
Tynes, John C., private
Veal, Joseph T., private
White, James R., private
Williams, Charles H., private
Williford, Joseph N., private
Worley, Robert D., private

Company D
Powell, John R., second lieutenant

FOURTH REGIMENT NORTH CAROLINA STATE TROOPS

Company E
Hoggard, William Thomas, private

FIFTH REGIMENT NORTH CAROLINA STATE TROOPS

Field and Staff
Garrett, Thomas Miles, colonel

Company D
Grant, Richard R. first lieutenant

Company F
Garrett, Thomas Miles, captain
Grant, Richard R., second lieutenant
Hays, Joseph S., first lieutenant
Perry, Marcus W., second lieutenant
Atkinson, John, private
Baker, George W., private
Baker, Joseph, private
Belch, John Ryan, private
Birch, John W., private
Blackstone, David George, private
Britton, James Peyton, private
Brogden, William T., private
Byrum, George W., private
Cofield, Henry, private
Conner, Joseph, private
Crummy, Kader B., private
Farmer, Thomas, private
Freeman, James H., private
Garrett, James F., sergeant
Green, Thomas H., private
Harrell, David, private
Haughton, Charles R., private
Hobbs, Charleton, private
Holloman, Josiah F., private
Hughes, Aaron, private
Hughes, David D., sergeant
Hughes, Grandison, musician
Hughes, James Ervine, corporal
Jenkins, Winborn, private
Jernigan, George W., private
Jernigan, Marcus L., private
Keeter, James, private
Keeter, Reuben L., private
Kennedy, Levi Solomon, private
Lane, William Preston, private
Lawrence, David H., private
Leicester, Jonathan J., private
McClaron, Benjamin, private
Meaks, John Benjamin, private
Miller, Isaac W., private
Miller, Nathaniel, corporal
Minton, Edward, private
Mizell, Matthew T., private

Mizell, Timothy, private
Mizell, Turner, private
Morris, Alexander, private
Morris, Alfred Jackson, private
Newbern, Henderson, private
Newbern, Hunter, private
Newbern, Thomas, private
Nurney, John H., private
Parker, Hardy W., first sergeant
Perry, James West, sergeant
Perry, Peyton A., private
Perry, Thomas, musician
Perry, William W., first sergeant
Phelps, James W., private
Pierce, Lodowick, corporal
Pierce, Quinton T., sergeant
Rogers, James, private
Stone, William Turner, private
Todd, Aquilla, corporal
White, Marcus A. private
White, Solomon, corporal
Williams, Joseph T., private
Willoughby, James, private

EIGHTH REGIMENT NORTH CAROLINA STATE TROOPS

Field and Staff
Cherry, Joseph B., adjutant

EIGHTH BATTALION NORTH CAROLINA PARTISAN RANGERS

Company A
Outlaw, Thomas E., private

Company C
Outlaw, Thomas E., private

NINTH REGIMENT NORTH CAROLINA STATE TROOPS (FIRST REGIMENT NORTH CAROLINA CAVALRY)

Company B
Earley, Abner, private
Earley, William N., private
Mizell, Silas, private

Company C
Williams, James M., private

Company E
Askew, Aaron O., sergeant
Best, James J., private
Gaskins, Joseph D., private

Lane, Harvey W., private
Outlaw, Britton, private
White, Rensellar C., private

TENTH REGIMENT NORTH CAROLINA STATE TROOPS (FIRST REGIMENT NORTH CAROLINA ARTILLERY)

Company H
Hobbs, Henry A., private

Company K
Oliver, George Wiley, private

ELEVENTH REGIMENT NORTH CAROLINA TROOPS (FIRST REGIMENT NORTH CAROLINA VOLUNTEERS)

Field and Staff
Bird, Francis Wilder, lieutenant colonel
Rhodes, Robert H., sergeant major
Mardre, William B., ordnance sergeant
Rayner, James T., ensign
Todd, Elisha, chief musician
Todd, Nehemiah J., musician

Company C
Bird, Francis Wilder, captain
Outlaw, Edward Ralph, captain
Cooper, Thomas Watson,
    first lieutenant
Craig, Clingman, second lieutenant
Rhodes, Edward Averett,
    second lieutenant
Todd, William H., first lieutenant
Winston, Patrick H., second lieutenant
Adams, James H., sergeant
Alexander, Thomas B., private
Baker, Gilbert R., private
Bazemore, Armstead L., sergeant
Bazemore, Henry, private
Bazemore, William H., private
Bazemore, William J., private
Blackstone, William R., private
Britton, Daniel W., sergeant
Brogden, William G., private
Burden, James M., corporal
Butler, John, private
Butler, Leven E., private
Butler, Thaddeus W., private
Butler, William H., corporal
Byrum, Jesse B., private
Byrum, Reuben L., private

Cale, Thomas F., private
Cale, William H., private
Carter, Benjamin, private
Carter, Joseph B., first sergeant
Casper, George M., private
Casper, James H., private
Casper, Joseph W., private
Casper, Justin, private
Casper, Thomas, private
Casper, William J., private
Castellow, James C., private
Cooper, Asa, private
Copeland, William D., private
Corprew, Jonathan, private
Cullipher, John C., private
Cullipher, Simon, private
Cullipher, William T., private
Davis, Alfred, private
Davis, Allen, private
Davis, Augustus, private
Davis, Edward, private
Davis, John, private
Evans, Aaron J., private
Floyd, James R., sergeant
Floyd, John G., first sergeant
Freeman, Jacob W., private
Gilliam, Francis, sergeant
Gilliam, John H., private
Goff, Thomas G., private
Gregory, John T., private
Gregory, Lemuel D., private
Gregory, William L., private
Harmon, James F., private
Harrell, George B., corporal
Hoggard, William, private
Hoggard, William M., sergeant
Holder, Thomas, private
Hughes, Henry, private
Jackson, Joseph C., private
Jenkins, Doctrine, private
Jernigan, Samuel, private
Keeter, James L., private
King, Joseph, private
Leggett, William, private
Mardre, William B., private
Mitchell, James E., private
Mitchell, Jeremiah P., private
Mizell, John N., private
Morris, William D., private
Myers, Nathan, private
Myers, Thomas L., private

Owens, Richard, corporal
Parker, Cullen, private
Parker, James B., private
Parker, John H., private
Parker, Thomas H., private
Parker, William G., sergeant
Peele, Thomas H., private
Phelps, Thomas, private
Phelps, W. J., private
Pierce, James H., private
Powell, William W., sergeant
Pritchard, Andrew J., private
Pritchard, James W., private
Pritchard, Joseph J., private
Rawls, James R., corporal
Rayner, James T., sergeant
Rhodes, Robert H., private
Rice, Napoleon B., private
Serlyn, Anthony, private
Simmons, William H., private
Skiles, Henry, private
Skiles, James W., private
Skiles, Robert M., private
Steely, Lafayette, private
Stewart, Thaddeus C., private
Stone, David G., private
Stone, John, private
Taylor, William H., private
Thatch, Stephen, private
Thomas, Joseph T., private
Thompson, David, sergeant
Todd, Augustus, private
Todd, Elisha, musician
Todd, Lewis, sergeant
Todd, Nehemiah J., musician
Trumbull, John D., private
Ward, Warren J., private
Ward, Whitmel T., private
Ward, William C., private
Ward, William T., first sergeant
White, Riddick, private
Williams, James H., private
Williams, William, private

Company D
Johnson, Daniel L., private

Company F
Conner, James Richard, private
Farmer, Joseph J., private
White, James B., private

TWELFTH REGIMENT
NORTH CAROLINA TROOPS

Company F
Allen, Thomas Turner, private

TWELFTH BATTALION
NORTH CAROLINA CAVALRY

Field and Staff
Sutton, William M., assistant quartermaster

Company A
Burkett, William Henry, private
Dunning, James W., private
Lassiter, Benjamin B., private
Morris, Zadock, private

Company B
Cherry, Joseph O., captain
Outlaw, David C., second lieutenant
Ward, George D., first lieutenant
Bird, William, private
Boswell, Edwin G., private
Bowen, James H., private
Bowen, Jesse T., private
Bowen, Marcus H., corporal
Brickle, J. D., private
Bulloch, Bythiel, private
Butler, William H., private
Cale, William Riley, private
Corbit, John, private
Farmer, Thomas, private
Farmer, William, private
Francis, Charles E., private
Francis, David B., private
Freeman, Charles, corporal
Freeman, William P., private
Gregory, Alfred, private
Harrington, James O., private
Johnson, John W., private
Jones, Reddick, private
Langdale, Jonathan J., private
Lipscomb, Joshua, private
Minton, Thomas, private
Mitchell, Franklin V., sergeant
Mizell, A. T., private
Myers, Ralph D., private
Nurney, William D., private
Oder, Nathaniel L., private
Parker, Pritchard, private
Peele, Joseph J., private
Perry, Martin, private
Powell, James K., private

Pugh, William J., private
Scott, William B. F., private
Todd, Doctrin E., private
Todd, Haywood, private
Tynch, Josephus, private
White, Augustus, private
White, Benjamin, private
White, David, private
White, H. W., private
Willoughby, Lamb H., private

Company C
Mardre, Thomas A., private
Simmons, Bartholomew H., private

THIRTEENTH REGIMENT
NORTH CAROLINA TROOPS

Company I
Bird, William W., private
Thomas, Joseph N., private
Williams, Henry H., private

FOURTEENTH REGIMENT
NORTH CAROLINA TROOPS

Company K
Everett, Thomas, private

FIFTEENTH REGIMENT
NORTH CAROLINA TROOPS

Company A
Matthews, John R., private
Phelps, Elisha, private
Phelps, Joseph, private

Company L
Winston, Patrick H., sergeant

FIFTEENTH BATTALION
NORTH CAROLINA CAVALRY

Field and Staff
Capehart, Balda Ashburn,
  assistant quartermaster

Company A
Britton, John G., private
Freeman, James, private
Northcutt, James, private
Northcutt, William T., private

Company B
Clarke, George B., private
Watford, Joseph J., sergeant

**SEVENTEENTH REGIMENT
NORTH CAROLINA TROOPS
(FIRST ORGANIZATION)**

Company D
Brooks, William Thomas, private
Madison, James M., private
Matthews, John R., private

Company E
Outlaw, William, private

Company F
Pugh, William J., private

Company H
Hodder, George W., private
Keith, James B., private

**SEVENTEENTH REGIMENT
NORTH CAROLINA TROOPS
(SECOND ORGANIZATION)**

Field and Staff
Keith, James B., hospital steward

Company C
Matthews, John R., private

Company D
Askew, William, private
Baker, John, private
Brooks, William Thomas, sergeant
Brown, Jacob, private
Brown, Starkey, private
Bunch, John A., private
Burress, James, private
Farmer, William, private
Freeman, Josiah, private
Freeman, William H., private
Green, George N., private
Harrell, David A., private
Hobbs, Henry A., private
Hoggard, Worley T., private
Holloman, James D., private
Miller, Charles, private
Morris, Eli, private
Nurney, William D., private
Odom, Richard B, corporal
Outlaw, Britton, private
Outlaw, Hezekiah, private
Pruden, Jacob, private
Wilder, Thomas R., private
Williams, Asa, private
Williams, Benjamin, private

Williams, John F., corporal
Williams, William R., private
Williford, John V., private
Williford, Joseph A., sergeant
Williford, Richard H., private
Wynns, George A., corporal
Wynns, James W., private

Company G
Ayers, Richard T., private
Hodder, George W., private

Company H
Keith, James B., first sergeant

Miscellaneous (No Company Reported)
Burse, James, private

**NINETEENTH REGIMENT
NORTH CAROLINA TROOPS
(SECOND REGIMENT NORTH
CAROLINA CAVALRY)**

Field and Staff
Spruill, Samuel B., colonel
Perry, Martin V., quartermaster sergeant

Company E
Thompson, Blount James, private

Company H
Bishop, George, first lieutenant
Bazemore, Thomas H., sergeant
Bishop, George, private
Brickhouse, Daniel B., private
Bunch, James H., private
Byrum, John, private
Capehart, William E., private
Casper, Calvin, private
Castellow, David, private
Copeland, William J., private
Cullipher, Augustus, private
Dixon, John K., private
Evans, James H., private
Hoggard, Abner L., private
Holder, James H., private
Howard, Elijah G., private
Hughes, Riddick, private
Liscomb, James W., private
Liscomb, Joseph J., private
Mardre, John W., private
Matthews, Jacob A., private
Matthews, Jesse R., private
Moore, William S., private
Parker, George R., private

Perry, Martin V., private
Perry, William D., private
Phelps, Elisha, private
Powell, Henry D., private
Powell, Solomon, private
Powell, William R., private
Pritchard, Docton, private
Pritchard, John W., private
Stephenson, George W., sergeant
Sullivan, Jesse, private
Tadlock, William J., corporal
White, George P., private

**TWENTY-SEVENTH REGIMENT
NORTH CAROLINA TROOPS**

Miscellaneous
Measler, W. G., private

**THIRTIETH REGIMENT
NORTH CAROLINA TROOPS**

Company A
Boswell, William H., private

**THIRTY-SECOND REGIMENT
NORTH CAROLINA TROOPS**

Field and Staff
Winston, Patrick H., sergeant major
Bridges, Joseph J., sergeant major
Webb, Robert W., ordnance sergeant

Company C
Furguson, Jesse L., third lieutenant

Company G
Whyte, Solomon H., captain
Hoggard, William H., first lieutenant
Mitchell, John H., second lieutenant
Morris, Granville G., second lieutenant
Pritchard, Calvin, first lieutenant
Tayloe, Francis Marion, third lieutenant
Bowen, James H., private
Bridges, Joseph J., first sergeant
Britton, Daniel W., sergeant
Butler, Jacob J., private
Byrum, James H., private
Byrum, Joseph O., private
Byrum, William J., corporal
Carter, James T., private
Casper, Thomas, private
Cowand, Joseph J., corporal
Drew, William H., private
Dudley, John T., sergeant

Earley, John H., private
Earley, Thomas J., private
Earley, William J., sergeant
Freeman, George, private
Gardner, John T., corporal
Gardner, Thomas E., private
Gardner, William H., private
Hagerthy, Thomas, private
Harris, John T., private
Harrison, Kader, private
Harrison, Reuben, private
Hawkins, William H., private
Hoggard, Jarvis B., private
Hoggard, John H., private
Hoggard, Joseph P., private
Hoggard, Thomas W., private
Hughes, Freeman H., private
Hughes, John, private
Hughes, John H., private
Hughes, Miles, private
Jernigan, James R., private
Jernigan, William H., first sergeant
Johnson, Littleton, private
Kellam, James T., corporal
Leary, James Edward, private
Miller, Henderson, private
Miller, John H., private
Miller, Levi, private
Miller, William C., private
Mitchell, Joseph S., private
Mitchell, Thomas H., sergeant
Mitchell, Thomas J., private
Mitchell, William J., private
Mizell, Henry C., private
Moore, Guilford, private
Newbern, James E., private
Outlaw, Joseph, private
Perry, James M., sergeant
Perry, Jeremiah, private
Perry, Joseph E., private
Perry, Joseph J., private
Perry, Lorenzo D., corporal
Perry, Thomas, private
Phelps, Willie G., private
Pritchard, Alsey H., corporal
Pritchard, Henderson, sergeant
Pritchard, Irvin, sergeant
Pritchard, William H., corporal
Pugh, Benjamin, private
Rayford, James H., private
Riggsby, Frank, private

Shadgate, Charles, private
Slade, James P., private
Speller, Hugh Hyman, private
Swinson, Anthony, private
Webb, Robert W., sergeant
White, Jonathan, private
White, Josiah, private
White, William W., private
Woodburn, Lucius L, sergeant

Second Company K
Winston, Patrick H., sergeant

Miscellaneous (companies not reported)
Hoggard, Thomas, private
Hoggard, William, private

**THIRTY-THIRD REGIMENT
NORTH CAROLINA TROOPS**

Company K
Adams, William A., private
Bunch, James, private
Bunch, N., private
Burch, Joseph J., private
Capehart, Richard, private
Cooper, Norfleet, private
Cooper, Thomas, private
Davis, William, private
Fraim, James W., private
Friar, Joseph W., private
Harrell, John H., private
Harrell, Richard C., private
Harrison, George, private
Hendricks, R. M., private
Hoggard, Jesse, private
Johnson, John R., private
Mangum, R., private
Miller, William, private
Minton, George T., private
Mitchell, Franklin V., private
Mizell, John B., private
Mizell, W. H., private
Morris, M. H., private
Nixon, Andrew, private
Odom, William W., private
Peele, Robert H., private
Perry, Joseph, private
Pierce, Ivy I., private
Pierce, J. A., private
Robertson, Eli, private
White, Alfred J., private
Williams, J. J., private

**THIRTY-FOURTH REGIMENT
NORTH CAROLINA TROOPS**

Company D
Kelly, James, private

**FORTY-FIRST REGIMENT
NORTH CAROLINA TROOPS
(THIRD REGIMENT NORTH
CAROLINA CAVALRY)**

Company G
Hyman, Aquilla P., second lieutenant
Cullipher, John W., private
Hancock, William J., private

Company K
Crichlow, John, private
Savage, William E., private

**FORTY-FOURTH REGIMENT
NORTH CAROLINA TROOPS**

Field and Staff
Sutton, Stark Armstead, adjutant

Company B
Parker, James H., private

Company F
Pritchard, John W., private

**FORTY-FIFTH REGIMENT
NORTH CAROLINA TROOPS**

Company C
Sutton, Stark Armstead, captain

Company F
Sutton, Stark Armstead, captain

**FIFTY-FIFTH REGIMENT
NORTH CAROLINA TROOPS**

Company A
Jones, Reddick, private

**FIFTY-NINTH REGIMENT
NORTH CAROLINA TROOPS
(FOURTH REGIMENT NORTH
CAROLINA CAVALRY)**

Field and Staff
Sessoms, Joseph W., assistant surgeon
Hardy, John H., quartermaster sergeant
Outlaw, George W., musician

Company D
Ruffin, Thomas, first lieutenant
Cotton, Cullen, private

Futrell, James W., private
Hardy, John H., private
Roundtree, Abner J., private
Tyler, Luther R., private

Company F
Cherry, Joseph B., captain
Cherry, George Outlaw, first lieutenant
Speller, Charles Broomfield, third lieutenant
Sutton, Louis B., second lieutenant
Watford, Joseph J., third lieutenant
Acre, William, private
Adkins, William D., corporal
Askew, David C., private
Askew, William L., sergeant
Barnes, Richard H., private
Bazemore, H., private
Bazemore, Joseph Perry, private
Bazemore, Kenneth, private
Bell, H. F., private
Bowen, Frederick C., private
Bowen, Holloway E., private
Bowen, James L., private
Bowen, Marcus H., private
Bowen, Thomas E., private
Bowen, William H., private
Bridger, Robert M., private
Brogden, William T., private
Bunch, William D., private
Burden, Zachob J., private
Butler, James M., private
Butler, John T., private
Butler, Joseph J., private
Butler, Kenneth D., private
Butler, Worley, private
Casper, Cullen, private
Cherry, Joseph O., private
Clark, Joseph B., private
Cobb, George W., private
Cobb, Jesse B., private
Cobern, Elezer, private
Cofield, A., private
Daughtry, Edward A., private
Dilday, Joseph J., private
Francis, James H., private
Freeman, James Calhoun, first sergeant
Freeman, Reddick N., private
Gill, Henry H., private
Gilliam, John B., sergeant
Grimes, William T., private
Hale, James R., private
Harmon, Eli, private

Harrell, Joseph J., private
Harrell, Wright, private
Hewson, John J., private
Hoard, Willie, private
Hobbs, Charles C., private
Hodder, James O., private
Holder, Docton P., private
Holder, William A., sergeant
Holloman, William E. private
Holloman, William J., private
Hughes, Whitmel H., private
Jenkins, Kader, private
Jernigan, James R., private
Lawrence, Jerry Baker, private
Leary, James Edward, private
Leary, John W., sergeant
Matthews, James A., private
Matthews, Jordan T., private
Mitchell, Joseph J., private
Mitchell, Rufus, private
Mitchell, William L., private
Mizell, George W., private
Morris, Alpheus, corporal
Morris, Andrew, private
Morris, Calvin J., sergeant
Morris, Edward, private
Morris, George, private
Morris, James W., private
Morris, William, private
Morris, William S., private
Myers, Ralph D., private
Myers, Samuel Lafayette, private
Newbury, George C., private
Northcutt, William T., private
Outlaw, David C., private
Outlaw, George W., private
Page, William B., corporal
Parker, Isaac, private
Parker, James R., private
Parker, Joseph B., private
Parker, Nazereth Whitmel, private
Peele, Joseph S., private
Peele, William E., private
Perry, Freeman, private
Perry, Jacob B., private
Perry, Shadrack J., private
Phelps, Henry P., private
Pierce, James R., private
Pierce, John W., private
Pitman, John D., private
Rayner, John A., private

Rhea, John, corporal
Rice, Dorsey, private
Rice, Lemuel S., private
Rice, William D., private
Robertson, E. J., private
Shadgate, Charles, private
Simmons, William J., private
Smithwick, John Thomas, private
Swain, Thomas E., private
Tayloe, George, private
Tayloe, Henry, private
Tayloe, James, private
Thomas, Lewis W., private
White, James W., corporal
White, Joseph W., private
White, Zachariah, private
Williford, Alanson, private
Willoughby, John R., private
Willoughby, John W., private
Willoughby, Winborn, private

Company I
Cherry, Joseph O., captain
Ward, George D., captain
Balfour, Charles H., private
Boswell, Edwin G., private
Bowen, Jesse T., private
Brickle, J. D., private
Bulloch, Bythiel, private
Farmer, Thomas, private
Harrington, James O., private
Lipscomb, Joshua, private
Minton, Thomas, private
Mitchell, Franklin V., sergeant
Myers, Ralph D., private
Outlaw, David C., sergeant
Perry, Martin, private
Scott, William B. F., private
Tynch, Josephus, private
White, David, private
White, H. W., private

Company K
Burkett, William Henry, private
Dunning, James W., private

**SIXTY-FIRST REGIMENT
NORTH CAROLINA TROOPS**

Company C
Only, William D., private

**SIXTY-THIRD REGIMENT
NORTH CAROLINA TROOPS
(FIFTH REGIMENT NORTH
CAROLINA CAVALRY)**

Company A
Rhodes, Robert H., private

**SIXTY-SIXTH REGIMENT
NORTH CAROLINA TROOPS**

Company D
Outlaw, Thomas E., private

**SIXTY-EIGHTH REGIMENT
NORTH CAROLINA TROOPS**

Field and Staff
Sessoms, John W., assistant quartermaster

Company D
Baker, John, private
Francis, William (rank unknown)
Morris, William W., private
Peele, Calvin (rank unknown)
Perry, James S. (rank unknown)
Razor, Guilford D., private
Simmons, R. R., private
Todd, Amos C., private
Todd, Moses, private
Todd, Roland P. (rank unknown)
Todd, Simon, private
Valentine, Elisha, private

Company E
Williams, Benjamin B., first lieutenant
Askew, Joseph A., private
Auston, James, private
Bazemore, James G. (rank unknown)
Bazemore, James R. (rank unknown)
Bond, John Thomas (rank unknown)
Bunch, Nehemiah, private
Burden, John L., fourth sergeant
Burden, William G., private
Byrum, David N., private
Cherry, J. R., private
Cowand, Romulous, private
Davis, Alpheus (rank unknown)
Earley, John A., private
Earley, Josiah, private
Farmer, Preston P., private
Freeman, John, private
Freeman, William H., private
Harris, John, private
Hill, John, private

Hollomon, Junius, private
Hollomon, Samuel W., private
Jenkins, William M. (rank unknown)
Myers, Joseph Haywood, private
Mitchell, James S. (rank unknown)
Nichols, Thomas L., private
Nurney, Eason (rank unknown)
Peele, Drew, private
Peele, Jackson (rank unknown)
Peele, James W., private
Perry, James W., third corporal
Pierce, Samuel M., private
Powell, John (rank unknown)
Rice, John, private
Ruffin, Joseph B., private
Saunders, James R., private
Slade, Harvey J., private
Swain, Thomas E., private
White, Ruffin M., private
Williford, James J. (rank unknown)
Wynns, William McDaniel, first sergeant

Company F

Mebane, John T., captain
Sutton, William M., captain
Bunch, Nehemiah, second lieutenant
Leary, James Edward., second lieutenant
White, VanBuren, second lieutenant
Baker, Gilbert R., private
Bayley, Miles, fourth sergeant
Bazemore, Alden, private
Bird, James, private
Bird, William W., private
Bowen, Al, private
Bowen, Frederick C., private
Bowen, George A. (rank unknown)
Britt, James M., private
Brown, William, private
Bunch, William, private
Butler, John T., private
Butler, Kenneth, private
Cale, Thomas F., private
Capehart, William A. (rank unknown)
Capps, John R. (rank unknown)
Cobb, George W., private
Cobb, James C., private
Cobb, James H., private
Cofield, Alfred B., private
Collins, William, private
Cox, Reuben H., quartermaster sergeant
Cullipher, Marcus T., private
Davis, Joseph O., private

Dawson, William A., private
Duers, Joseph R., third corporal
Francis, Benjamin S., private
Francis, James H., private
Garrett, Richard, private
Gaskins, George L., fifth sergeant
Gaskins, John S., private
Gaskins, William T., private
Hale, Joseph H., private
Harrell, Asa T., private
Henry, John W., private
Hodder, James O., private
Hoggard, John R., private
Holliday, William A., private
Howard, Reddick H., private
Hughes, Whitmell H., private
Hyman, Joel (rank unknown)
Jenkins, Abner H., private
Jernigan, Granderson, private
Jernigan, Worley M., private
Johnston, Thomas, private
Jordan, Alfred, private
Langdale, James W. (rank unknown)
Langdale, Jonathan J., private
Mardre, George L., private
Mardre, Thomas A., first corporal
McGlaughon, John R., private
Mebane, Alexander Wood, sergeant
Miller, Josiah B., private
Miller, William R. C., private
Minton, David H., private
Minton, William H., private
Mitchell, George, second corporal
Mitchell, William N., private
Mizell, William T., private
Moore, Calvin, private
Morris, Edward S., private
Morris, Granville G., third sergeant
Morris, William T. (rank unknown)
Mountain, William E., second sergeant
Myers, William Henry, private
Newbern, Hunter, private
Newby, John, private
Parker, Asa (rank unknown)
Peele, Henry D., private
Perry, Isaac P., private
Perry, James Etherton, private
Perry, James T., private
Perry, John W., private
Perry, Marcus W., first sergeant
Perry, Shadrack J., private

Perry, William T., private
Perry, William T., private
Phelps, Asa Biggs, private
Phelps, Joseph, private
Phelps, Richard A. (rank unknown)
Pierce, James R., private
Pierce, John W., private
Pierce, William R., private
Rayner, Joseph R., private
Rhodes, William T. (rank unknown)
Robertson, William A., private
Shaw, George Washington, private
Shaw, John, private
Simmons, Bartholomew H.,
  fourth corporal
Skinner, Thomas B., private
Smith, James, private
Smith, James E., private
Swain, Thomas E., private
Thomas, Joseph N., private
Thrower, Lafayette, private
Webb, John N., private
White, Dorsey, private
White, J. J. (rank unknown)
White, Kader, private
White, Watson L. (rank unknown)
Williams, Henry H., private
Winborn, Joseph W., private

Company H
Butler, Cader, private
Peele, Alexander (rank unknown)
Watford, Joseph J., private

Company K
Capehart, Cadmus, second lieutenant

Miscellaneous
Hoggard, L., private
Williams, James T. (rank unknown)

SEVENTIETH REGIMENT NORTH CAROLINA TROOPS (FIRST REGIMENT NORTH CAROLINA JUNIOR RESERVES)

Company K
Tadlock, William W., private

Captain Abner W. Moseley's Company North Carolina Troops (Sampson Artillery)
Newbern, William T., private

TENTH REGIMENT VIRGINIA CAVALRY

Company E
Lassiter, Benjamin B., private

CONSCRIPT BUREAU

Skirven, George F., second lieutenant
Speller, James J., first lieutenant

CONFEDERATE STATES ARMY MEDICAL DEPARTMENT

Capehart, William Rhodes, assistant
  surgeon
Gilliam, Francis, assistant surgeon
Sutton, William T., surgeon
Watford, William B., assistant surgeon

CONFEDERATE STATES ARMY ADJUTANT AND INSPECTOR GENERAL DEPARTMENT

Williams, James Marshall, first lieutenant

CONFEDERATE STATES NAVY

Gray, Benjamin, powder boy
Outlaw, William (rank unknown)

OTHER CONFEDERATE SERVICE

Gill, William E. (rank unknown)

EIGHTH REGIMENT NORTH CAROLINA MILITIA

Allen, Thomas J., captain
Andrews, John A., first lieutenant
Bass, Augustus, first lieutenant
Bazemore, Edward, second lieutenant
Bishop, William J., second lieutenant
Bond, James, captain
Bond, John Thomas, first lieutenant
Bowen, Humphrey H., second lieutenant
Bridgers, Joseph J., second lieutenant
Brown, Joseph H., third lieutenant
Brown, William T., captain
Bunch, Nehemiah, first lieutenant
Capehart, Balda Ashburn, assistant
  quartermaster
Castellow, Thomas Q., third lieutenant
Cherry, George Outlaw, captain
Cobb, George Washington, first lieutenant
Cowand, Robert A., captain
Earley, James A., second lieutenant
Ferguson, William A., assistant commissary

Gillam, Thomas, major
Gilliam, John B., second lieutenant
Harrison, Kader, second lieutenant
Heckstall, John W., lieutenant
Hughes, Giles, captain
Hughes, Whitmell H., first lieutenant
Jenkins, Abram, captain
Jenkins, Charles T., third lieutenant
Leary, John W., second lieutenant
Lee, John H., third lieutenant
Miller, Charles, second lieutenant
Miller, Robert B., second lieutenant
Mitchell, John L., third lieutenant
Mizell, Jonathan T., first lieutenant
Mizell, Joseph, captain
Moore, Charles J., third lieutenant
Moore, John Aquilla, first lieutenant
Morris, Granville G., captain
Mountain, William E., third lieutenant
Northcutt, Joseph A., second lieutenant
Outlaw, William D. (rank unknown)
Perry, Marcus W., third lieutenant
Pugh, Whitmel L., second or third
   lieutenant
Rayner, Marcus J., third lieutenant
Rhodes, Jonathan Jacocks, colonel
Rodgers, James E., captain
Shoulars, George J., second lieutenant
Simons, Edward P., third lieutenant
Skinner, Thomas B., first lieutenant
Smallwood, Robert, first lieutenant
Smallwood, Thomas, surgeon
Smith, Starkey B., surgeon
Sutton, Louis B., captain
Sutton, William M., adjutant
Sutton, William T., surgeon
Thompson, Augustus H., second lieutenant
Todd, John D., second lieutenant
Todd, Lewis, first lieutenant
Ward, James H., second lieutenant
Weston, Mutico, second or third lieutenant
White, Hezekiah, captain

White, VanBuren, captain
Williams, James, captain
Williford, Asa, first lieutenant
Wynns, William M. (rank unknown)

NINTH REGIMENT NORTH CAROLINA MILITIA

Andrews, John A., first lieutenant
Bazemore, Edward, second lieutenant
Bishop, William J., second lieutenant
Brown, Joseph H., second lieutenant
Brown, Thomas S., lieutenant colonel
Brown, William T., captain
Bunch, Jesse H., major/adjutant
Bunch, Nehemiah, first lieutenant
Cherry, George Outlaw, captain
Cowand, Robert A., captain
Earley, James M., second lieutenant
Harrison, Kader, second lieutenant
Jenkins, Abram, captain
Norfleet, Stephen A., colonel
Perry, James S., first lieutenant
Pierce, Samuel M., captain
Pugh, Whitmel L., second or third
   lieutenant
Rayner, Marcus J., captain
Rhodes, Jonathan Jacocks, colonel
Rodgers, James E., captain
Shoulars, George J., second lieutenant
Smallwood, Robert, first lieutenant
Taylor, William H., first lieutenant
Todd, John D., second lieutenant
Todd, Lewis, first lieutenant
Weston, Mutico, second or third lieutenant
Williford, Asa, first lieutenant

BERTIE COUNTY MILITIA/HOME GUARD

Miscellaneous
Fraim, John G., captain
Smallwood, Charles (rank unknown)
Williams, John, captain
Wilson, John, major

1. Confederate soldiers from Bertie County were identified primarily from various volumes of Manarin and Jordan, *North Carolina Troops*, and supplemented by Compiled Service Records of North Carolina's Confederate Soldiers; Compiled Service Records of Confederate Officers; Civil War Collection, entries 16 and 63 (for members of the 68th Regt. NCT), Division of Archives and History; Bertie County census records for 1860; and a handwritten roster of some of the county's soldiers on file in the Register of Deeds Office, Windsor. The county's militia officers were identified from the AGO Militia Officer Roster and Bradley, *Confederate Militia Officers Roster*.

APPENDIX 2

Bertie County Federal Servicemen[1]

**FIRST REGIMENT NORTH
CAROLINA UNION VOLUNTEERS**

Company A
Mitchell, Joseph J., private

Company B
Hoggard, Jesse, private
Oliver, George Wiley, private

Company C
Mizell, Jonathan T., first lieutenant
Ayers, Robert E., private
Brown, Andrew J., private
Brown, Starkey, private
Burrows, James, private
Butler, Marcus, private
Butler, William H., private
Cale, William H., corporal
Castellow, George D., private
Castellow, Isaiah, private
Conner, James Richard, corporal
Cowan, William B., private
Dundelow, Josiah, private
Flood, John B., private
Flood, Joseph A., private
Flood, Thomas A., private
Flood, William D., private
Freeman, Charles, corporal
Freeman, Thomas H., private
Green, George N., private
Green, James R., private
Hall, John L., private
Harrison, Early K. D., private
Hoggard, George T., first sergeant
Hoggard, Timothy, private
Johnson, David, private
Johnson, Hardy, private
Johnson, Marcus R., private
Luton, James D., private
Mhoon, James T., sergeant
Miller, David R., private
Miller, Elisha, private
Miller, John C., private

Miller, Jonathan, corporal
Miller, Jordan, private
Mizell, Jeremiah, private
Mizell, John T., corporal
Mizell, Joseph, private
Mizell, Miles, private
Mizell, Zeddock M., private
Pugh, William J., private
Ray, William, private
Simmons, William H., corporal
Thomas, Joseph, private
Todd, Doctrin E., corporal
Todd, John F., private
Todd, John M., private
Todd, William, private
White, Augustus, private
White, Bryant, private
White, George N., private
White, Joseph A., private
White, Matthew W., private
White, Noah A., private
White, William N., private
White, William W., private

Company D
Livermon, William Council,
    second lieutenant
Atkinson, John, private
Baker, Joseph J., private
Bass, James T., private
Butler, James, private
Butler, John, private
Butler, Joseph J., private
Byrd, James, private
Byrd, William H., private
Capehart, Thomas J., private
Corbit, James, private
Cowand, James R., private
Cullipher, Marcus T., private
Evans, James H., sergeant
Gregory, Alfred J., private
Harrell, Isaac, private
Harrell, William Harrison, sergeant

Hobbs, George W., private
Hobbs, Henry A., corporal
Hoggard, Jesse, private
Jernigan, William, private
Johnson, George W., private
Johnson, Haywood, private
Johnson, John W., corporal
Langdale, John N., corporal
Miller, Joseph J., private
Miller, Nathaniel, private
Miller, Solomon, private
Mitchell, William L., private
Mizell, Thomas T., private
Skiles, James W., private
Taylor, George, private
Todd, Grandison, private
Todd, Marcus, private
White, James, corporal
Williford, Jonathan, private

Company E
Livermon, William Council,
    second lieutenant
Brogden, William T., private
Castellow, Truston, private
Clark, William E., private
Harrell, John B., private
Harrell, Mathias, private
Harrell, Whitman, private
Hobbs, Charleton, sergeant
Hoggard, Worley T., private
Jernigan, Charles J., private
Jones, Samuel, private
Lawrence, William A., private
Minton, James M., private
Minton, Richard H., private
Minton, Thomas J., private
Morris, Andrew, private
Morris, Gabriel T., private
Morris, Lawrence, private
Morris, Zadock, private
Parker, Isaac, private
Parker, Nazereth Whitmel, private
Ward, William, private

Company F
Outlaw, Thomas E., private

Company G
Burse, Joseph, private
Castellow, David, private
Castellow, Truston, private
Smith, Richard, private

Company H
Bowen, James H., private

Company I
Myers, William Henry, private
Rice, George W., private
Thomas, Lewis W., private
Thomas, William David, private
Williams, Doctrin, private

Company L
Ayers, Richard E., private
Lawrence, William A., private
Miller, Elisha, private
Mizell, Joseph, private
Thomas, William David, private
Todd, John M., private
Todd, William, private
White, George N., private
White, Kenneth, private
White, Noah A., private
White, William N., private
White, William W., private
Willoughby, John R., private

SECOND REGIMENT NORTH CAROLINA UNION VOLUNTEERS

Company A
Barnacastle, Charles C., first lieutenant
Mitchell, Joseph J., private
Outlaw, Thomas E., private

Company B
Johnson, Littleton, captain
Atkinson, John, private
Baker, Joseph J., private
Bass, James T., private
Bazemore, Alden, private
Bowen, James H., private
Butler, James, private
Butler, John, private
Butler, John, private
Butler, Joseph J., private
Butler, Kenneth, private
Butler, Worley, corporal
Byrd, James, private
Byrd, William H., private
Cale, John T., private
Cale, William Riley, private
Capehart, Thomas J., private
Castellow, Reddin, private
Castellow, Thomas Q., private
Castellow, Truston, private

Conner, Abner P., private
Corbit, James, private
Cowand, Alfred E., private
Cowand, James R., private
Cullipher, Marcus T., private
Dundelow, John, private
Evans, James H., sergeant
Evans, Yancey, private
Gregory, Alfred J., private
Harrell, Isaac, private
Harrell, William Harrison, sergeant
Hobbs, Charleton, sergeant
Hobbs, Demitrius, private
Hobbs, Henry A., corporal
Hoggard, Timothy, private
Hoggard, Worley T., private
Hollomon, William E., private
Jernigan, Alfred, private
Jernigan, William, private
Johnson, George W., private
Johnson, Haywood, private
Johnson, John W., sergeant
Jones, Samuel, private
Langdale, John N., corporal
Lawrence, William A., private
Miller, Henderson, private
Miller, Joseph J., private
Miller, Nathaniel, corporal
Miller, Solomon, private
Mitchell, William L., private
Mizell, Thomas T., private
Morris, George, private
Morris, William, corporal
Myers, William Henry, private
Oliver, George Wiley, private
Powell, Henry D., private
Pritchard, Joseph J., private
Rice, Edward, private
Rice, George W., private
Skiles, James W., private
Smith, Richard, private
Taylor, George, private
Thomas, Lewis W., private
Thomas, William David, private
Todd, Grandison, private
Todd, Lewis, private
Todd, Marcus, private
Todd, Samuel J., private
Ward, William, private
White, Benjamin, private
White, James, corporal

Williams, Doctrin, private
Williford, Jonathan, private

Company C
Harrell, Asa T., private
Hoggard, Jesse, private
Johnson, Thomas, private
Myers, William Henry, private
Rice, George W., private
Smith, Richard, private
Thomas, Lewis W., private
Ward, William, private

Company E
Hoggard, Calvin, captain
Keeter, James L., second lieutenant
Bowen, William E., sergeant
Byrum, Hardy L., private
Capehart, Richard E., private
Capps, John R., private
Castellow, Starkey, private
Castellow, Truston, private
Cobb, John A., private
Cobb, Samuel, private
Cofield, George, private
Cullipher, Jackson, private
Cullipher, James, private
Cullipher, John W., private
Cullipher, Marcus T., private
Cullipher, William E., private
Cullipher, William T., private
Davis, Henry C., private
Davis, Jonathan Taylor, corporal
Dempsey, John H., private
Dempsey, Joseph, private
Gregory, Alfred J., private
Harrell, George J., private
Harrell, Isaac, private
Harris, Thomas, private
Hoggard, Frazier, sergeant
Hoggard, Timothy, private
Hollomon, William B., private
Hughes, Jacob E., private
Jernigan, Thomas Edward, private
Johnson, George W., private
Johnson, John Thomas, private
Johnson, John W., sergeant
Keeter, Humphrey, private
Keeter, Reuben L., private
Langdale, John N., sergeant
Lawrence, Jeremiah, private
Liecester, James A., private

McDaniel, William, private
Mitchell, Joseph D., private
Mizell, Charney Gillam, private
Mizell, George, private
Mizell, Henry C., sergeant
Mizell, Henry T., private
Mizell, Thomas T., private
Oliver, George Wiley, corporal
Phelps, James H., private
Phelps, Joseph, private
Ray, John T., private
Razor, Gilford D., private
Rice, George W., private
Shaw, John, private
Thompson, James R., corporal
Umphlett, Reddick, private
Ward, Shelton, private
White, George T., private
White, James, corporal
White, Lorenzo, private

Company F
Stone, John Augustus, private

Miscellaneous
Cobb, James H., private
Hughes, Reddick, private

EIGHTY-FIFTH REGIMENT NEW YORK INFANTRY

Company C
Pugh, Henry, colored cook
Rolack, John, colored cook

ONE HUNDRED THIRD REGIMENT PENNSYLVANIA INFANTRY

Company I
West, Richard, colored cook

Company K
Garrett, Dolphus, colored cook

ONE HUNDRED FOURTH REGIMENT PENNSYLVANIA INFANTRY

Company H
Hoggard, William Thomas, private

FIRST REGIMENT LOYAL EASTERN VIRGINIA VOLUNTEERS

Company A
Hoggard, Kenneth R., private
Harris, John, private

FIRST REGIMENT UNITED STATES VOLUNTEER INFANTRY

Company A
Belch, John Ryan, private

Company B
Hughes, James Ervine, private

Company D
Casper, James H., private

Company F
Farmer, Joseph J., private
Parker, John H., private
Stone, John, private

Miscellaneous
Harris, John T., private

UNITED STATES COLORED TROOPS: FIRST REGIMENT UNITED STATES COLORED CAVALRY

Company A
Ergerson, Asking, private

Company I
Beasley, Arther, private

SECOND REGIMENT UNITED STATES COLORED CAVALRY

Field and Staff
Robbins, Parker D., sergeant major
Robbins, Augustus, quartermaster sergeant

Company B
Capehart, Henry, private
Holly, Dallas, private
Outlaw, Wright, private
Pierce, Watson, private
Robbins, Augustus, first sergeant

Company D
Britton, Thomas, private
Cooper, Ceasar, private
Floyd, Harry, private
Freeman, General, private
Freeman, Samuel, private
Robbins, John H., private
West, Henry, private
Williams, Richard, private

Company E
Askie, Alexander, private
Askie, Blunt, private

Askie, Simon, private
Baker, Andrew, private

Company G
Cheaton, Coran, private
Griffin, Irvin, corporal
Mitchell, Alfred, private

Miscellaneous
Murch, George L., private

**THIRTY-FIFTH REGIMENT
UNITED STATES COLORED
INFANTRY**
(originally the First Regiment
North Carolina Colored Infantry)

Company A
Eason, Haywood, corporal

Company B
Cotton, Randall, private

Company D
Banks, Ceasar, private
Bell, Edward, private
Bishop, Allen, private
Lawrence, Canny, private
Rayner, Clark, private

Company E
Bunch, David, private
Cherry, Arthur, private
Cherry, Noah, private
Mountain, Cato, private
Wiggins, Joseph, private
Wilson, Blunt, private

Company F
Askew, Daniel, private
McCrae, Hardy, private
Northcutt, Starking, private
Winn, Archibald, private

Company G
Blunt, Andrew, private
Bullock, Charles, private
Freeman, David, private
Harrison, Bartlett, private
Jordan, George, private
Jordan, Kenney, private
Long, Jerry, private
Morning, Joseph, private
Pugh, Champ, sergeant
Pugh, Freeman, private
Roberts, Edward, private

Ruffin, Charles, private
Taylor, Simon, private
Winn, John, private

Company I
Cherry, Andrew Jackson, corporal
Garrett, Joseph, private
Mountain, Peter, private

**THIRTY-SIXTH REGIMENT
UNITED STATES COLORED
INFANTRY**
(originally the Second Regiment
North Carolina Colored Infantry)

Company A
Bond, Alexander, private
Carter, Dorsey, private
Ellison, Joshua, private
Freeman, Isum, private
Gillam, Primus, private
Henry, Richard, musician
Raby, Edward, private
Rolack, David, private
Taylor, Dorsey, private
Taylor, Jule, private
West, Britton, private
White, George, private
Williford, Thomas, private
Wilson, Jones, private
Wilson, Lewis, private
Wilson, Robert, private

Company B
Breckus, Robert, private
Buck, Robert, private

Company C
Cherry, David, private
Eskey, George T., private
Hoggard, William, private
Jefferson, John C., sergeant
Powell, William, private
Tadlock, Isaac, private
Watson, Joseph, private
Watson, Rhoden, private
Wilson, Peter, private
Winn, Bryant, private
Winn, Rolack, private

Company D
Cherry, John Wright, private
Norfleet, Saunders, private
Northcutt, Alfred, private

Company F
Bember, Ephraim, private
Skinner, Jacob, private

Company G
Cherry, Elijah, private
Reed, George, W., private

Company H
Bazemore, George, private
Bond, West, private
Bunch, Alexander, private
Cherry, Daniel, private
Cherry, Noah, private
Holly, Benjamin, private

THIRTY-SEVENTH REGIMENT UNITED STATES COLORED INFANTRY
(originally the Third Regiment
North Carolina Colored Infantry)

Field and Staff
Miller, Nelson, commissary sergeant

Company A
Perry, Turner, private
Ruffin, Joseph, private
Simons, Arthur, private

Company B
Cherry, Austin, private
Cherry, Dorsey, private
Cherry, Freeman, private
Cherry, George, private
Cowan, Senna, private
Fanning, Frank, private
Freeman, Miles, private
Harmon, Henry, private
Horn, Henry, private
Miller, Nelson, sergeant
Miller, Silas, private
Newsome, Thomas, private
Powell, George, private
Powell, Lewis T., private
Roulhac, Lewis, private
Smith, John J., corporal
Stevenson, Edward, private
Thomas, Henry, private
Todd, Slade, private

Company C
Askie, Bryant, private
Askie, Charles, private
Askie, George, private

Askie, Henry, private
Askie, Isaac, private
Askie, Jackson B.
   (also known as Bryant Jones), private
Askie, James, private
Askie, Lawrence, private
Askie, Murphree, private
Askie, Stephen, private
Askie, Thomas, private
Barnes, John, private
Bunch, John, private
Cherry, Alexander, corporal
Weston, Henry, private

Company D
Burdin, George, private
Cherry, Noah, private
Evans, Webb, private
Hoggard, John, private
Hyman, Andrew, private
Miller, David, private

Company E
Britton, Jerry, private
Burdin, George A., private
Cooper, Amos, private
Cooper, Miles, private
Cooper, Rhoden, private
Etheridge, Wright, drummer
Miller, Madison, private
Simmons, Daniel, private
Smith, Turner, private
Taylor, Spencer, private
White, Bryant, private
Yearley, Andrew, private

Company F
Burdin, John, private
Miller, Jackson, private
Smiddick, William, private
Smithwick, David, private
Turner, Francis, private
Ward, John, private
Watford, Alexander, private

Company I
Gordon, William, private
Ward, Frank, private
White, Watson, private

Company K
Bachus, Madison, private
Britton, Michael, private
Douglas, Thomas, private

Mullen, John, private
Perry, Daniel, private
Perry, Nelson, private
Powell, John, private

Miscellaneous
Ruffin, Peter, private

FOURTEENTH REGIMENT
UNITED STATES COLORED
HEAVY ARTILLERY
(originally the First Regiment
North Carolina Colored Heavy Artillery)

Field and Staff
Cherry, Wright, commanding sergeant

Company A
Beasley, Jesse, private
Cherry, Wright, private
Erket, Richard, private
Freeman, Toney, private
Gould, Jack, private
House, Peter, private
Jones, Anderson, private
Jones, Henry, private
Northgard, Noah, private
Outler, Joseph, private
Outler, Norfleet, private
Sessoms, Dorsey, private
Tyne, Jacob, private
White, Abram, private
White, Payton, private
Wilson, Payton, private

Company B
Bond, Wright, private
Earley, Allen, private
Elliott, Albert W., sergeant
Jacocks, John, private
Pugh, Isham, private
Taylor, Benjamin, private

Company C
Douglas, William, private
Measles, Haywood, private
Outler, King, sergeant
Watford, Benjamin, private
Watford, Joseph, private
White, Lawson, private
White, Lewis, private
Williams, Thomas, private

Company D
Davis, Jacob, private

Madison, James, private
Ranner, Joseph, private
Shark, Bastian, private
Shark, Bryant, private
Smith, Nelson, private
Taylor, Watson, private
Williams, Hardy, private

Company E
Bazemore, Joseph, private
Bazemore, Simon, private
Bazemore, Willis, private
Gillam, Armstead, private
Gillam, Stewart, private
Gillam, William, private
Gould, Jack, private
Jones, Anderson, private
Jones, Henry, private
Northgard, Noah, private
Outler, Norfleet, private
Thompson, Abraham, private

Company F
Clark, Carid, private
Dewell, Henry, private
Dewers, Samuel, sergeant
Douglas, William, private
Gillam, Henry, private
Gillam, Hill, private
Hardy, Mike, private
Hasty, Jesse, private
Madison, James, corporal
Ranner, Joseph, private
Rascoe, Britt, private
Sewell, Henry, private
Shark, Bastian, private
Shark, Bryant, private
Smallwood, Jesse, private
Smith, Collins, private
Taylor, Watson, private
Thompson, Robert, private
Vew, Charles, private
Watford, Benjamin, private
Watford, Joseph, private
White, Andrew, private
White, Lawson, corporal
White, Lewis, private
Williams, Benjamin, private
Williams, Hardy, private
Williams, Shade, private
Williams, Thomas, private
Wilson, Thomas, private

Company G
Askew, Andrew, private
Askew, Benjamin, private
Askew, York, private
Bond, Harry, private
Bond, Henry, private
Bond, Isaac, corporal
Bond, Jordan, corporal
Bond, Wright, private
Drake, Kine, private
Freeman, Samuel, private
Gillam, Austin, private
Green, John, private
Gurley, Dolphin, private
Hamlin, Isaiah, private
Hill, Frederick, private
Lee, John, private
Lee, Scott, private
Mitchell, Wright, private
Pugh, Aaron, private
Pugh, Adam. private
Pugh, Robin, private
Pugh, Robin, private
Pugh, William, private
Rascoe, Haywood, private
Rascoe, Joseph, private
Rascoe, Rhoden, private
Ruffin, Abner, private
Ruffin, Edward, private
Ruffin, George, private
Ruffin, John, private
Ruffin, Richard, private
Smallwood, Daniel, private
Smallwood, Hampton, private
Smallwood, Knowledge, private
Smallwood, Nathaniel, private
Smallwood, Silas, private
Smallwood, Wilson, private
Thompson, James, private
Thompson, John Henry, corporal
Thompson, Phillip, private
Thompson, Samuel, private
Williams, Dempsey corporal
Williams, Henry, corporal
Williams, Jack, private
Williams, James, private
Williams, Lewis, private
Williams, Samuel, private
Williams, Sharp, private
Williams, Willie, private

Company H
Ashmond, Joseph, private

Barnhill, Blount, private
Bond, Carter, private
Bond, George, private
Bond, Nelson, private
Bunch, Gane, private
Extall, Canaan, private
Falk, John, private
Gaskin, Luster, private
Hoggard, Alfred, private
Miller, Matthew, private
Morris, Thomas, private
Smallwood, Peter, private
Smallwood, Stephen, private
Steward, Daniel, private
Taylor, Nelson, private
Thompson, Abraham, private
Thompson, Eli, private
Thompson, John, private
Thompson, Nelson, private
Thompson, Thomas, private
Williams, Alfred, private
Williams, Burrell, private
Williams, Drew, private

Company I
Cherry, Hill, corporal
Craig, John, private
Highman, Lonnow, private
Osburn, Friley, private
Pugh, Andrew, private
Pugh, Solomon, private
Ruffin, Ephraim, private
Ruffin, Turner, corporal
Sanderlin, Preston, private
Smallwood, Austin, private
Smallwood, Jacob, private
Smallwood, Luke, private
Smallwood, Primus, private
Smallwood, Robert, private
Smallwood, Starkey, private
Smith, Allen, private
Smith, Jordan, private
Thompson, Abraham, private
Thompson, Faden, private
Thompson, Ham, private
Thompson, Mark, corporal
Thompson, Nathaniel, sergeant
Thompson, Neptune, private
Thompson, Pompy, private
Thompson, Robert, corporal
Thompson, Washington, private
Thompson, William, private

Thompson, Willis, private
Walton, Lewis, private
Williams, Freeman, private
Williams, Hilliard, private
Williams, William, corporal

Company L
Cherry, Alfred, private

Company M
Bond, Wright, private
Davis, Jacob, private
Earley, Allen, private
Pugh, Isham, private
Skinner, Richard, private

Miscellaneous
Pugh, Charles
Ruffin, Joshua, private
Smith, Randall, private
Washington, George, private

United States Navy:
Askew, William, landsman
Barnes, Michael, landsman
Bell, Dolphin, first class boy
Bell, Freeman, first class boy
Blunt, Thomas (rank unknown)
Burdin, Lawrence, first class boy
Butler, William Hill, first class boy
Easton, Wright (rank unknown)
Etheridge, Alpheus, first class boy
Etheridge, Ansie, first class boy
Etheridge, Bailey, first class boy
Evans, Thaddeus W., first class boy
Garrett, York, first class boy
Hardy, Joseph (rank unknown)
Harrell, George E., landsman
Harrell, Thomas J., first class boy
Hardy, Henry, second class boy

Hill, Robert, landsman
Hoggard, William, first class boy
Holly, Albert, first class boy
Johnson, James R., first class boy
Johnson, John, first class boy
Johnson, John W., landsman
Kelley, Thomas, Coal Heaver
Livermon, Lewis, landsman
Livermon, Thomas, landsman
Lyers, Isham, first class boy
Mebane, David, second class boy
Moore, Dirson, first class boy
Overton, Willliam, landsman
Poole, Samuel, third class boy
Pugh, James, first class boy
Reddick, Amos, first class boy
Reddick, Joseph, first class boy
Rolack, Henry, first class boy
Sanderlin, Asa, first class boy
Scisson, Wiley, first class boy
Shark, Andrew, first class boy
Shark, Isham, first class boy
Sharp, Haywood, coal heaver
Sharp, Henry, first class boy
Sharp, John, first class boy
Sharrock, Isham, first class boy
Sprewell, Peter, landsman
Taylor, Noah, first class boy
Todd, Worley, landsman
Walton, Merida, first class boy
Watford, Cassius, landsman
Watson, Abraham, first class boy
White, Drew, first class boy
White, Henry, first class boy
White, Manassa, landsman
White, Toney, first class boy
Wilson, Jacob, landsman
Wilson, Norfleet, first class boy
Wood, John, second class boy

1. Federal soldiers and sailors from Bertie County were identified from the following sources: Compiled Service Records of North Carolina's Union Soldiers (1st and 2d Regts. N.C. Union Vols); Compiled Service Records of New York's Union Soldiers (85th Regt. Inf.); Compiled Service Records of Pennsylvania's Union Soldiers (103d and 104th Regts. Inf.); Compiled Service Records of Virginia's Union Soldiers (1st Regt. Loyal Eastern Vols); Compiled Service Records of U.S. Volunteer Infantry (1st Regt.); Compiled Service Records of U.S. Colored Troops (1st and 2d Regts. Cav; 35th, 36th, and 37th Regts. Inf.; and 14th Regt. Hvy. Arty.); and muster rolls for gunboats of the North Atlantic Blockading Squadron (supplemented by Index to Rendezvous Reports, Civil War [U.S. Navy]). Additionally, information was obtained from available pension files for soldiers and sailors.

BIBLIOGRAPHY

Unpublished Records, Diaries, Correspondence, Manuscripts and Other Primary Sources

Manuscript Sources:

ARCHIVES, NORTH CAROLINA DIVISION OF ARCHIVES AND HISTORY, RALEIGH

Adjutant General's Militia Officer Roster (AG-129).
Adjutant General's Office (Militia) Letter Book, 1862–1864.
Bertie County Convention Vote Returns, February 28, 1861.
Bertie County Court of Pleas and Quarter Sessions Minutes, 1853–1867.
Bertie County Estate Records.
Bertie County Presidential Election Returns, 1860.
Bertie County Superior Court Minutes, 1858–1869.
Bertie County Tax Lists, 1860.
Governors Papers (Henry T. Clark and Zebulon B. Vance).
Muster and enlistment bounty rolls, and clothing accounts for Sixty-eighth Regiment N.C. Troops (entries 16, 63), Civil War Collection.
Records of the Adjutant General's Office, Civil War Collection.

Private Collections:

Heckstall, Thomas, Papers.
Parker, William G., Papers.
Pittman, Thomas Merrill, Papers.
Vance, Zebulon B., Papers.
Winston, P. H., Papers.

BERTIE COUNTY REGISTER OF DEEDS OFFICE, WINDSOR

Roster of Bertie County Confederate Soldiers.
Bertie County Marriage Certificates.

LIBRARY OF CONGRESS, MANUSCRIPTS DIVISION, WASHINGTON, D.C.

Gibson, Samuel J., Diary.
Knox, Dudley W., Papers.
Lee, Samuel P., Papers.

NATIONAL ARCHIVES, WASHINGTON, D.C.

Compiled Records Showing Movements and Activities of Volunteer Union Organizations (microfilm, M594): 2nd Regt. Mass. Hvy. Arty.; 27th Regt. Mass. Inf.; 103rd Regt. Penn. Inf., Record Group 94.

Compiled Service Records of Confederate General and Staff Officers, and Nonregimental Enlisted Men, Record Group 109.

Compiled Service Records of Confederate Soldiers Who Served in Organizations from the State of Georgia, Record Group 109.

Compiled Service Records of Confederate Soldiers Who Served in Organizations from the State of Kentucky, Record Group 109.

Compiled Service Records of Confederate Soldiers Who Served in Organizations from the State of North Carolina, Record Group 109.

Compiled Service Records of Confederate Soldiers Who Served in Organizations from the State of Texas, Record Group 109.

Compiled Service Records of Former Confederate Soldiers Who Served in the First Through Sixth U.S. Volunteer Infantry Regiments, 1864–1866, Record Group 94.

Compiled Service Records of Union Soldiers Who Served in Organizations from the State of Massachusetts, Record Group 94.

Compiled Service Records of Union Soldiers Who Served in Organizations from the State of New York, Record Group 94.

Compiled Service Records of Volunteer Union Soldiers Who Served in Organizations from the State of North Carolina, Record Group 94.

Compiled Service Records of Union Soldiers Who Served in Organizations from the State of Pennsylvania, Record Group 94.

Compiled Service Records of Volunteer Union Soldiers Who Served in Organizations from the State of Virginia, Record Group 94.

Compiled Service Records of Volunteer Union Soldiers Who Served with the United States Colored Troops, Record Group 94.

Confederate Vessel Papers, Record Group 109.

Eighth Census of the United States, 1860: Bertie County, North Carolina, Population, Slave, and Agriculture Schedules.

Index to Navy Rendezvous Reports, Civil War, Record Group 24.

Logbooks for gunboats of the North Atlantic Blockading Squadron (USS *Ceres*, USS *Chicopee*, USS *Commodore Perry*, USS *Delaware*, USS *Lockwood*, USS *Mattabessett*, USS *Miami*, USS *Tacony*, USS *Valley City*, USS *Whitehead*), Records of the Bureau of Naval Personnel, Record Group 24.

Muster rolls for Union gunboats of the North Atlantic Blockading Squadron (USS *Barney*, USS *Ceres*, USS *Chicopee*, USS *Commodore Hull*, USS *Commodore Perry*, USS *Eutaw*, USS *Henry Brinker*, USS *Lockwood*, USS *Malvern*, USS *Mattabessett*,

USS *Miami*, USS *Otsego*, USS *Shawsheen*, USS *Southfield*, USS *Valley City*, USS *Whitehead*, USS *William Badger*, and USS *Wyalusing*), Records of the Bureau of Naval Personnel, Record Group 24.

Pension Case Files of Bureau of Pensions and Veterans Administration, 1861–1942, Record Group 15 (pension files for Federal soldiers and sailors from Bertie County).

Records of the Adjutant General's Office, 1780s-1917, Record Group 94.

Records of Confederate Movements and Activities (microfilm, M861): Thirteenth Battalion N.C. Cavalry; Sixty-second Georgia Cavalry; Forty-second Regiment N.C. Troops, Record Group 109.

Records of the United States Army Continental Commands (pt. 1, entry 3229—Departments of North Carolina and Virginia, Letters Sent, January-May 1863, July 1863-June 1865; pt. 2, entries 1809 and 1815—U.S. Forces at Plymouth, N.C., Department of Virginia and North Carolina, Letters Sent, January-May 1865; and Record of Passes Issued by the Union Provost Marshal, Plymouth, N.C., 1865), Record Group 393.

Regimental Papers and Books), Second Regiment North Carolina Union Volunteers, Record Group 94.

United States Military Academy Cadet Application Papers, 1805–1866, Record Group 94.

PORT O' PLYMOUTH MUSEUM, PLYMOUTH

Dunn, William E., Letters.
Stafford, Thomas J., Letters.

SOUTHERN HISTORICAL COLLECTION, UNIVERSITY OF NORTH CAROLINA LIBRARY, CHAPEL HILL

Capehart Family Papers.
Confederate Miscellaneous Papers.
Smallwood, Charles, Diary.
Winston, Robert W., Papers.

SPECIAL COLLECTIONS LIBRARY, DUKE UNIVERSITY, DURHAM

Colerain Baptist Church Records, 1821–1909.
Holly Grove Baptist Church Minutes, 1822–1878.

OTHER

Angley, Wilson. "A Brief History of the North Carolina Militia and National Guard" (unpublished research report, North Carolina Division of Archives and History, 1985).

Bartlett, J. Hobart, letter to author, August 27, 1983.

Bower, Byron B., et al., letters (courtesy Ms. Adelaid Wolf).

Connaritsa Baptist Church Records, 1851–1884, North Carolina Baptist Historical Collection, Wake Forest University, Winston Salem.

Flusser, Charles Williamson Papers, Navy Historical Foundation, Washington, D.C.

Mizell, Mary, letter, personal collection of the author.

"Resolution Against the Policy of Arming Slaves" by the North Carolina House of Representatives, March 4, 1865.

Walker, Susan P., United States Military Academy Archives, West Point, N.Y., letter to author, May 14, 1992.

NEWSPAPERS

New Bern North Carolina Times
Raleigh North Carolina Standard
Raleigh Register (weekly and semi-weekly)

INTERVIEWS

Hoggard, Hubert, August 9, 1984.
Hoggard, James Philip, September 15, 1979.
Rose, Nora Thomas, August 18, 1979.

BOOKS, PAMPHLETS, AND OTHER PUBLISHED MATERIALS

Barrett, John Gilchrist. *The Civil War in North Carolina.* Chapel Hill: University of North Carolina Press, 1963.

———. *North Carolina as a Civil War Battleground, 1861–1865.* Raleigh: Division of Archives and History, North Carolina Department of Cultural Resources, 1980.

Blakeslee, B. F. *History of the Sixteenth Connecticut Volunteers.* Hartford: Case, Lockwood and Brainard Co., 1875.

Bradley, Stephen E. *North Carolina Confederate Militia and Home Guard Records.* Vol. 2, *Militia Letter Book 1864–1865 and Home Guard Orders.* Virginia Beach: privately printed, 1995.

Bradley, Stephen E., ed. *North Carolina Confederate Militia Officers Roster.* Wilmington: Broadfoot Publishing Company, 1992.

Bridges, Hal. *Lee's Maverick General, Daniel Harvey Hill.* New York: McGraw-Hill, 1961; Lincoln: University of Nebraska Press, 1991.

Brown, Dee Alexander. *The Galvanized Yankees.* Urbana: University of Illinois Press, 1963.

Cathey, Cornelius O. *Agriculture in North Carolina before the Civil War.* Raleigh: State Department of Archives and History, 1966.

Cheney, John L., Jr., ed. *North Carolina Government, 1585–1979: A Narrative and Statistical History.* Raleigh: North Carolina Department of the Secretary of State, 1981.

Clark, Walter, ed. *Histories of the Several Regiments and Battalions from North Carolina in the Great War, 1861–'65.* 5 vols. Raleigh and Goldsboro: State of North Carolina, 1901.

"Confederate Tax Census" for Bertie County, North Carolina, 1862. (Windsor: United States history class, 1975–1976, Roanoke Chowan Academy, n.d. [p. 2 of Windsor District tax list]).

Crabtree, Beth Gilbert and James W. Patton, eds. *"Journal of a Secesh Lady": The Diary of Catherine Ann Devereux Edmondston, 1860–1866.* Raleigh: Division of Archives and History, North Carolina Department of Cultural Resources, 1979.

Crofts, Daniel W. *Reluctant Confederates: Upper South Unionists in the Secession Crisis.* Chapel Hill: University of North Carolina Press, 1989.

Dillard, Richard. *The Civil War in Chowan County, North Carolina.* Edenton: the author, 1916.

Donaghy, John. *Army Experience of Capt. John Donaghy, 103d Penn'a Vols., 1861–1864.* Deland, Fla.: E. O. Printing Co., 1926.

Durrill, Wayne K. *War of Another Kind: A Southern Community in the Great Rebellion.* New York: Oxford University Press, 1990.

Dyer, Frederick H. Dyer. *A Compendium of the War of the Rebellion.* New York: Sagamore Press, 1959.

The Episcopal Church in Bertie County, 1701–1990: From Its Anglican Roots to the Twentieth Century. Windsor: St. Thomas' Episcopal Church, n.d.

Glatthaar, Joseph T. *Forged in Battle: The Civil War Alliance of Black Soldiers and White Officers.* New York: Free Press, 1990.

Graham, Matthew John. *The Ninth Regiment New York Volunteers (Hawkins' Zouaves).* New York: E. P. Coby and Co., 1900.

Hamilton, Joseph G. de Roulhac. *Reconstruction in North Carolina.* New York: Columbia University, 1914; Freeport, N.Y.: Books for Libraries Press, 1971.

Harris, William C. *North Carolina and the Coming of the Civil War.* Raleigh: Division of Archives and History, North Carolina Department of Cultural Resources, 1988.

Jacocks, William Picard. *Descendants of Thomas Jacocks who died in 1692 in Perquimans Precinct, North Carolina.* N.p., n.d.

Johnson, F. Roy. *Tales from Old Carolina.* Murfreesboro: Johnson Publishing Company, 1965.

Johnson, Robert Underwood, and Clarence Clough Buel, eds. *Battles and Leaders of the Civil War.* 4 vols. New York: Century Co., 1884–1888.

Johnston, Frontis W., ed. *The Papers of Zebulon Baird Vance.* Raleigh: State Department of Archives and History, 1963.

Kruman, Marc W. *Parties and Politics in North Carolina, 1836–1865.* Baton Rouge: Louisiana State University Press, 1983.

Long, E. B. *The Civil War Day by Day: An Almanac, 1861–1865.* New York: Da Capo Press, 1971.

Lonn, Ella. *Desertion during the Civil War.* New York: Century Company, 1928.

McCallum, James H. *Martin County during the Civil War.* Williamston: Enterprise Publishing Company, 1971.

McCormick, John G. *Personnel of the Convention of 1861.* Chapel Hill: University of North Carolina Press, 1900.

McPherson, James M. *Battle Cry of Freedom: The Civil War Era.* New York: Oxford University Press, 1988.

Manarin, Louis H., and Weymouth T. Jordan Jr., comps. *North Carolina Troops, 1861–1865: A Roster.* Raleigh: Division of Archives and History, North Carolina Department of Cultural Resources, 1966—. 13 volumes to date.

Merrill, J. W., comp. *Records of the 24th Independent Battery, N.Y. Light Artillery, U.S.V.* New York: Ladies Cemetery Association of Perry N.Y., 1870.

Norton, Clarence Clifford. *The Democratic Party in Ante-Bellum North Carolina, 1835–1861.* Chapel Hill: The University of North Carolina Press, 1930.

Official Records of the Union and Confederate Navies in the War of the Rebellion. 30 vols. Washington, D.C., 1880–1927.

Pearce, T. H., ed. *Diary of Captain Henry A. Chambers.* Wendell: Broadfoot Publishing Co., 1983.

Phisterer, Frederick. *New York in the Rebellion.* 5 vols. Albany: Weed, Parsons and Co., 1890.

Price, William H. *Civil War Handbook.* Fairfax, Va.: L. B. Prince Co., 1961.

Public Laws of the State of North Carolina Passed by the General Assembly at its Session of 1862–63. Raleigh: W. W. Holden, Printer to the State, 1863.

Shaw, William L. *The Confederate Conscription and Exemption Acts.* Sacramento: California Civil War Centennial Commission, 1962.

Shiman, Philip. *Fort Branch and the Defense of the Roanoke Valley, 1862–1865.* N.p.: Fort Branch Battlefield Commission, 1990.

Sitterson, Joseph Carlyle. *The Secession Movement in North Carolina.* Chapel Hill: University of North Carolina Press, 1939.

Stewart, Charles W. *Lion-Hearted Flusser.* Annapolis: United States Naval Institute, 1905.

Taylor, Rosser Howard. *Slaveholding in North Carolina: An Economic View.* Chapel Hill: University of North Carolina Press, 1926.

Tolbert, Noble J. *The Papers of John Willis Ellis.* 2 vols. Raleigh: State Department of Archives and History, 1964.

Trotter, William R. *Ironclads and Columbiads: The Civil War in North Carolina—The Coast.* Winston Salem: John F. Blair, 1989.

The War of the Rebellion: A Compilation of the Official Records of the Union and Confederate Armies. 128 vols. Washington, D.C., 1880–1891.

Watson, Alan D. *Bertie County: A Brief History.* Raleigh: North Carolina Division of Archives and History, 1982.

Wesley, Charles H., and Patricia W. Romero. *Afro-Americans in the Civil War: From Slavery to Citizenship.* Washington, D.C.: Association For the Study of Afro-American Life and History, 1976.

Wilcox, Arthur M., and Warren Ripley. *The Civil War at Charleston.* Charleston, S.C.: *News Courier* and *Evening Post,* 1991.

Winston, Robert Watson. *It's a Far Cry.* New York: Henry Holt and Company, 1937.

Yearns, W. Buck, and John G. Barrett, eds. *North Carolina Civil War Documentary.* Chapel Hill: University of North Carolina Press, 1980.

ARTICLES

Brown, T. J. "Forty-second Regiment." In *Histories of the Several Regiments and Battalions from North Carolina in the Great War, 1861–'65,* edited by Walter Clark. Raleigh and Goldsboro: State of North Carolina, 5 vols., 1901.

Cushing, W. B. "The Destruction of the Albemarle." In *Battles and Leaders of the Civil War,* 4 vols., edited by Robert Underwood Johnson and Clarence Clough Buel. New York: Century Co., 1884–1888.

Delaney, Norman C. "Charles Henry Foster and the Unionists of Eastern North Carolina." *North Carolina Historical Review* 37 (July 1960).

Elliott, Gilbert. "The Ram 'Albemarle.' " In *Histories of the Several Regiments and Battalions from North Carolina in the Great War, 1861–'65*, edited by Walter Clark. Raleigh and Goldsboro: State of North Carolina, 5 vols., 1901.

Evans, J. W. "Sixty-eighth Regiment." In *Histories of the Several Regiments and Battalions from North Carolina in the Great War, 1861–'65*, edited by Walter Clark. Raleigh and Goldsboro: State of North Carolina, 5 vols., 1901.

Graham, W. A. "Nineteenth Regiment (Second Cavalry)." In *Histories of the Several Regiments and Battalions from North Carolina in the Great War, 1861–'65*, edited by Walter Clark. Raleigh and Goldsboro: State of North Carolina, 5 vols., 1901.

Hawkins, Rush C. "Early Coast Operations in North Carolina." In *Battles and Leaders of the Civil War*, 4 vols., edited by Robert Underwood Johnson and Clarence Clough Buel. New York: Century Co., 1884–1888.

Holden, Edgar. "The *Albemarle* and the *Sassacus*." In *Battles and Leaders of the Civil War*, 4 vols., edited by Robert Underwood Johnson and Clarence Clough Buel. New York: Century Co., 1884–1888.

Marley, A. P. "Note on the Destruction of the Albemarle." In *Battles and Leaders of the Civil War*, 4 vols., edited by Robert Underwood Johnson and Clarence Clough Buel. New York: Century Co., 1884–1888.

Parramore, Thomas C. "The Burning of Winton in 1862." *North Carolina Historical Review* 39 (January 1962).

Parramore, Thomas C., et al. "Jack Fairless and the Wingfield Buffaloes." *Ahoskie Roanoke-Chowan News* Civil War Supplement, 1960.

Sauers, Richard A. "Laurels for Burnside: The Invasion of North Carolina, January–July 1862." *Blue & Gray* 5 (May 1988).

INDEX

A

Adams, William A., 54

Albemarle (Confederate ironclad ram): controls navigation on Roanoke River, 129; damaged in naval battle, 131; fired on by Union gunboat, 140; participates in Confederate attack on Plymouth, 127, in naval battle, 130; pictured, 126, 130; rumored to be ready for service, 125; sinking of, 144; targeted for destruction by Federal troops, 139, 140–141, 143

Albemarle Sound, 28, 29, 48, 50, 73, 78, 128, 129, 143; provides navigational access to much of state, 24; region of, vulnerable to attack by Federal forces, 38, 86; utilized by Federal forces, 37, 39, 84

Alice (Confederate steam vessel), 17, 47, 48

Allison (Federal steam vessel), 149, 150

Anderson, George, 13

Andersonville, Ga.: Confederate prison at, 128, pictured, 128

Ashby Harbor, 36

Askew, David C., 113

"Aunt Harriet" (slave of Winston family): pictured, 91

B

Badham, William, Jr., 32

Baker, Laurence, 57

Baldwin, Charles, 140, 141

Barnacastle, Charles C., 102–103; quoted, 103

Barron, Samuel, 26

Basnight, Lemuel, 87

Battle of Batchelor's Bay, 130

Battle of Roanoke Island, 51

Bazely (Union tugboat), 146

Beasley, Joseph W., 157

Beaufort, N.C., 43

Beecher, James Chaplin, 83

Bell, Mr. _____, 78

Bell, John, 1, 5, 7, 8, 9

Belle (Union tugboat), 146

Benjamin, Judah P., 28, 29, 38, 39

Benson, William, 81

Bertie County home guard, 109, 141, 153

Bertie County, N.C.: citizens of, begin to return home following exile in Federal lines, 150, contribute various resources toward war effort, 157, elect delegates to state secession convention, 17, flee county, 109, 110, 125, 142, oppose conscription for Confederate service, 45, 54–57, 69, 87, pledge support for its Confederate soldiers, 16, prepare for war, 16–17; Confederate deserters from, enlist in Union army, 71, 90, 99–100; Confederate soldiers from, sustain battle casualties, 46–47, 99; cotton production in, 1860, 5; deteriorating conditions in, 60–61, 66, 67–69, 70, 86, 90–91, 92–93, 131; Federal raids into, 37, 112, 113, 115, 125, 139, 145, 154, 157–158; guerrillas in, 153; issues bonds to finance organizing of soldiers, 24; landowners in, 1860, 2; martial law imposed in, 43; men of, enlist for Confederate service, 22, 31, 44, 72, 100, 155, for Federal service, 54, 72, 73, 129, 154, 157; officials of, attempt to assist needy citizens, 110; population of, 1860, 3; pro-Union sentiment in, 5, 8, 9, 10–11, 12, 13, 55; remains under Confederate influence, 50; slave ownership in, 1860, 4, 5; slaves and former slaves in, encouraged by proximity of Federal vessels, 52–53, enlist in Federal military service, 53, 83, 102, 109, 110, 125, 152, flee to Union lines, 83, 92,

Planters, 5; flee Bertie, 91

Plymouth, N.C., 38, 40, 47, 56, 59, 73, 105, 115, 155; controlled by Confederate forces, 129, 139, by Federal forces, 48–49; recaptured by Union navy, 145; refuge for Bertie Buffaloes, Union sympathizers, 107, 125; site of Federal naval headquarters, 50, of recruiting for service in Union army, 53–54, 110; targeted for Federal naval show of force, 46; Union sympathizers in, 48, 52

Pool, John, 6, 9, 10, 70, 82, 158; fishery of, attacked by Federal marines, 81, 82; quoted, 67–68, 69, 91, 101; recommends measures for relief of dangerous conditions in Bertie, 68–69; writes to Governor Vance concerning conditions in Bertie, 88–89

Poor, Walter S.: quoted, 131

Poor relief, 110

"Poor whites," 5

Poplar Point, 147

Porter, David D., 151

Powell, J., 53

Powell, John R., 32

Presidential election of 1860, 2, 6, 8, 11

Pugh, Thomas J., 13

Pugh, William A., 92, 157

Pugh, William J., 71, 72

Q

Quackenbush, S. P., 46

R

Railroad bridges: targeted for Federal incursion, 40

Rainblow Bluff, 126, 146, 147, 148

Randolph, John, 23, 68

Ransom, Matt W., 122

Rascoe, Bill, 123

Rayner, Kenneth: quoted, 11–12

Recruitment: for Confederate service, 23, 31, 43, 71; for Federal service, 28, 54, 102–103, 104, 151

Reed, John A., 117; quoted, 118

Refugees (white). *See* Conscription evaders

Republican Party, 1

Rhodes, Edward Averett, 32

Rhodes, Jonathan Jacocks, 73, 78, 89; granted permission to conduct armed

militia patrols, 44; orders muster of Bertie County militia, 27; quoted, 16; requests permission to organize militia patrols in Bertie, 69–70; urges young men of Bertie to enlist for Confederate service, 17

Roanoke Island, 28–29, 30, 31, 37, 38, 41; capture of, by Union forces, 36, 39

Roanoke River, 38, 40, 47, 48, 50, 58, 61, 73, 129, 140, 141, 143, 145, 155, 156; provides navigational access to much of state, 24; under Confederate control, 139; utilized by Federal forces, 37, 84, 86

Robbins, Parker D.: pictured, 84

Robertson, Beverly H., 73

Roulhac, Mary: quoted, 83

Rowan, Stephen C., 36, 40, 41; appoints C. W. Flusser commander of Union naval forces in North Carolina sounds, 50; decides to station Federal naval vessel at Plymouth, 50; quoted, 46, 50; visits Plymouth, 50, 53

Ruffin, Mr. _____, 53

Runaway slaves, 44, 51, 53, 70, 74, 78, 87, 107–109, 129, 139, 152, 157. *See also* Slaves

Ryan, Emily, 24

S

Salmon Creek, 79, 82, 86, 87, 153, 154

Sassacus (Union gunboat), 130–131

Sea Bird (Confederate steam vessel), 22, 23, 36

Secession: convention to consider, authorized by General Assembly, 16; "convention" held to consider, 7; by North Carolina, 17; by South Carolina, 9, 11, 12; by states of lower South, 12, 13; by Virginia, 15

Seddon, James A., 124

Shamrock (Union gunboat), 145

Sharp, Haywood, 53

Sharp, Henry, 53

Sharp, John, 53

Sharpe, Starkey: quoted, 57

Sharrock, Whitmel T., 24

Shawsheen (Union gunboat), 48, 58, 75; pictured, 49

Skirven, Thomas, 119

Slagle, Lemuel, 113